David Dale graduated in psychology from Sydney University, but decided he would do less harm to the cause of mental health if he went into journalism. He has worked for the ABC, *The Australian*, *Cleo*, *General Practitioner*, *The National Times*, *RAM*, and *The Sun-Herald*. He created the daily 'Stay in Touch' column in *The Sydney Morning Herald*, and has just returned after two years as the *Herald's* correspondent in New York. He is currently Editor of *The Bulletin*.

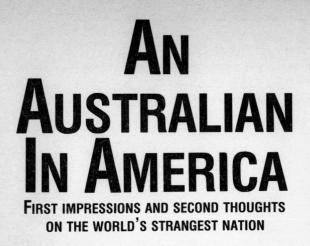

An Australian In America

First Impressions and Second Thoughts on the World's Strangest Nation

David Dale

Cartoons by Matthew Martin

Collins
PUBLISHERS
AUSTRALIA

COLLINS PUBLISHERS AUSTRALIA

First published in 1988 by William Collins Pty Ltd,
55 Clarence Street, Sydney, NSW 2000
Reprinted 1988
Copyright © David Dale 1988

National Library of Australia
Cataloguing-in-Publication data:

An Australian in America: first impressions and second
thoughts on the world's strangest nation.
Includes index.
ISBN 0 7322 2425 X.
1. United States — Social life and customs —
1971–   . I. Title.
973.927

Typeset in 11/12 pt Bodoni Book by Love Computer Typesetting, Sydney
Printed by The Book Printer, Victoria

CONTENTS

INTRODUCTION

This is a book of first impressions and second thoughts about America. It begins 11 days after my arrival in the country, with a bunch of instant generalisations. It ends two years later, in January, 1988, with a farewell train journey across the continent. In between, it tries to make sense of the wonderful diversity of America's people and places.

To write this book I talked to panhandlers, politicians, Mormons, communists, racists, restaurateurs, actors, gamblers, Californians, Bostonians, Cajuns, unionists, preachers, farmers, mayors, Mafia bosses, FBI agents, piano players, Jewish comedians, chili fanciers, advertising executives, bimbos, and couch potatoes – all of them card-carrying Americans. I became a card-carrying American myself: I was issued social security number 100–70–3629. I'm not supposed to give that number to any unauthorised person, so please keep it to yourself.

This is not a travel book in the normal sense, although it could be useful if you're planning to visit the USA (check the index). It doesn't list what to see or where to stay, except indirectly. Its purpose is to stimulate your thoughts about what kind of people Americans are, and how Americans differ from Australians – as we are or as we might become.

Much of this book is based on research done during my term as *The Sydney Morning Herald's* correspondent in New York. That job gave me the most entertaining 21 months of my life. I had no strictly defined brief, except to try to explain America to Australians. I could travel wherever story ideas took me, within reasonable expense limits. I could write whatever I liked, except that the *Herald* would insert polite dashes into common American expressions like 'motherfucker'.

I must thank the *Herald* for that opportunity. In particular, my thanks go to Chris Anderson and Eric Beecher (now editing the other *Herald* in Melbourne.) I must also cringe in gratitude to Mike Carlton (Australia's top TJ) and his producer Warwick Adderley for letting me explore the weirder aspects of American life through my weekly appearances on Mike's 2GB wireless program. My young friend Susan Anthony was a constant source of information and inspiration in New York. And Lisa Highton was perceptive enough, or silly enough, to think it would make a book worth reading.

David Dale
1988.

1

FIRST IMPRESSIONS

The longer you've been in a country, the harder it becomes to make generalisations about it. I have been in America only 11 days now, most of them in New York, so I can cheerfully assert the following propositions:

1. The Chrysler Building is the most beautiful feat of architecture in the 20th century.
2. All Americans are selling something.
3. All Americans are so polite it's scary.
4. You can get anything you want in New York (and a lot of things you don't want), except an early morning wake-up call and a public toilet when you most need it.

I suppose you expect me to produce evidence. Okay, but allow me a few digressions on the way.

The Chrysler Building, corner of Lexington Avenue and 42nd Street, has a spiky silver tower like a vintage car radiator and chrome gargoyles like leopards thrusting out of its sides. It was the tallest building in the world for a few months after it was built in 1929. The Empire State Building took over that dubious honour, and was, in turn, topped during the 1960s by two repulsive boxes called the World Trade Center. But the Chrysler Building remains Manhattan's loveliest structure, a monument to an era when architects could put beauty ahead of economics. That was because capitalists at that time wanted to be remembered for more than how many companies they swallowed.

Every detail is impeccable. The lobby, of red marble and inlaid wood with a ceiling mural of ancient modes of transport, leads to lifts decorated with silver and gold filigree. The building's doormen have stopped me both times I tried to take the lifts to the top floor ('you need an appointment with someone there, sir'), so I haven't been able to establish whether the wonders of the Chrysler Building continue to the upper floors. But I will.

As to point two: last Saturday I was leaving The Complete Traveller Bookshop on Madison Avenue, having discovered, among other curiosities, a guide to Sydney published in 1950, with photos of the harbour without an opera house (the American tourist who buys that is in for a shock). Immediately I was assailed by a small and dirty female child shouting: 'Getcher dolls here, two dollars. Getcher handbags here, one dollar.' She was sitting on the pavement near a blanket, upon which she had laid out three broken dolls, a teddy bear and two purses.

She was the youngest street capitalist I'd seen in Manhattan, but far from the first. On fine days, every street corner around Times Square is occupied by a tall black man selling sunglasses. On overcast days, the corners are occupied by tall black men selling fold-up umbrellas. I'm told that in winter, the corners contain tall black men selling fake cashmere scarves. These peddlers give New York the look of a Third World city rather than the richest metropolis on earth.

The Third World appearance is compounded by the queues every-where (New Yorkers love lining up for movies, for food and for imagined bargains), by the hundreds of street beggars, by the big rusty cars that bounce through the potholed streets blasting their horns, and by the pervasive odour of urine, especially near the subway stations (see point four, above).

Among the most enterprising street traders are the buskers, who are selling their talent, or in some cases, just An Idea. Apart from the usual guitarists, violinists and saxophonists, there are magicians, breakdancers, standup comics, even pianists (who wheel around up-right pianos and stop to do requests). One night I saw a long queue at Columbus Circle, and, tracing it to its source, discovered a busker who was selling views of Jupiter. He had on a trolley what he described as 'the world's most powerful portable telescope'. For a dollar you could look through it while he gave a brief talk on the characteristics of the planet. He was making a fortune.

Then there are the human windshield wipers. If you're driving round the centre of Manhattan and stop at traffic lights, you can expect a ragged man to leap out from the sidewalk, spray your windscreen with soapy liquid, smear a sponge round a bit and ask you for a dollar.

These entrepreneurs even try it on with New York taxi drivers, surely the hardest human beings in the world. When a wiper leapt out while I was taking a cab through Soho, in southern Manhattan, the driver shouted: 'Who astya ta do dat?' The wiper replied: 'Everybody,' and continued smearing. Driver: 'Just stop, willya. You ain't geddin anyting. Why doncha gedda job?' Wiper. 'Sorry, I don't have time to stand round talking to you. Bye.'

Which leads me, somewhat tenuously, to my point about the politeness of Americans. Beggars approach and say, 'Pardon me, sir,' before quietly seeking either money or a cup of coffee (which I rarely carry). When you say no, they say, 'Thank you. Have a nice day', with no apparent trace of irony.

New Yorkers revel in their reputation as the rudest people in America. They like to tell stories against themselves, like the one about the Canadian tourist who goes up to a New Yorker and says; 'Excuse me, could you tell me the way to Times Square or should I just go fuck myself now?' and the light bulb joke – 'Q: How many New Yorkers does it take to change a light bulb? A: What's it to you buddy?' But the reputation is undeserved. New Yorkers may push and shove and talk loudly and blow their horns a lot, but they cannot escape their American conditioning to be helpful, friendly and cute.

Phone operators are the worst. Their life's mission is to prove they are nicer than you. When you're phoning international long distance, the operator says. 'Thank you for calling A T and T' (as if you had any choice). I decided to test politeness to its limits with a phone operator, while waiting for a reverse charges call to go through, and this conversation ensued . . .

Operator: 'Thank you for using A T and T.'

Me: 'Thank you.'

Operator: 'You're welcome.'

Me: 'Thank you.'

Operator: 'You're entirely welcome, David, have a nice day.'

Me: 'Thank you.'

Operator: 'Thank YOU, sir.'

I gave up. You can't win against these people. They must have the last word.

As for the fourth proposition with which I began this ramble (You can get anything you want, etc), it might also be expressed in these terms: America is the land of excessive choice. Try lunching in one of New York's famous delis. You'll spend more time having to make decisions about your food than eating it. Do you want your sandwich on a roll, white bread, pumpernickel bread or rye? Do you want a pickle on the side, and if so, sliced or unsliced? Mayonnaise or mustard on your corn beef? What kind of coffee (which is served at the beginning of the meal): regular, espresso, capuccino, decaffeinated regular, decaff espresso, decappucino? What kind of dressing on the salad: French, Italian, Blue Cheese or Thousand Island? (What the hell is Thousand Island dressing, anyway?) And of course the transactions must be carried out with constant injections of thank yous and you're welcomes. Enough, already.

This is a nation where you can obtain a seat belt for your pet (or a massage or a course of psychotherapy); where you can buy kosher dog food ('because you never know if your dog is Jewish'); where you can watch a television network that does nothing but weather reports 24 hours a day; where you can ask the phone company to install a device that will block calls from particular numbers, but where the phone company is astonished when you ask for an early morning wake-up call, and the operator suggests you buy an alarm clock.

Some luxuries are useful, as I discovered when I got into a discussion with a friend on what the world would have been like if President John Kennedy had lived. My friend said there was no difference between Kennedy and Richard Nixon. If I wanted to be convinced of this, he said, I could watch the famous 1960 debates between Kennedy and Nixon anytime I liked. They are available on request at the Museum of Broadcasting on 53rd Street near Fifth Avenue. In fact, I could experience just about any great moment in US media there: the first episode of *Twilight Zone* or *Sergeant Bilko* or *Mr Ed*, the Beatles' appearance on *The Ed Sullivan Show*, or Orson Welles's *War of the Worlds* hoax.

So I went to the museum and watched the first Kennedy–Nixon debate. It's astonishing how right-wing Kennedy sounds. Ronald Reagan would have been proud of his declaration that America must be the top nation in the world, and win the arms race against the Soviets. Kennedy left Nixon with nothing to do but agree.

I took care to use the toilet at the Museum of Broadcasting before I went back into the streets. As far as I can tell, there are no public toilets in New York. And if you ask to use the toilet in a bar, without buying a drink and tipping the barman, the fabled American politeness suddenly vanishes.

Postscript: Those thoughts appeared in an article I wrote for *The Sydney Morning Herald* immediately after I arrived in the United States and took up residence in apartment 7A, 12 West 72nd Street, Manhattan. The rest of this book is based on my experiences in the 21 months that followed.

Some of the themes I discussed here reappear in later chapters. Politeness pops up in Chapter 3, about the way Americans talk. David Hill, former railway expert, notices the urine problem in Chapter 15. The street beggars begin Chapter 5. I discover that American food means more than Thousand Island dressing in Chapter 12. The full gamut of unnecessary choices is explored in Chapter 8. And whether the New York experience is any basis for judging America is examined in chapters on other cities I visited, like Los Angeles, Chicago, New Orleans, Boston, and San Francisco.

2

RITUALS

Some tribal customs: the ball game; the Senate debate; the power lunch; Italians on parade; Thanksgiving; the card game.

The baseball game has been going for half an hour, and so far there's been no contact between bat and ball. Mostly the batter doesn't even swing at it, and when he does, he always misses. Americans have a nerve saying that cricket is boring.

This isn't some amateur show I'm watching. It's Sunday afternoon at Yankee Stadium and I'm attending a game between the New York Yankees and the Minnesota Twins, two of America's top teams.

Finally the batter manages to make contact with the ball. The crowd roars. The ball flies up very high, and descends towards the stand. Members of the crowd start scuffling with each other to reach it. Several kids produce what would have been called butterfly nets in days gone by, and one of them snares the ball. The electronic scoreboard flashes a sign saying: 'The Yankees are happy for you to keep any balls thrown into the stand'. The umpire declares it a foul. The score remains at zero/zero. Another half hour goes by before a ball is hit again.

By the end of the day, the score is Yankees four, Twins one. More balls have been caught by crowd members than by players. Out of a game that lasts two hours, the highlights are, in order of excitement:

1. The rest break after the seventh inning, when the huge flashing scoreboard invites the crowd to 'take a stretch and join in singing *Take me Out To The Ball Game* with Eddie Layton on the electric organ', and they do.

16

2. A loud fight between two people in the crowd over seat numbers, resolved by a policeman who tells one of the arguers: 'Lady, open your mouth again and we'll see you home'. (She moves to another seat, but audibly refers to the policeman by a long American expletive that sounds like 'mofo'.)

3. The warmup, when majorettes in shiny green and white uniforms spin flags to the theme from *Rocky*.

4. The moment when one of the Yankees 'steals a base', which means that while all the opposing players are concentrating on the batter, the Yankee who has previously been batting sneaks from first to second base. The problem is that this happens very quickly, and, by definition, no-one notices till it's too late, so the excitement is in suddenly realising it, rather than in actually observing it. Your discovery of what has happened is assisted by the signboard flashing 'SPEED STAR'.

5. The arrival on the field of a Minnesota player named Roy Smalley. The crowd boos and snarls viciously. I ask the man behind me what's wrong. He says: 'The guy used to be a Yankee. He changed teams because he wanted to get out of New York. He should stay out.' (In general, the level of sportsmanship is not high. The crowd slow handclaps whenever a Minnesota player is at bat, to distract him from hitting properly. And the men running between bases always slide towards the men guarding the bases in such a way as to knock their legs out from under them, so they're too disabled to throw the ball to another base.)

What do Americans see in this slow game? It's not even as if the hot dogs taste any good. Yes, spotty youths with great contraptions round their necks do still wander down the aisles dispensing frankfurt, roll and your choice of mustard or tomato sauce. But the frankfurts are indistinguishable from the rolls.

And yet it attracts mass hysteria. All round the stadium are souvenir stalls selling Yankees caps for $6 and clear plastic 'ballholders' for $2.75. Each Sunday about 30,000 New Yorkers pay around $10 a head to get into a game. Half the members of the Yankees team are earning a million dollars a year.

The day after the Yankee–Twins game, I read the newspaper accounts of it. You'd think something had actually happened. *The New York Post* said:

'For five innings, Ron Guidry dominated. Vicious sliders slapping the dust around home plate. Blistering fastballs exploding past helpless hitters . . . Ron Guidry made the Minnesota Lumber Company look like the hole in the bat gang. Guidry, knowing he could throw as hard as he could, for as long as he could, had good velocity in his fastball, but it was his down-and-in slider that had the home-run mashing Twins swinging like rusty gates.'

I guess I must have been missing something. But I'm not in a hurry to return to Yankee Stadium and find out what it was.

'Grab grab, suck suck'

It's five past midnight, Thursday morning, in the United States Senate chamber, and in strolls Teddy Kennedy. He waves a hand to indicate he supports an amendment, nods cheerfully at John Glenn, and strolls out.

The US Government ran out of money at midnight. The president has threatened to send the public servants home. Nobody in this room is showing any sense of urgency about the Senate's supposed task of passing a new budget.

Kennedy is short and fat, and has long, grey hair. Glenn is tall, ramrod straight, blotchy skinned, and bald. Viewed from the public benches above the Senate floor, neither looks like presidential material. But then again, nor does any of the other 96 men wandering around the blue and yellow room or sitting behind the tiny school desks. Nevertheless, this gathering represents the cream of American politicians, the superstars of public debate – in their own description, 'the world's greatest deliberative body'.

Most of the men in this chamber have at least once sought to become president or vice-president of the United States. Those who haven't tried yet, are planning to try in the years to come. Some of them, like Kennedy, Glenn, Hart and Goldwater, are living legends in America. The US Senate is a political groupie's paradise.

This is the time of year when the Senate is at its most bizarre. The senators are trying to finalise the details of how the government should spend its money over the next 12 months. This annual ritual is rendered more confused by the fact that one-third of the senators are up for re-election (an event which happens every two years). So their aim is to demonstrate to their constituencies that they have achieved something.

This means every one of them, for the past two weeks, has been trying to add his or her own pet project to the budget legislation. The Senate term for these personal amendments is 'cats and dogs' – the strays that would be considered too trivial to be debated at any other time of year. There are 1,300 of these animals to be considered.

In a series of sittings that have lasted well into the dawn's early light, the Senate has passed an Ohio senator's amendment to restore William Howard Taft's birthplace in Ohio; allocated $US4 million for the building of a peace academy in West Virginia (a project which West Virginia senator Jimmy Randolph has been pushing since 1933); agreed to a California senator's motion for an increase of $US8.3 million in funds for AIDS research, and excused the Kennedy Center in Washington from paying $US33 million in interest owed on its debts.

It's all been done with a genteel grace that would amaze and embarrass any politician from the parliament in NSW or Canberra. The rudest the atmosphere gets is when Daniel Moynihan, a Democrat who used to be United States Ambassador to the United Nations, says he will try to block a water subsidy for some California farmers because it will go to the kind of people who come to Washington to 'grab grab, suck suck, grab grab, suck suck'.

Once in a while an amendment exceeds the very broad limits of tolerance of what is deemed appropriate to add to a budget, and the Republican Majority Leader, Howard Baker declares that it is not 'germane'.

Senator Baker is a short man who struts around the chamber with his hands in his pockets and a broad grin on his face. He is about to leave the Senate because he wants to devote himself to campaigning to become the Republican presidential candidate in 1988, when Ronald Reagan must retire. Whenever Senator Baker seeks to veto an amendment, the mover complains at length but politely. Thus a Democrat who was seeking a ban on the importation of armour-piercing bullets says: 'The National Rifle Association is outside the door here telling people not to vote for this.' (I checked this. It was true.)

Barry Goldwater, who was the Republican presidential candidate in 1964 but lost to Lyndon Johnson, tries to speed matters up with a procedural motion. When someone claims this is unfair, Goldwater says: 'Every once in a while I find it possible to rise above principle. This happens to be one of those times. I think the Senate is beginning to look like a bunch of jackasses.' A Republican named Malcolm Wallop interjects: 'Why in the world would the senator say we are beginning to

look like a bunch of jackasses? We have been there for some time.'
Goldwater: 'Oh, I'm sorry, I wear glasses.'

Now it's 8 am on Thursday, after the sitting has gone on for 21 hours and most of the senators have spent an hour or two on the cots that have been set up in the corridor outside the chamber. Senator John Heinz, a dark, handsome Pennsylvania Republican who is expected to find himself on a presidential ticket one day, is moving that the government should pay a special grant of $US190,000 to a Pennsylvania poultry farmer who had to destroy all his hens because of an outbreak of avian flu.

Senator Heinz's name should be familiar to you because he is, indeed, the owner of all 57 varieties. Perhaps because of his family interest in agricultural matters, nobody seems to think that his amendment is not germane, and it looks like Senator Heinz has sewn up the chicken vote.

At 9.30 am the Senate agrees to break for a few hours. The senators emerge into Washington's morning drizzle to find the papers quoting the president as saying he will send half a million public servants home because he doesn't have the money to pay them. They know very well it's just a bit of melodrama. But when they return at 2 pm, they somehow find it possible to rush through the remaining amendments in an hour.

Senator Heinz is not visible when his amendment comes around for a final vote. Someone shouts: 'Hey what about the chickens?' Senator Baker, hands in pockets, looks around and then says, 'We've waited long enough.'

The budget bill passes the Senate, crammed with cats and dogs, but devoid, for this year anyway, of chickens.

Postscript: Howard Baker did, indeed, leave the Senate soon after this. But he never ran for the presidency. Instead, he became Ronald Reagan's chief of staff after Don Regan, the former chief of staff, was forced to resign because Nancy Reagan didn't like him.

Baker was replaced as Republican leader in the Senate by Bob Dole, who did run for the presidency. Senator Gary Hart ran for the presidency too, but he was forced to give up his campaign when the media reported that he'd been playing around with a beautiful model (and possibly others). Later he decided he'd withdrawn prematurely and re-entered. They breed them tough in the world's greatest deliberative body.

The view from Siberia

There are those who say that the power lunch is dead in New York, because business executives have become too busy to eat, and prefer to do their negotiating in their offices. A visit to the Bar Room of The Four Seasons restaurant on any weekday disposes of that theory.

As you mount the staircase from the marble lobby into the vast wood-panelled dining chamber, the power lunchers are arrayed before you ... Manhattan's princes of real estate, publishing, television, finance, fashion, sport and politics.

Mort Zuckerman, property developer, might be squeezed into one leather-lined booth with Henry Kissinger (whose two bodyguards sit quietly on the other side of the room). Richard Snyder, boss of Simon and Schuster publishing, may be rising from his chair to greet his guest Barbara Walters, America's highest paid newsreader.

John Fairchild, fashion magazine publisher, might be in close communion with Bill Blass, a clothing designer. (Fairchild has only recently resumed his patronage of The Four Seasons, having boycotted it for a year after hearing the Maitre D describe one luncheon companion, Perry Ellis, as 'that faggot'.)

Peter Ueberroth, the chief administrator of American baseball, might be laughing with Norman Lear, TV producer. And at the right-hand corner table, by himself, might be Philip Johnson, the architect who designed The Four Seasons and who has been modifying it regularly over the past 27 years.

All of these people eat in the Bar Room at least once a week. Their seating is allocated in accordance with strict rules worked out by Paul Kovi, one of the two owners of The Four Seasons. The best five tables are at the back of the room, below the balcony. This area is 'paradise'. If Kovi seats you there, you know he judges you to be one of the most important guests of the day.

Up on the balcony is 'Siberia'. If Kovi seats you there, either he doesn't know you, or he rates you a failure. Suicide would be an appropriate response.

I suppose Sydney's nearest equivalent to The Four Seasons would be Chez Oz, and Melbourne's equivalent would be Fanny's. But there are two significant differences between those Australian lunch powerhouses and New York's lunch powerhouse: the total wealth assembled in The Four Seasons could buy and sell the customers of Chez Oz or Fanny's 100 times over; and Chez Oz and Fanny's have interesting food.

It seems to be a peculiarity of Manhattan's rich and famous that they have abominable culinary taste (or that they deliberately choose bad restaurants to demonstrate their originality). The model of this is Elaine's on the Upper East Side. Late at night, all of showbiz flocks there to be insulted or ignored by the waiters, and to consume Italian food that rarely rises above the disgusting. The Four Seasons isn't as bad as Elaine's. Its waiters are merely snooty. Its food is merely pretentious and mediocre.

I've eaten at The Four Seasons three times now. The first two occasions were dinners in an area called the Pool Room, which has shimmering metal curtains and a kind of giant hot tub in the middle. From those meals I recall eating something that looked like an upmarket Big Mac, consisting of layers of thick pancake, smoked salmon, sour cream, and caviar, and something called 'crisped shrimp with mustard fruits', which came surrounded with a cold fatty batter that any suburban Chinese restaurant would be ashamed to put around its prawn cutlets.

On my third visit, I ate in the Bar Room, to chronicle the lunching habits of the powerful. When I gave my name at the reception desk, the head waiter consulted the seating map and handed a piece of paper to a red-uniformed 'host', who led us towards our table.

I wasn't surprised when we crossed the room and headed up the stairs to the balcony. But we continued to a small room behind the balcony, in which we were the only guests and from which we had no view of the restaurant. 'This must be Outer Siberia,' my friend whispered. I asked if we could move to a table on the balcony, and after much deliberation with the head waiter, our 'host' agreed. We had a good view of the main chamber, decorated with a hanging metal sculpture and three red-leaved trees in pots, and full of men and women in grey suits.

My friend recognised Michael Korda, novelist and editor-in-chief of Simon and Schuster, and thought she recognised several other heavy business types. I recognised Barry Gibb, singer and composer, at a table of people who looked as if they'd just flown in from Hollywood.

A pretty blonde in a burgundy suit and silk scarf approached our table, and I decided she was Shelley Long, the star of the TV comedy *Cheers*. She wasn't. She was our waiter. (Note that the word 'waitress' is no longer used in New York. Waiter is a gender-neutral word, like writer, conductor and flight attendant.) I don't think she has much of a future at The Four Seasons, because she was very pleasant and helpful.

The Four Seasons says it specialises in a new healthy cooking style called 'Spa Cuisine' (the name is copyright, though I can't imagine any other restaurant wanting to steal it). This seems to involve putting a lot of water on the plate with the food. Thus a starter called 'wild mushroom won ton' ($14) had some little dumplings stuffed with a tasty mushroom mince floating around in water with slices of capsicum and snowpeas.

The wild mushroom won ton was the best of our dishes. I was particularly depressed by my rack of lamb with peanut sauce and chilli rice ($30). The lamb was flavourless, the peanut sauce had no spice to it and the rice was claggy. Our bill, including one bottle of New York State Chardonnay, 8 per cent tax and 15 per cent tip, was $150.

But this isn't a restaurant review, so let me mention a few characteristics I noticed about the power lunchers.

1. Most people arrived in chauffeur-driven stretched limousines (like the one in *Crocodile Dundee*), which waited outside, double parked, throughout the lunch.

2. Barry Gibb was the only man in the room not wearing a tie.

3. In the toilet, there was a man whose job was to hand each customer a towel after he had washed his hands. For this service, you were expected to leave a tip. All the men I saw departing the loo left $1 notes.

4. Throughout the lunch, I never heard anyone in the restaurant laugh. But this may have been because of the excellent acoustics.

5. The Four Seasons has a wine list with about 400 varieties on it. But the vast majority of tables had no wine on them.

6. The Bar Room was full at 1 pm and almost empty by 2.15.

The power lunch may not be dead in New York, but it certainly isn't much fun.

Postscript: After I expressed these sentiments about The Four Seasons in an article in *The Sydney Morning Herald*, I received a letter from one of the owners of the restaurant. Someone in Australia must have sent him a copy of my story. This was what the letter said:

'Dear Mr Dale, My partner, Paul Kovi, and I, and our entire staff were somewhat saddened by your report in *The Sydney Morning Herald*. We are sorry you did not find one redeeming feature about our restaurant. Not the food, not the service, nor the clientele, but especially we were surprised you didn't like our employees, either, right down to the Men's Room Attendant.

'Come now, Mr Dale, we do serve 250,000 covers a year and this is our 29th year that we are in business. We must be doing something right some of the time. Mr Dale, how about making friends? If you come right down to it, we are not bad folk and what's more our bark (or in our case, bite) like yours, is not as bad as you make it sound.

'How about giving us a call and giving us and yourself another chance either as our guest or a paying guest, if you prefer. Cordially, Tom Margittai.'

I haven't been back. There are too many good restaurants in New York to waste time on a snobby second-rater.

Lost in Little Italy

New Yorkers love a parade. If you're walking round Manhattan on any Saturday or Sunday, you'll keep running into streets blocked off for floats or stalls or marchers or dancers.

If it's not the Irish, it's the South Koreans. If it's not the Poles, it's Organised Labor. If it's not the Retired Police Officers, it's the Gay Pride Movement. If it's not the Italian Columbus Day Parade, it's the Spanish Columbus Day Parade (they are held on separate days, presumably to avoid unseemly scuffles between competing claimants to descent from the great discoverer).

The weekend that falls in the middle of October achieves some sort of record. It's the turn of the Italians, the booklovers, the Hare Krishnas, the runners and the Yuppies. The diversity of American culture is on full display. I thought I was very brave in venturing outdoors to see how these groups celebrated around each other.

I started with the New York Runners Club, which took over 20 blocks of Fifth Avenue on Saturday morning and, in typical New York style, handed out brochures saying why they are wonderful people: 'The world's original elite mile road race run on a straight course, combining the most dynamic event in track and field with the most charismatic avenue in the world.'

Apparently that wasn't persuasive enough, because when I went to have a look, there were about 30 people lining the barricades, watching twice as many runners, organisers and police.

When the runners cleared out, the street was taken over by hordes of Hare Krishnas pulling three tall carts covered with red, green and navy canopies. This is called the Rathayatra Parade. During these events in India earlier this century, it was not uncommon for fanatical devotees to hurl themselves under the vast wooden wheels of the floats, but the New York event went off without injury.

On Sunday, the central two kilometres of Fifth Avenue were blocked off again for the annual booklovers' fair. Publishers set up stalls designed to promote their latest products, and literati in carefully shabby clothes hung around hoping to be recognised. One stall had a trivia quiz based on the case of Bernard Goetz, who shot four youths he thought were trying to rob him on the subway. You won a copy of *Quiet Rage*, a book about Goetz, if you could correctly answer true or false to statements like 'The four youths knew each other well' and 'The alleged assailants were carrying sharpened screwdrivers'.

By far the most spectacular event of the weekend was the Festival of San Gennaro, which commemorates a Neapolitan saint who was beheaded by the Romans in the year 350 AD. The festival fills 12 blocks of Mulberry Street in south Manhattan, with food stalls, sideshows, and fortune tellers. It has happened every year since 1925.

The Festival of San Gennaro demonstrates some of the fascinating paradoxes of the Italian community in New York. It's held in an area called Little Italy, which was the first home of many of the four million Italians who migrated to America between 1880 and 1920. But now, 70 per cent of the buildings in Little Italy are owned by Chinese, and less than a third of the residents have any Italian background. The Italians have integrated so successfully into American society that there's no need for a ghetto any more.

American politics, arts, sports and business are full of Italian names. The Governor of New York is Mario Cuomo, who was a serious contender for the US presidency in 1988. One of New York State's two senators is Alfonse D'Amato. Geraldine Ferraro ran for vice-president. The chairman of Chrysler is Lee Iacocca. Then there's Sylvester Stallone, Frank Sinatra, Joe Di Maggio, Annette Funicello, Madonna (last name Ciccone), etc.

(Stop reading for a minute and try to think of some famous Australian politicians, performers or business people whose origins are Italian. Maybe you came up with George Paciullo. Anyone else? Perhaps it takes more time than the Italians have so far had in Australia.)

Italian-Americans are proud of their heritage, and cram into Little Italy for the San Gennaro Festival (to the bemusement of the workers in the Chinese groceries, which now far outnumber the Italian cafes).

The oddity is that most of the returning crowds don't speak Italian any more, or even pronounce their names the way a modern Italian would. I watched a tourist from Italy (Big Italy, I should say) walking up and down the stalls having a terrible time finding anyone who could understand him.

I'd set myself the task of eating every Italian dish that I had never heard of before, and, seeing a sign saying 'Braciolle' above one stall, I carefully asked for a serving of 'bra-chee-oh-leh'. The man behind the counter, who wore a T-shirt branded 'Invarone Bros', said: 'Whad you say? Whad you wan?' I repeated my best Italian vowels, but he had to come out from behind his counter and look at the sign before he understood me. 'Oh,' he said, 'you wan brashol.'

I realised what Mario Cuomo means when he says sadly that the modern Italian-Americans have swapped 'the rolling rounded rhythms' of their grandparents for 'the short sharp bite of English'.

'Brashol' turned out to be a big lump of pork, barbecued on a skewer. At other stalls I tried calzone (fried dough stuffed with ricotta cheese), baked ziti (tube pasta with red sauce), scungilli (rubbery slices of some sort of seafood), and zeppole (pastry puffs deep fried and sprinkled with icing sugar). Zeppole was the dish common to every stall.

At one stall I had this exchange:
Me (reading from a sign): 'What is Stigliole?'
Stallworker: 'Sweet bread.'
Me: 'And what is Gimirelli?'
Stallworker: 'Same ting.'
Me: 'Oh. Could I have some?'
Stallholder: 'We doan gaddit today.'

It's hard to imagine a greater contrast than that between the San Gennaro Festival and the final event of the weekend, the Columbus Avenue Festival.

Thirty years ago, Columbus Avenue was the centre of the area where *West Side Story* was filmed, a battleground for gangs of poor Irish origin and poor Puerto Rican origin. Now it's the centre of what has been nicknamed 'The Yupper West Side', where upwardly mobile Anglo-Saxons and upwardly mobile Jews cohabit in restored brownstones and elegant apartment blocks.

The Columbus Avenue Festival is a celebration of purchasing power and health-consciousness. Instead of the messy foodstalls and palm-readers of Mulberry Street, you find aerobics demonstrations and tables bearing antiques, silk shirts, sushi, bonsai plants, air-ionisers, frozen yoghurt, earrings and macrame watchbands.

For one moment I thought I'd found an element in common between San Gennaro and Columbus Avenue. One stall contained rows of bubbling frying pans, and the workers were throwing dough into them, scooping it out, and sprinkling it with icing sugar. Zeppole on the Upper West Side? No. The sign on the stall said firmly that these were 'Pennsylvania Dutch funnel cakes'.

Grateful invaders

Forget Christmas. The most important holiday of the American year is Thanksgiving, because it unites almost everybody, regardless of economic status, religion, or national origin.

At Christmas, the rich are too busy buying presents for themselves to think about the poor, but at Thanksgiving there's almost an embarrassment of food handouts. Jews who feel a bit uneasy about celebrating December 25, need have no qualms about stuffing themselves with turkey and pumpkin pie on November 27.

Any religious elements of Thanksgiving have long since been discarded. Last century, New Yorkers used to get up at 9 am on Thanksgiving morn and go to church before committing the sin of gluttony all afternoon. Now they get up at 9 am to watch the Macy's Thanksgiving Parade, an awe-inspiring procession of inflated rubber figures about seven storeys high. The figures include all the icons of American popular culture. I got up late, but in my 20-minute perusal of the parade, I saw Woody Woodpecker, Olive Oyl, Kermit the Frog, the Wright Brothers, and Superman, whose five-metre-long hand fell off after the wind blew him into some trees in Central Park.

Christmas is a time for families, but at Thanksgiving even foreigners like me get invited to the feast, so that we can show our gratitude for being allowed into this great country. I ate turkey and played charades by the fire at a large home in Westchester, the leafy suburb of large houses from which the insider traders daily commute to Wall Street.

(Digression: Westchester is normally a placid retreat, but I learned that the residents have a crisis, in the form of incursions onto their lawns by local geese who have decided not to fly south for the winter. Many of the houses are now surrounded by miniature electrified fences, designed to keep the geese away. The fences don't kill the geese, merely stun them, and apparently the geese are too stupid to fly over them. So you see, it's not easy being a rich suburbanite in New York.)

Only one section of American society does not enter wholeheartedly into the joy of Thanksgiving, and they are the people who invented it – the Indians. The first Thanksgiving was in November, 1621, when a group of Pilgrim settlers and a group of Wampanoag Indians got together at Cape Cod to celebrate the first harvest by white people in America. To welcome the newcomers, the Indians brought turkeys, corn and native vegetables. Their enthusiasm has declined since then. Nowadays the 1.5 million native Americans, with an unemployment rate of 45 per cent, have feelings about Thanksgiving that are not unlike those of Aboriginal people about Australia Day.

Some Indian organisations mark it as a day of mourning. Rudy Martin, a spokesman for the American Indian Community House in Manhattan, said Thanksgiving signified 'the beginning of the almost total genocide of a culture'. William Winterstone, a New York sculptor of Chippewa Indian descent, holds a dinner for his friends on Thanksgiving Day each year, but says this is because the date coincides with a Chippewa harvest festival. He says: 'As a traditional Indian, Thanksgiving holds no particular significance for me, but as a human being living in this world like everyone else I'm affected by Thanksgiving.

'There's a pain and ambiguity there. You have to peel through the hate, the bitterness, the negative self-image and just look at the truth of the Indian and Thanksgiving, and there's a big question mark. Indians feel that the non-Indian world has unfinished business with us, and in the meantime we're dying.'

It's all in the cards

'What do they do at New York cocktail parties?' I asked a friend when I got my first invitation to one. 'They give you their cards,' she replied.

She wasn't exaggerating. I've now learnt that within two minutes of getting into a conversation, New Yorkers ask if you have a business card (I don't) and, regardless of your answer, pull out their wallets and give you theirs.

I stayed at the party about 90 minutes and came away with five cards. Since then I've become a collector. I never throw away any card that's given to me, and I have allocated a special drawer in my desk for them. When I look through that drawer every couple of weeks, I find the cards make up a portrait of New York life.

Let me run through a selection from the collection.

Steve Reichl, publicity consultant.

I notice I've scribbled on the back of this card 'soap opera PR'. Reichl, who is tall and elegant, told me he works with the detergent company Procter and Gamble, which sponsors daytime television serials with names like *The Young and the Restless* and *As the World Turns*.

He pointed out that the name 'soap opera' is derived from Procter and Gamble's sponsorship of such shows throughout the history of US radio and television. Now they're trying to sell these shows to Australian daytime TV with a sponsorship deal involving Procter and Gamble's subsidiaries there. You're in for a treat if that happens.

Marcello Sili, Marcello

This card is fawn and oval-shaped, reflecting a trend towards making cards more memorable. It won't be long before we have to get circular wallets to hold them. Marcello Sili was wearing an orange suit when I met him, possibly for the same reason his card is oval. He runs an Italian restaurant called Marcello on First Avenue. It has been open since mid-1986, and although it's getting plenty of customers, Sili is sad. He says New Yorkers are terribly conservative about Italian food, and won't try any unusual dishes he offers them. I told him about some of the Italian food I've eaten in Sydney, and he said: 'Australians must be very progressive, huh?' I told him to keep pushing.

He said another of his problems was that a not very important New York criminal had started eating in his restaurant lately. The man recently threatened to have a waiter beaten up because a veal chop was undercooked. Sili, who has worked in lots of Italian restaurants in New York, points out that a top Mafia person would never behave like that. Once they find a restaurant they like, the important criminals behave impeccably. He fears that this man is just stupid enough to act on his threats, and hopes that somebody more senior in 'the Mob' will discover his restaurant soon, because this will ensure the more stupid criminal does not make trouble.

But then again if important Mafia figures start eating at Marcello, it might suffer the same fate as Spark's Steakhouse, where, a few months back, a criminal was gunned down in the doorway by a rival faction as he was leaving after an excellent lunch.

The Manhattan restaurant business isn't easy.

Morton Burger, DDS, PC.

Burger is a dentist, though with his long hair and lopsided glasses, he looks more like a mad professor. He proved the value of handing out cards, because I took a visiting Australian friend to him when she got a sore jaw. Burger diagnosed an impacted wisdom tooth, cleaned out the infection, prescribed antibiotics and charged only $30, which demolished a myth I'd heard about American dentists being expensive.

Betty Greenberg, Director, Dyansen Gallery.

Greenberg's gallery is in Soho, Manhattan's trendiest 'nouveau poor' area. Some of the Soho galleries specialise in the work of young men who were 'discovered' doing graffiti on subway trains. Their paintings, which look like the graffiti on subway trains, sell for as much as $5,000 each, which beats getting arrested for defacing public property. Greenberg's gallery has most recently been displaying bronze and onyx reproductions of 1920s art nouveau sculptures which were originally made of bronze and ivory. The reproductions cost about $15,000 each. The originals cost about $16,000 each.

Yvonne Tauleross, duck our speciality, roasted plain or with fruit sauces, confit or smoked, rabbit, goat, venison, tripe, steak, wild boar, cassoulet, bear, chicken, speciality and home cooking, unusual desserts.

As you may imagine, this card has very little empty space on it. It belongs to the owner of a restaurant called Yvonne's in the Catskill Mountains about two hours' drive from New York City. Tauleross, a French lady in her 50s, told me she gets her bear meat frozen from a meat supplier, and she thinks the bears are Canadian. Her venison comes from New Zealand and her wild boar from Australia. I ate goose.

Pardon Me I AM A DEAF MUTE I Sell This Card For A Living Pay What You Wish May God Bless You Thank You.

A neatly dressed man walked through New York subway trains handing out this card. I paid 25 cents for it. His method of begging has the great advantage of being silent, in contrast to most subway beggars who stand at the end of each carriage and shout about their plight, or shuffle through, rattling cups.

Richard Torres. Accounting and Auditors.

A friend recommended this small dark man to do my taxes at the end of my first year in New York. His services were necessary because in America you have to submit three tax returns a year – one to the federal government, one to the state and one to the city.

I was very worried about Richard Torres at first. He does not seem to have an office, and works out of his apartment. His shelves are filled with books about Adolf Hitler and the rise of nazism, but whether Torres regards Hitler as a model or as a warning, I was too scared to ask. He works weird hours and is likely to phone you at midnight if he has a question about your income. He finished my forms barely an hour before the last deadline for submission. But six weeks later, I got rebates from the city and state tax authorities totalling $2,500. Then, six months later, they asked me for documentary proof of every claim Torres had made.

Frederick C. Gershon. Carr Gershon. c/- CBS Records.

Freddy Gershon used to be the chief operating officer of the Robert Stigwood Organisation, which means he planned the careers of performers like the Bee Gees, Eric Clapton, Bette Midler, John Travolta, and Peter Allen. He retired in 1981, at the age of 42, and now produces occasional stage musicals (like *la Cage Aux Folles*). He also writes books about the music business.

I learned a useful expression from Gershon. He was discussing how difficult it was to get funding for the film *Saturday Night Fever*. 'De guys in de cabanas wouldn't go for it,' he said. 'Some film about some wop who dances on Saturday nights, what use is dat, dey said.'

I asked what he meant by 'the guys in the cabanas'.

Gershon: 'You know – wit de pinky rings.'

Dale: 'I'm sorry?'

Gershon: 'You know, wit de cigars and de pinky rings. De guys in de cabanas at the Beverly Hills Hotel.'

I learned that a lot of rich people who invest in films like to rent cabanas by the swimming pool at the Beverly Hills Hotel, and hold court there for supplicant producers. So 'de guys in de cabanas' has become the general term for the kind of people who might put up money for a movie or musical. Use it in good health.

Patricia Reed Scott, Director, Mayor's Office of Film, Theatre and Broadcasting. New York.

If you want to make a film in New York, you need to talk to Pat Scott. She'll issue you· a permit, and then stop traffic for you, persuade building owners to let your cameras onto their property, even arrange stunts for you. She has at her disposal a squad of 35 New York police, permanently assigned to help moviemakers.

New York's mayor, Ed Koch, created Pat Scott's position because moviemaking gives jobs to thousands of New Yorkers, and encourages millions of visitors. Her task is to wrest the title of 'America's movie capital' away from Los Angeles. Listening to Pat Scott, it's hard to imagine why anyone wants to make films in LA at all: 'In a vertical city like New York you can't step round the corner without running into 20 other people who have another idea or another point of view. In a horizontal city like LA, where you have to get into your little capsule and drive 45 minutes to get anywhere, none of that is going on. It is not stimulating. This city is so stimulating it burns people out, but that is a wonderful atmosphere for the making of films or any entertainment.'

Dolores M. Wills. Press Officer. Foreign Press Center. US Information Agency.

Dee Wills is employed by the US Government to make life, or at any rate work, easier for foreign correspondents based in New York. She is one of a group of enthusiastic public servants who organise interviews and tours designed to show how America works.

Every couple of weeks, buses loaded with polyglot lots of hacks leave the Foreign Press Center headquarters on East 50th Street, for destinations like Philadelphia, Harlem, the Hudson Valley, Wall Street, the Museum of Natural History, and the high schools of the Bronx. At these destinations the correspondents absorb information about the US Constitution, black history, farming, finance, taxidermy, and education.

In some countries the Foreign Press Center would be a propaganda agency, but I've never detected any indication that Dee Wills and her colleagues care whether the correspondents end up with a positive or negative view of the US system. Mine, as it happens, has been mostly favourable.

3

LANGUAGE

From have a nice day to sonofabitch.

Americans don't speak English, as you know, so there is no reason to expect them to understand Australian. The trouble is that their areas of ignorance sneak up on you and disrupt your life when you think you're communicating normally.

My first linguistic mistake in America was to say to a waiter 'I'm not very hungry. I think I'll just have two entrees.' He replied, 'Well, the servings are pretty large here, sir.' When the confusion ended, I had discovered that in America, the word 'entree' means main course. A first course is called an 'appetiser'.

Americans don't understand the word fortnight (they just say two weeks), or jumper (sweater), or torch (flashlight, unless it's what the Statue of Liberty is holding), or queue (line), or footpath (sidewalk), or pram (baby carriage or baby buggy), or petrol (gas), or car boot (trunk).

If you tell Americans you were pissed, they'd think you were angry (for our meaning, they would say tanked). And they are uncertain about our term 'over the top' (as in tasteless, exaggerated). This is probably because they have no need of such a concept, since there's no limit to the excesses Americans will tolerate, particularly in the name of patriotism.

But communication is worse the other way, when an Australian tries to understand everyday American. The damn language keeps changing, from month to month, from social group to social group, from region to region. In New York, a long bread roll filled with ham, cheese and salad is called a hero. In New Orleans it's a po' boy; in Philadelphia, it's a hoagie; in Pittsburgh a submarine; in Boston a grinder; in Los Angeles a torpedo and in Miami a Cuban sandwich.

Preppie, jock, flake, geek, nerd and wimp have peaked and passed. There are two new usages I'm still grappling with: 'bimbo' and 'attitude' (which, in this context, must be pronounced 'addatood').

Consider these sentences: 'He just stood there giving me attitude' and 'That girl's got attitude'. As far as I am able to grasp it, 'attitude' is a kind of arrogant, supercilious, know-all method of dealing with people. It doesn't seem to be a compliment, although sometimes I think I detect the idea that a person with 'attitude' is street-smart, a trendy type who is 'very New York'.

The most interesting usage came from someone describing to me how breakdancers on the street start their act. She said they always have a piece of cardboard, which they place on the ground. 'They walk round the cardboard all the time staring at it, giving it attitude.'

The *Wall Street Journal* declared 1987 to be 'The Year of the Bimbo', mainly because of the activities of Donna Rice (a model who sat on the knee of the presidential candidate Gary Hart); Fawn Hall (secretary to the military strategist Oliver North); Tammy Bakker (wife of the disgraced evangelist Jim Bakker); and Jessica Hahn (church secretary who fell victim to Jim Bakker's lusts and then posed nude for *Playboy*).

A bimbo may be loosely defined as an attractive woman who is preoccupied with pleasing her man. But according to the *Wall Street Journal*, men can be bimbos too: 'Assorted male models, certain actors, – a bunch of rich guys with famous last names but fluff for brains – all have been referred to as bimbos. Sometimes, it seems, bimbos marry bimbos (and produce a bambino).'

Some of the linguistic problems of people like me are addressed in a course offered by the Resident Associate Program of the Smithsonian Museum in Washington. The course is called 'American English', and it's for diplomats and other long-term visitors from overseas. The theory is that foreigners who speak perfect academic English could still provoke international incidents by missing the nuances of local usage.

The course has lessons on four distinct American dialects and focuses on particular words and phrases in each. First there is Media English, with terms like 'showbiz', 'glitz', 'anchorperson', 'X-rated', 'easy-listening', 'prime time', 'punk' and 'dee-jay' (and the more recent 'veejay', for presenters of rock videos).

This is followed by Business English, with 'three-martini lunch' (a discussion over a meal on expenses – very rare in these hardworking days, and more likely to be replaced by a 'power breakfast'), 'fine print', 'Muzak', 'let me give you my card', and 'put it on my tab'.

Then comes Government English, which covers such concepts as 'grassroots', 'stuffing the ballot box', 'to cut your teeth', 'landslide', 'mudslinging', 'political suicide', 'to cry uncle' (one of Ronald Reagan's favourite expressions, indicating what he wants the Nicaraguan government to do), 'lame-duck President' (nearing the end of his final term), 'on the stump' (campaigning locally), and 'Watergate' (as a concept synonymous with political corruption, rather than just a historical event).

And, finally, Party English, with 'networking' (giving people your card, I think), 'finger food', 'mingling', 'breaking the ice', 'Yuppie' (surely more appropriate in the Business lesson?), and 'fashionably late'.

The final exam takes the form of a cocktail party at which fake guests mingle with the students, throw out typical American expressions, and assess how they cope. Presumably the graduates will then have no trouble responding to such typical New York invitations as: 'Yo, scumbag, get the fuck out the way fo I bus yo ass!'

Behind nice

I heard this conversation in a bus in Atlantic City:

Driver (to old lady getting off): 'Have a nice day.'

Old Lady: 'What was that, honey?'

Driver: 'You heard.'

It crystallised a suspicion about Americans that had been growing in me for some time – that their relentless politeness is not evidence that they have warmer, more thoughtful natures than the citizens of other countries. I wonder if the verbal rituals – the repetition of 'You're welcome' and 'Have a nice day' (now often adapted to 'Have a nice one', leaving you the choice of what to enjoy) – are a facade, designed to cover up aggression, resentment and inefficiency.

Australians sometimes remark on how smoothly things seem to function in America. Actually, they don't. It only sounds that way. When you're trying to get a delivery, a repair, a long-distance connection, an installation, an alteration, or an explanation, you think the people you're dealing with are efficient because they keep saying things like 'We'll get right onto that', 'That'll be ready by Friday', 'Okay, David, I'll get back to you today'. They are always lying. Getting things done in America is no easier than getting things done in Sydney or in London. The language is the only thing that works smoothly.

Even some Americans have started to worry about what is behind the facade of friendliness. Jill Norgren, a professor of government at a New York college, wrote to *The New York Times* complaining that people she'd never met kept using her first name. She said she went into a bank and was addressed thus by the teller: 'Now Jill, let me explain how this works.'

Norgren wondered why this annoyed her, since it was theoretically 'a sign of acquaintance, informality and warmth'. She felt the problem was that it was fake. She continued: 'In an era of mass society and anonymity, the business community attempts to stroke and manipulate us with feigned friendliness. What's in it for business? Do most customers actually like it? Does it increase sales? Or does it intimidate?'

Clifton Daniel, a former editor of *The New York Times*, wrote in agreeing with Professor Norgren and wondering if the robotically sweet people dealing with the public have been 'told by some public relations type that this relaxes the sucker and makes him an easy mark'.

Daniel continued: 'I can't otherwise understand why every harassed, underpaid, irritable and crotchety person in the whole country should simultaneously adopt the habit of addressing me by my first name and expressing the fervent hope that I'll have a nice day. Frankly, I don't think they care at all what kind of day I have, and they have already forgotten my first name.'

Does the Pope shit in the woods?

It's hard to believe that a nation as obsessed with politeness as America could sustain a magazine devoted exclusively to insults. But *Maledicta – the Journal of Verbal Aggression* has been appearing now for 10 years, and is the sole source of income for its editor and publisher, Dr Reinhold Aman of Waukesha, Wisconsin.

Mind you, *Maledicta* comes out only once a year, and has a mere 5,000 subscribers, so we can hardly say that the forces of 'Have a nice day' have been vanquished. *Maledicta* does, however, provide evidence that beneath the saccharine surface of American society, there seethes a layer of fierce and creative malice.

Reinhold Aman says the ability to devise interesting insults is a sign of a mature community. He quotes Sigmund Freud: 'The first human who hurled a curse instead of a weapon against his enemy was the founder of civilisation.' Aman sees his role in life as providing a scholarly chronicle of modern abuse.

Most Americans limit themselves to what Aman calls 'the dirty dozen' insults. The most popular of these is 'sonofabitch', which seems pretty tame to Australians but which is banned from use on US television and radio. The rest show a preoccupation with sex or excretion that is familiarly Australian. Aman says that Catholic countries prefer insults based on blasphemy, while Asian countries prefer ancestor abuse, and Arab countries have some nice twists on animals ('may the fleas of a thousand camels invade your armpits'). But various sub-groups within the United States are doing their best to widen the vocabulary of vituperation.

For American blacks, the favourite epithet is an accusation of incest, which, in the usual pronunciation, comes out sounding like 'mofo'. Aman says it originated in Africa and was brought to America by the slaves. There are humorous variations on this theme, for example 'mammy-jammer' and 'granny-jazzer', and in some combinations, the term can indicate admiration rather than criticism, as in 'he's one bad-ass motherfucker'.

Motherhood is a recurring theme in black abuse. You may hear black teenagers exchanging observations like 'Your mother is like a birthday cake – everyone gets a piece', or 'Your mother is like a bowling ball – always getting laid in alleys'. But other members of the family are not immune. One of *Maledicta's* contributors reported this line from a black schoolyard: 'Your brother's like a grocery store – he takes meat in the back'.

Californians have come up with some typically mellow maledictions, mostly synonyms for stupidity or drug-induced vagueness, as in 'airhead', 'dipstick' and this common construction: 'She's, like, a total space cadet'.

People of Yiddish background have a style of insult which uses the 'good news, bad news' formula: 'May you be famous – they should name a disease after you'; 'May you receive three shiploads of gold – and they shouldn't be enough to cover your doctors' bills'.

There's also a Jewish tradition of using sarcastic questions to show contempt for comments judged to be inappropriate. The most often heard is, 'What am I, chopped liver?' but the range includes: Does a snake have knees? Does a chicken have lips? Does the Pope know Latin? Is the Pope a Catholic? Is the hole close to a donut? Does a bear shit in the woods? Is a pig's ass pork? Is a four pound robin fat?

Rural America offers a smorgasbord of scatology: He's so dumb he couldn't pour piss out of a boot with the directions printed on the heel; He can't tell owlshit from putty without a map; Your breath's so foul it'd knock a buzzard off a manure wagon; He'd steal a rotten donut out of a bucket of snot; They are living so far out in the boondocks that you have to wipe the owlshit off the clock to see that time it is; He's so low he can kiss a tumblebug's gilliewinkie without bending his knees; He's got a smile that could sell used snuff.

(Don't these put Australian slang slingers to shame? Concoctions like 'As flash as a rat with a gold tooth' sound less impressive than we thought.)

Then there's the verbal aggression we develop in our professions. Well-informed contributors to *Maledicta* have catalogued the kind of terms doctors and nurses use when they think their patients can't hear or understand . . .

Albatross: a patient with multiple problems, unlikely to be cured (see Dump).

Banana: a jaundice patient.

Blimp: an overweight patient.

Camel Driver: a doctor of foreign origin, especially Middle East (also called 'flying carpet salesman').

Dump: A patient nobody wants who has been transferred from another hospital or department.

FLK: a young patient with unusual appearance or behaviour (stands for 'Funny Looking Kid').

Fruit Ranch: psychiatric unit (also called 'International House of Pancakes').

PPPPPT: a patient needing complex treatment (stands for Piss Poor Protoplasm Poorly Put Together).

SHPOS: a patient who gives trouble and whose condition worsened because of his failure to take care of himself (stands for 'Sub-Human Piece Of Shit).

Plumber: a urologist.

Soapbox Derby Syndrome: a rapidly progressing illness.

Three Toed Sloth: a slow talking, slow acting patient, such as a degenerated alcoholic.

Maledicta has also provided a valuable insight into what government officials consider to be offensive language, by obtaining and publishing the list of letter combinations which cannot appear on licence plates issued in New York and California. Apart from obvious words starting with F and C, the list of licences you'll never see includes BUT, CIA, CON, CUL, GAY, GOD, HEL, HUN, JIG, JUG, LSD, NIG, PEE, PET, POT, PUD, RUN, and YID.

Aman calls *Maledicta* 'the journal the world swears by'. He says its subscribers, from 28 countries, are mostly anthropologists, linguists and psychologists, with a smattering of doctors and journalists.

Aman's own specialities are linguistics and mediaeval literature, which he taught at the University of Wisconsin until 1974. At that point he was told to seek employment elsewhere, because the university officials – 'those biodegradable nitwits in cacademia', as he calls them – regarded his research as 'undignified' (it had become focused on the offensive, the violent and the scurrilous aspects of human languages over the past 5,000 years).

So Aman continued his research privately, and in 1977 issued the first edition of *Maledicta*, decorated with a hieroglyphic used on ancient Egyptian legal documents as a warning against breach of contract (it means 'May you be fucked by a donkey').

Publishing the journal and giving lectures around the country provides a meagre living for Aman, who is 50, but he wishes there were more scholars like him. 'Every day around the world, tens of thousands of people are humiliated, demoted, fired, fined, jailed, injured, killed or commit suicide because of insults, slurs, curses, threats, blasphemies, vulgarities, and other offensive words,' he says. 'Such events emphasise the importance of this type of language and cry out for more research on verbal aggression and its effects.'

If you wish to assist Reinhold Aman's researches, or subscribe to his journal, write to *Maledicta*, 331 South Greenfield Avenue, Waukesha, Wisconsin 53186, USA.

4

CITIES

Los Angeles (how to be Very LA) and Atlanta (free at last).

Steve, a lawyer, and Dave, an architect, are going to take me out and introduce me to Los Angeles. They know that since I've come from New York, I must hate LA, but they're going to change my mind.

Steve and Dave have been recommended to me as being 'Very LA' by my friend Barbara. Although she lives in New York, Barbara is Very LA herself. She's into crystals and reincarnation. She believes that her crystals help her to focus her emotional energy, and that everything that happens to us is the result of what we did in past lives. Steve and Dave must have been virtuous in their past lives because they are having a great time in this one.

They pick me up at 9 pm at my hotel, which is a renovated art deco structure called the Shangri-la. A magazine clipping in the hotel lobby says it is the favourite retreat of budget-conscious celebrities. Past guests have included Stan Laurel (of Laurel and Hardy), Diane Keaton, Bill Murray, Natassia Kinski, and Randy Newman.

I don't see any of them, but in the carpark I do pass Donovan Leitch, who once sang hits like *Sunshine Superman* and *Mellow Yellow*. He is having an altercation with two teenage girls who appear to be his daughters.

Steve and Dave assure me that star-spotting is Very LA. Dave mentions that tomorrow he is having lunch at Universal Studios with Steven Spielberg's story editor.

We drive to Steve's office (which was designed by Dave, in green and pink postmodern style) to have 'a hit'. Steve puts a little mound of marijuana into a pipe, lights it, and offers it around. I politely decline, explaining that chardonnay is my drug of choice. Steve and Dave puff away.

They feel that while cocaine may still be the fashionable drug for Yuppies in New York, Los Angeles is once again leading the way by reverting to a safer, more mellow mind-altering chemical. New York will probably pick up the marijuana trend in 6 months or so.

We go for a drive round Santa Monica, a mixed suburb where homeless derelicts sleep on the beach a few metres from ritzy mansions. In the novels of Raymond Chandler, the detective Philip Marlowe used to take occasional trips to a place near Los Angeles called Bay City, where the cops were even more corrupt than in LA. That was Santa Monica.

These days it is the kingdom of Jane Fonda and her husband Tom Hayden, who is the local member of the State Congress, and it is famous for having a left-wing council which has imposed the strictest rent control rules in the nation.

Some landlords object. We pass a group of empty tumbledown shacks which have a large painted sign outside saying 'Amerika is already here in Soviet Monika. Tom Fonda Big Brother and his rent control have stripped away the rights of property owners. Why has the mess you see here not been torn down. Big Brother has already taken my rights, are yours next?'

We eat in not one but two restaurants on Main Street, which is a fashionable clothing and art gallery area where, among others, the Australian designer Ken Done has set up his store. We don't see any celebrities in either restaurant, but in the first we eat nouvelle Mexican food and in the second we eat oysters and a pizza made with grilled chicken and cilantro (the Californian word for coriander). Steve drinks Bloody Marys and Dave drinks Corona, a light beer from Mexico.

(Incidentally, new wave pizzas, with thin crust and healthy ingredients, are Very LA, having been introduced in 1984 by the city's hottest chef, Wolfgang Puck. Everyone recommends Puck's restaurant, Spago, as a guaranteed celebrity-spotting establishment, but when I go there two nights later the only face I recognise is Gregory Peck's.)

Steve talks about some of his murder cases. There was a Filipino man who looked out of his window one night and saw some guys robbing cars outside. He picked up his revolver and shot one of the guys, a black, who had a car radio in his arms at the time.

The owner of the car, a Mexican, came up and attempted to retrieve

Los Angeles Man (descending into the hot tub)

his radio, but a crowd of black people gathered and blamed him for shooting the thief. A scuffle broke out and somebody threw the radio across the road, where it smashed. Then somebody else came out with a shotgun and fired in the air, but hit the Mexican. The police arrived to a very confusing scene. 'Only in LA . . . ' Steve said proudly. The black man later died in hospital. Steve represented the Filipino until he ran out of money, and then the public defender took over.

It has been a very informative evening. Next day, guided by advice from Steve and Dave, I try some tourism. I drive along Wilshire Boulevard through Macarthur Park (yes, the song was named after it, but no, it is not melting in the dark) to the La Brea Tar Pits. This is a journey in time to the primordial ooze – a lake half covered with black tar and methane bubbles gurgling to the surface. A sign says the tar in the lake has trapped animals since time immemorial, and more than 100 tonnes of fossil bones have been dug up in the area. To convince you, the guardians of the tar pits have placed a life-size fibreglass mammoth in the lake, apparently trumpeting for help while two other fibreglass mammoths look on helplessly from the bank.

Then on to a place where one is sure to find celebrities – Hollywood Cemetery. If you can't catch them live, get them after they've stopped moving. Cecil B. DeMille has a huge grey marble casket which is less vulgar than you expect, and Douglas Fairbanks has his own pool of remembrance and a temple engraved 'Good night sweet prince, and flights of angels sing thee to thy rest'.

It's quite a contrast to Marilyn Monroe's memorial, over in Westwood Cemetery, which consists of a single brass plaque with only her name and dates (1926–1962). A fresh pink rose is in a vase attached to her plaque.

I go out to dinner with Roxanne, an old friend from New York. We're in a restaurant at Venice Beach called 72 Market, owned by Dudley Moore and Liza Minelli. They aren't there, but Roxanne recognises a man who has a regular role in *Dynasty*.

Roxanne says it is currently Very LA to go on game shows and try to win money or resaleable objects. Since Los Angeles is the head-quarters of the TV networks, they film most of their game shows there and are always looking for new contestants. Several of Roxanne's co-workers have taken days off to take part in game shows, and one of them won $13,000.

Roxanne has always been a level-headed person. She grew up in middle America, got a degree in business administration, and spent 7 years in New York. When her company transferred her to LA she said, 'I hope I don't turn into an airhead.'

I ask if she has become Very LA after 6 months on the West coast. She laughs and says No, then adds tentatively, 'Well, I do have an altar.' She says a friend took her to a Buddhist meeting. It was Very LA. Tina Turner was there.

They gave Roxanne a miniature shrine on three months' trial. She has to put a fresh bowl of water in front of it every day. If she doesn't find some meaning in her life after three months, she can return the altar and try something else.

Ugly and historic

Raymond Chandler once said that Los Angeles was a city with all the personality of a paper cup. Well, Los Angeles is the Holy Grail compared to Atlanta.

The Yankees, showing great good sense, burned Atlanta to the ground in 1864, and it would seem that nobody built anything much on the site for 100 years until a whole lot of skyscrapers, car parks and freeways were plonked onto the wasteland in the early 1960s. There is no discernible city centre – just rows of office blocks, surrounded by slums mainly inhabited by black people, and then, on the outskirts, townships and shopping malls inhabited by wealthy whites.

If you're white, you drive to work. If you're black, you use the limited subway system called MARTA. MARTA stands for Metropolitan Atlanta Rapid Transit Authority, but the whites have sensitively nicknamed it 'Moving Africans Rapidly Through Atlanta'.

Atlantans will tell you that their city is the most sophisticated in the south, and that it has a large gay population. So much for the myth that gay people have good taste.

Such artistic endeavours as exist, are the result of bursts of generosity by Coca-Cola, Atlanta's richest company. Coke, which also owns Columbia Pictures, is a major sponsor of local talent (in the early 1970s it backed an obscure Georgia politician named Jimmy Carter), and a builder of art complexes. When Coke's owner, Robert Woodruff, gave $28 million in 1981 to create two art museums in Atlanta, he told associates that it was an investment for the company. He said he never bought paintings himself, but the galleries would make Atlanta a more attractive habitat for the kind of Coke executives who liked art.

In the light of all this, you may ask why anyone would wish to visit Atlanta. The answer is that Atlanta is an essential chapter in modern American history, because it was where the black civil rights movement began, and because it gives cause for optimism that if you push hard enough, you can overcome oppression.

Atlanta contains the Ebenezer Baptist Church, where Martin Luther King first preached against segregation, and the Centre for Non-Violent Social Change, founded by King, which now adjoins his tomb. King's sarcophagus is engraved: 'Free at last, free at last, thank God Almighty, I'm free at last.'

Most poignant of all, there is the Woolworth's lunch counter in Forsyth Street. I was taken to see it by John Lewis, a local member of the US House of Representatives. There's nothing unusual about it – it's just a counter with stools occupied by white and black customers eating sandwiches. But when John Lewis first saw that lunch counter 26 years ago, the stools were occupied only by whites. He was a trainee for the Baptist ministry, and he had walked into Woolworth's with 10 other nervous young blacks who were determined to challenge the counter's 'whites only' rule. They sat on the stools all day. No-one would serve them. During the afternoon a group of whites from the local Ku Klux Klan came and tried to drag them off the stools. The police arrived and arrested the blacks for disturbing the peace.

It was the start of a long career of being arrested for John Lewis, who became chairman of the Student Non-Violent Co-ordinating Committee of Martin Luther King's Southern Christian Leadership Conference. Between 1960 and 1966 he was put in jail 40 times. His crimes included riding on a bus, walking down a street, and ordering a hamburger. Those activities also earned him repeated bashings, two of which put him in hospital with concussion.

John Lewis is an unlikely looking hero. He is short, plump and bald, and he speaks so matter of factly about his experiences that it takes you a couple of minutes to realise what courage was involved. Here he describes one occasion when he had organised a freedom ride through the south:

'The bus pulled into the bus station and we got off. Then suddenly this mob, maybe 2,000 people, seemed to just come out of nowhere. They had baseball bats, iron pipes, chains, and there were men, women and children among them. There was a group of reporters and the mob started taking them apart and smashing their cameras.

'When they had beaten the reporters down they turned on us and started beating us. Our baggage was taken from us and burned right there in the street. I was hit and left unconscious there in the street for about 45 minutes. But I remember as I was lying there on the street and just bleeding, the attorney-general of Alabama came up and served an injunction on me for travelling through the state of Alabama as part of an inter-racial group.'

Nowadays John Lewis looks on a very different Atlanta. He is the elected representative in the US Congress for a substantial part of the city. Black aldermen control the city council which once enforced the rules requiring segregated schools, restaurants, and public toilets. They work with a black Mayor, Andrew Young, formerly the US Ambassador to the United Nations.

Atlanta even has a number of black millionaires, like Herman Russell, president of H. J. Russell Constructions; Jesse Hill, president of Atlanta Life Insurance; and Cornell McBride, president of M and M Cosmetics, which makes products for straightening hair and whitening skin.

There's still a long way to go. Fred Taylor, an organiser with the Southern Christian Leadership Conference, observes:

'90 per cent of the political power in Atlanta is in the hands of blacks, but 90 per cent of the economic power is in the hands of whites. So now we are allowed into the top restaurants, but we still can't afford it. And the city's two top social clubs, the Piedmont Driving Club and the Capitol City Club, still don't let blacks or Jews in. The schools are desegregated, but the schools in central Atlanta are 90 per cent black because the whites pulled out their kids and put them into private schools.'

John Lewis remains optimistic. He wouldn't have stayed in the civil rights struggle if he didn't believe change was possible. He says: 'Some people ask me "Don't you get bitter, don't you get hostile, after all the suffering and going to jail and so on?" I say no.

'You have to say it was worth it. The struggle is ongoing and it's evolving. The first problem is to get rid of the current administration in Washington. Then I'm hopeful that the remaining boundaries will come down.'

5

EXTREMES

*Glimpses of America's rich and poor: the homeless and the
hopeless; the shop for the top; a theory of masochism.*

Not so long ago in America there was a craze for what were called
'panhandler jokes'. The idea was to think of clever variations on
conversations with people seeking money in the street. The basic joke
went something like: 'Buddy, how about a dime for a cup of coffee?'
'No thanks, I prefer tea.'

I asked a sample of Americans at a Christmas party if they could
remember any others, and, with much stretching of memories, they
came up with these:

'Mister, could you spare five dollars for a cup of coffee?' 'Five
dollars for coffee? That's ridiculous.' 'Can I help it if I'm a big
tipper?'

'Lady, please help me, I haven't eaten for two days.' 'Goodness, I
wish I had your willpower.'

'Mister, could you give me a quarter for a cup of coffee?' 'Here's 75
cents, buy yourself three cups.' 'Oh no thanks, I wouldn't sleep a
wink.'

'Sir, I haven't eaten in three days. Could you let me have one cent?'
'What can you do with one cent?' 'I'm anxious to weigh myself.'

Those jokes originated in the 1930s, when the Depression had
thrown hundreds of thousands of Americans out of work. The word
'panhandler' was the euphemism in a society that couldn't admit it had
beggars. The jokes were a way of making light of a situation that
everyone knew was unusual and temporary.

Nowadays, the streets of New York are full of beggars again. Outside the department stores on Fifth Avenue, Christmas shoppers in fur coats stride past ragged figures holding signs that say 'Please help me. No job'. As I walk from the subway station to my apartment each evening, thin men and women thrust hands out at me every half block or so. They mumble or shout, and the ones I can understand use all the traditional lines – 'A quarter for a cup of coffee?', 'I haven't eaten in two days', 'Can you spare some change for food?'.   But nobody tells panhandler jokes these days. This time around, the situation is embarrassingly permanent.

The richest city in the world tolerates within it some of the worst poverty in the world. It is estimated that 30,000 New Yorkers currently have no home or even temporary accommodation. You see them sleeping in subway stations, on the benches in Grand Central Station, in cardboard packing cases in doorways. During the day they wander the streets and beg. At night, as the temperature drops below zero, some of them die.

The problem is not confined to New York. It is estimated that Los Angeles has 30,000 homeless (with only 5,000 beds available in shelters and welfare hotels). Chicago estimates its homeless population as 25,000. But the Reagan administration has been gradually reducing the funds it provides to the cities for homeless accommodation, arguing that the state governments, not the federal government, should take on the responsibility of housing the poor. The state governments say they have no money.

New York City Council has started using old hotels in central Manhattan as emergency accommodation. About 50 establishments with names like The Latham, The Martinique and the Prince George, which have gone from 20s grandeur to 80s squalor, now house 5,000 families and 10,000 individuals. This exercise is massively expensive, because, in the best capitalist traditions, the council pays the hotel owners the normal rate for the rooms. Sheltering one homeless family can cost the council $30,000 a year.

A recent survey of the people in the welfare hotels showed that the vast majority were black or Hispanic. The average age was 35. Among the single adults, one-quarter were 'chronically mentally ill'. Among the families, most consisted of three children and a single mother who had never had a home of her own. Of the single males, more than half were Vietnam veterans. The average length of stay was 233 days.

Some of those in the welfare hotels must wonder if they'd be better off in the streets. Drug dealing is rife in the corridors. Late in 1986, two security guards hired to patrol welfare hotels were charged with stabbing two homeless men to death.

Because the hotels are badly maintained and overcrowded, the residents often get injured. Four children were burned to death in their room at the Brooklyn Arms Hotel in July, 1986. A month later, in the same hotel, an 18-year-old youth fell to his death in an elevator shaft.

Efforts by the city to expand and improve accommodation for the homeless seem to have bogged down in legal action. Showing a wonderful Christmas spirit, several community groups have started a lawsuit to stop the council from moving homeless people into their areas, because 'they hang around and commit crimes and harm the neighbourhood'.

Robert Hayes, counsel for a group called Coalition For the Homeless, says the lawsuit is simply a case of real estate interests trying to keep property values high. 'Our view is that the hotels are disgraceful places to put mothers and children,' Hayes says. 'But these families will be more severely damaged if these hotels are taken from them before there are other alternatives.'

The city council is suing the federal government for the restoration of food grants for the homeless. The Reagan administration has reduced its food benefits to anyone living in a welfare hotel, claiming that the room rental paid by the city is part of the homeless person's income. In 1986, a destitute family of four received $143 a month from the federal government, in 1987, a family of four living in a welfare hotel received $62 a month for food.

Meanwhile, Ed Koch, mayor of New York, has started a program of rounding up homeless people who appear to be mentally ill, and putting them in hospitals. He says the problem of homelessness partly arises from a new attitude to mental illness that became fashionable in the 1970s. Thousands of people who were judged to be no danger to themselves or others were released from mental hospitals, on the theory that they would be better off rejoining the community and receiving their treatment in day clinics. Many of them never re-appeared for treatment, but were incapable of working.

Koch now wants to put the worst cases back in hospitals. The New York Civil Liberties Union is fighting this in court, arguing that people are entitled to live on the streets if they want to, and that Koch is purely concerned with a cosmetic exercise of removing beggars from the sight of wealthier citizens.

Mayor Koch has also proposed a grand scheme to eliminate the need for welfare hotels and solve the homeless problem by 1990. He wants to spend $100 million building four huge shelters on vacant lots in each of New York's five boroughs.

As soon as Koch announced the details of the scheme, the presidents of all five boroughs rejected it. Two borough presidents refused even to negotiate about having homeless shelters in their areas. The other three said they wanted to come up with alternatives, and clearly intend to take a very long time about it.

No-one is saying it, but the subtext in all this is clear – homeless people don't vote, while middle class homeowners do. No politician is going to get re-elected by being kind to panhandlers. Those on the street in the world's richest city can look forward to many more cold Christmases.

'These men don't NEED anything'

On the afternoon I visited the Bijan department store for men, number 699 Fifth Avenue, New York, there'd been only two customers all day. The day before, there'd been no customers at all.

Jeffrey Starr, who runs Bijan's New York store, wasn't panicking. He knows that when a customer does come in (by appointment only), the chances are he'll spend about three hours and at least $20,000.

For that money, he'll have picked up a couple of shirts (silk at $550 each, or cotton at $425 each, with the Bijan name on the buttons) and a raincoat (silk, lined with mink, $19,000). Or possibly a couple of suits (minimum $2,200 each) and a gold-plated .38 calibre revolver with suede handle ($10,000, including a mink pouch). Or perhaps he'd want to pay a little more to be sure of staying snug on winter nights, and choose a $98,000 chinchilla bedspread. It probably caught his eye as he entered the store, draped tastefully over the bannister of the spiral staircase, under the Baccarat crystal chandelier (not for sale).

'To be my customer, you must earn $100,000 a month,' says the man who created all this, Bijan Pakdad, born in Iran 48 years ago, trained in engineering in Germany and fashion in Italy, now owner of two men's stores in America which earn $40 million a year.

Bijan's New York manager, Jeffrey Starr, tends to be rather less flamboyant in his comments than his master, but will allow that Bijan's 'showrooms', in Los Angeles and New York, are the most expensive men's stores in the world. 'The people who come here, because they're generally rich, powerful, well known, don't NEED anything,' he says. 'They already have everything. But they come here because they want the quality, the attention to detail, the service. They want Bijan's perfectionism.'

Dr Starr (he likes to be called Doctor because he used to be an eye specialist before he accepted Bijan's offer to go into trade) says Bijan has 16,000 regular clients, and needs no more – 'Either they come to him or Bijan flies to them in his private jet,' Starr explains.

These regular clients include Ronald Reagan (there's an auto-graphed photo of him in the New York store, wearing a jeans outfit designed by Bijan), Frank Sinatra, Henry Kissinger, Cary Grant, Julio Iglesias, most of the heads of the royal families in the Arab states, and a host of third world dictators, past and present.

'Bijan had the pleasure of making many suits for President Jean-Claude Duvalier of Haiti,' says Starr, demonstrating the store's scrupu-lous aloofness from political concerns. Bijan emphasises his bi-partisan approach: 'I am watching television and I see Mr Reagan and Mr Mondale debating. One says: "This policy of yours is bad". Then the other says, "No, yours is bad". I watch them and suddenly I think: The suit at the left is Bijan, the right one is Bijan also. At least they agree on something. Ah, but this one's shirt is Bijan and this one's is not.'

The fortunes of Bijan's customers rise and fall. A couple of years ago, 20 per cent of his customers were based in Texas. Now, with the oil glut, the Texans aren't so apparent, but the Wall Street money movers have taken their place.

'Forgive me for sounding snobbish,' Starr says, 'but for the people who come here, the price is not the point. If we raise our prices because of inflation, it doesn't make any difference. No-one has ever told us something is too much.'

This generous attitude on the part of his customers has made Bijan Pakdad, in his own words, 'very, very rich'. 'My customers know how to live,' says Bijan. 'Me too. I live royally. I enjoy myself. I have a collection of cars. I love cars. I have my own planes. I have homes in Beverly Hills. I have homes in Italy. I have a very beautiful penthouse in New York.'

But Starr points out firmly that Bijan's personal flamboyance – some might say it borders on the vulgar – is not reflected in his clothing designs. 'He really is the essence of sensitivity,' Starr says. 'I've never seen anyone so fastidious and right on when it comes to colour, or scale, or sense of proportion or balance.'

I cautiously raised the possibility that some of the clients might buy Bijan clothes purely because they are the most expensive, as a display of their wealth, and might be putting themselves at risk of robbery. Starr disagreed.

'Bijan's clothing has a very quiet, understated elegance,' he said. 'The items that we have don't really telegraph the quality to people who aren't also well dressed. Your average burglar or mugger is not really conscious of quality.

'Bijan's jewellery, the chains, are designed to be worn under your shirt. There's a ring with diamonds on the inside. Our people just want the inner comfort of knowing they have the best.'

But just in case this theory isn't sufficient protection, Bijan will happily put bulletproof lining into a customer's overcoat at no extra charge. And a customer can also protect himself in style with the Bijan gold-plated revolver. 'Bijan designed the gun in collaboration with Colt, as a tribute to the United States,' Starr says. 'He is very proud of the United States. It's given him the opportunity to be as successful as he has since he started here 15 years ago. He wanted to make something that was truly American. He made a limited edition of 200 pieces, each numbered and signed. We've sold 186 of them at $10,000 each.'

Having succeeded with guns, suits, shirts, ties, shoes, socks (the store's cheapest item at $55 each), and luggage (a set of five crocodile skin cases costs $75,000), Bijan is now moving into designing perfumes.

He started with a spicy fragrance for men, at $1,500 for 6 ounces in a 'very masculine' Baccarat crystal container. Now Starr says he is excited to announce that there will be a fragrance for women, and it will be the first Bijan product to be sold outside his own stores.

'People have asked Bijan for a long time,"Can we have a bite of your apple without paying so much money",' Starr says. 'With the clothes we have always said no, because we could not supply in large numbers and maintain the quality. But with this new fragrance, we will be able to sell the products in a limited number of upscale speciality stores throughout the world. I'm sure Australia will be included in that.'

The cost of the perfume will be a mere $90 an ounce. It means, Bijan says, that for the first time, he will be able to sell something to people who have 'taste but no money'.

Monetary madness

You have to pity the rich of America. Apparently many of them are wracked by neurosis, and the neurosis is caused by having money which they didn't earn. The syndrome is nicknamed 'affluenza'.

Naturally, it has given rise to a new speciality within the field of psychiatry. According to Dr John Levy, director of the C. G. Jung Institute in San Francisco, 'affluenza' has these symptoms: lack of motivation and self-discipline; suspiciousness (finding it hard to believe people like you for yourself); boredom (because you've done it all, and any activity seems pointless); guilt and low self-esteem.

Another of the pioneers in treatment of the rich, Dr Dennis Pearne of Watertown, Massachusetts, says his patients suffer chronic depression. 'They're edgy, have trouble sleeping, can't eat, and they don't know why,' he says. 'It's hard for people to imagine that conflict comes from anything to do with money.'

Pearne says his clients often act out their confusion in ways which only confirm society's stereotypes of the idle rich. He treated one man who kept trying to throw away his inheritance by manic spending on trivialities. The man said that this gave him 'a thrill, a rush in the instant of making the purchase, the instant when the money changed hands, a very powerful feeling, almost like a sexual orgasm'.

In New York I've noticed what must be another major symptom of affluenza: an outbreak of masochism among the monied classes. Presumably it is caused by guilt. How else can one explain the terrible way Manhattan's monied classes treat themselves? The older rich patronise restaurants and clubs that offer them disgusting food and supercilious service. The younger rich queue up outside nightclubs and discos where there's every chance they'll be refused admittance on the whim of the doorman. 'Treat me like dirt,' their subconscious minds seem to be saying. 'I must be punished because I don't deserve my wealth.'

Americans like to believe they live in a classless, equal opportunity society. The homeless people lying in the streets of the big cities are an all too obvious contradiction of that. As they scurry from their stretched limousines into their high security apartment blocks, the rich may not see many of the homeless, but they know they exist. They know that one per cent of Americans own half the country's wealth. For some, that means guilt.

It used to be that the rich could be sure of getting a rotten meal at an establishment called The 21 Club, where they would be made to wait half an hour for a table, even when the place was empty, and be served glutinous concoctions like 'chicken hash a la creme' ($21), and 'linguine with white clam sauce' ($25).

But in mid-1987, a new chef arrived at 21 and dared to improve the food, so the regulars were forced to flee to another establishment, named Mortimer's, on the ritzy Upper East Side. When I went there, in the spirit of journalistic investigation, I joined a packed house of tweedily dressed elderly ladies, and struggled through something called 'designer meatloaf', which tasted like wet cardboard. Vegetables cost extra, and only 'snap peas' were available. They arrived (cold) just as I was swallowing the last mouthful of meatloaf.

But for the most exquisite masochism, you need to lunch in Manhattan's grandest retreat of the upper classes – The Metropolitan Club. This was founded in 1890 by the financier J. Pierpont Morgan, and does not allow blacks, Jews or women to join. It's a magnificent mansion with sweeping staircases, chandeliers, murals and tapestries. In the dining room, its members and innocent guests like me get even worse food than at Mortimer's, and even surlier service. And how happily the Metropolitan's members pay their dues of $3,000 a year.

Meanwhile their children, along with the upwardly mobile new money cocaine sniffers from Wall Street, enjoy a different form of self-abuse. They line up outside dingy semi-renovated warehouses filled with the sound of monotonous disco music, and anticipate the thrill of being humiliated by a doorman who earns a tenth of their salary. The doorman will let some in and refuse others. He will not explain why. If you're a rock star or a film star, your chances are good. But simply having money is no help at all.

The places the young rich want so desperately to enter (or, if my theory is right, want so desperately to be rejected by) change every three months or so. For a while, the queues were outside a place called Nell's, which is named after and managed by an Australian woman whose only identifiable claim to fame is that she had a bit part in the film of *The Rocky Horror Show*. But at other times during 1987 the scene has been at The Tunnel, a high tech disco, and a place called 1018, which describes itself as 'a cha-cha parlour'.

It's tough keeping up with the club of the moment. But this gives a rich kid an added opportunity for agony – what if you got admitted to a nightclub, and then learned that you'd picked the wrong one, and THIS month's hot spot was actually around the corner? How embarrassing.

Of course, not all the children of America's top families exorcise their guilt by being social butterflies. A group of more serious young rich folk have joined together in an organisation called the Haymarket People's Fund. Its founder, George Pillsbury (heir to one of America's biggest baking companies), describes Haymarket as 'a therapy group for people with inherited wealth'. The organisation runs seminars on how to keep your money and your honour, and how to spend responsibly.

Haymarket is unashamedly left wing in the causes it supports – unions, anti-nuclear activists, ecology watchdogs, consumer protection. Another Pillsbury heir, David Becker, who gives about $100,000 a year to the Haymarket Fund, happily admits that a lot of its activities work towards the elimination of the economic system which produced the wealth of its members.

'This is an important part of my adjusting to my money,' he says. 'I grew up in the '60s, when there was a lot of guilt tripping on the part of people I went to school with about "bad corporate money". Now in a lot of ways, I'm proud of what I am. I'm glad my money comes from cake mixes and not napalm. But still, as cousin George says, we're rich because people in the flour mills weren't paid enough.'

Haymarket's members are not only recipients of inherited wealth.

'Even people who make their own money can be confused by its power,' says George Pillsbury. 'They've thought a lot about how to go about earning it, but very little about how to handle it once they've got it. Haymarket helps people understand how money works, how to do something positive about it.'

Most of Haymarket's activities and its membership are secret, because the rich kids who support it don't want to be accused of charity for self-aggrandisement or tax avoidance. That charge could easily be made against their parents and grandparents.

America has more than 25,000 charitable foundations set up by individuals and companies since the steel magnate Andrew Carnegie first thought of the idea in 1900. Most are named after their creators – the biggest are the Hughes Institute, the Ford Foundation, the Getty Trust, the Kellogg Trust, the Macarthur Foundation and the Rockefeller Foundation. All get big tax concessions.

America's foundations have assets totalling $100 billion, and give away $6 billion a year to causes ranging from poetry-publishing to the Nicaraguan contras. But somehow with all this private money being given away, America's city streets are still lined with beggars. So off go the rich to Mortimer's.

6

ENTHUSIASTS

*An assortment of passionate Americans: the communist,
the hot dog scholar; the rock crusader; the collector of
failed products; the minstrel of Manhattan; Ladies Against
Women.*

Carole Marks, assistant of the general secretary of the Communist Party of the United States of America, was telling me what America will be like when her party is elected to power. It was very reassuring.

'A lot of the structures would be just the same,' said Ms Marks (yes, she does get a lot of jokes about her name). 'You would still have the Republicans and the Democrats, at least initially, but they would be in the minority in congress. There would still be the Bill of Rights and the Constitution. The American people would never give those up. The main difference would be that the opposite class would be in power.'

I couldn't help asking what, in retrospect, seems a silly question – 'Would there still be baseball?' Ms Marks smiled. 'Of course there would,' she said. 'Nothing like that would change. Why would we want to lose anything from such a rich culture?

'People really do have strange ideas about us. They're always asking things like "Would you take away my bank account?" "Would I have to give up my house?"

'It has nothing to do with personal property. It simply means that the resources and wealth of the nation, such as the factories, the land, would not be privately owned. Boats, cars, savings accounts, homes, that's all personal property, that cannot be touched. People are flabbergasted when I tell them that.'

At the moment, Ms Marks says, the Communist Party USA has 28,000 card-carrying members, plus the active support of another million people who have their own reasons for not joining up officially. The party is about to start a mass membership drive, to take advantage of what it sees as public disillusionment with capitalism under Ronald Reagan.

Ms Marks isn't going to predict a date when the American people will elect a communist government, but she is sure it is inevitable. In the meantime, 150 paid party officials like her work industriously from their national headquarters on West 23rd Street, New York. The slightly dilapidated 10 storey edifice also houses the party's newspaper, called *The People's Daily World*, the Young Communist League, and the school of Marxist Studies.

Ms Marks says proudly that the party owns the building, and has been offered $5 million for it. It won't sell. Apart from the sentimental attachment, moving headquarters would make life difficult for the FBI, which has a permanent post in the Chelsea Hotel across the road, from which it takes photos of people entering and leaving the communist offices.

The US Communist party has never been illegal in its 68-year history, but it has had its difficulties with the authorities. During the 1950s, the party chairman, Henry Winston, and the general secretary, Gus Hall, each spent 8 years in jail on a charge of 'conspiring to teach the overthrow of the US government'. Nowadays, Ms Marks says, life in the Communist party is much more pleasant. The FBI takes photos and bugs the phones, but there's no direct harassment. In fact, working for the Communist party is the most exciting job Ms Marks can imagine. 'It's really a great life,' she says. 'It has a sense of purpose. You're constantly involved with movements to create change. We're on TV and radio shows. And we travel. We go all over the world all the time, as invited guests at all kinds of international peace meetings.'

As she spoke, I decided Carole Marks was the most optimistic human being I'd ever met. She is a motherly lady in her 40s, who came to communism from civil rights and peace movements she joined in the 1960s. 'In those movements, it seemed to me that we would make an advance in one area and then be set back in another,' she says. 'Nothing was coming together. Then I went to the Soviet Union, and I was amazed. I saw no poverty to the extreme that it exists here. Health care, housing, education, child care, all these things are managed so well.

'And later I heard Gus Hall speaking, and that was it. It just so happened that the first internal party publication I saw had on the back of it "Secretary needed in the headquarters of the Communist Party" and I got that job 13 years ago.'

Ms Marks greatest achievement has been signing up her 80-year-old mother as a party member. 'I come from a Jewish working class family,' she says. 'My father was union, but conservative. He died unable to face the fact that I had joined the party. My mother read the stuff, and she listened to the speakers, and she came around. She said she was reluctant because she didn't know if she could contribute anything. She will, she'll do letters to the editor, she'll help us with mailings.'

Ms Marks says that while Gus Hall does stand for the US presidential elections every four years (he got 36,386 votes in 1984, compared to Ronald Reagan's 54,418,689) the party's main work is on a small scale. It runs its own candidates in some local elections ('we raise the issues, and we start to convince people that we are a viable alternative'), it campaigns against 'ultra-right Reaganite' candidates in other elections, and it consults with unions and peace groups.

'Our role amongst the unions and the movements is to propose ideas that are a bit ahead of what is happening,' she says. 'So we are proposing now a law that would prevent the corporations from just closing down factories and moving to another country like Korea. This might lead on eventually to nationalising the factories under the control of the workers and the local community.'

I asked if unions were wary of talking to known communists, given the party's bad image in America over the years. 'There is some of that, but the unions are in a position where they need new solutions,' Ms Marks said.

'They don't advertise it, but they do talk to us. Now more than ever, people feel they are not risking much by getting help from us, because they see that the country is in trouble, with the crisis in the presidency, the economic situation, homelessness and hunger, the farming collapse. People are looking for more basic solutions.'

I asked another silly question – do you get any money from the Soviet Union? Ms Marks smiled patiently again. 'No, I wish we did, but there is no Moscow gold,' she said. 'We are not representatives of the Soviet Union in any way. We often defend the Soviet Union, because we believe in a lot of the things they are doing, but our role is to be the party that represents the working people of America.

'Communism will come to America when the majority of the American people, the working people, not the wealthy class of course, when they decide that it is a viable alternative. And we think America has never been more ripe for a socialist revolution than it is now.'

Wet, salty, and democratic

'The bun is *supposed* to get mushy,' said the greatest living expert on the history, sociology and symbolism of the hot dog. 'Your thumb is *supposed* to go into it.'

Bruce Kraig, lecturer in history at Roosevelt University, was rejecting my complaint that the roll was dissolving in my fingers. If the roll had stayed firm, this would have been clear evidence that I did not have a white Rosen Bun, which is the essential accompaniment to the Vienna all beef frankfurter. And then Kraig would have failed in his duty to demonstrate the full hot dog experience.

It is appropriate that Bruce Kraig, as world authority on the hot dog, lives in Chicago. Chicago is always described as 'the most American city in America', and the hot dog is America's best known symbol.

Stroll around the streets of Chicago and you see that McDonald's wouldn't stand a chance. There are sleek shiny doggeries everywhere, offering not just the basic beef frankfurt in a roll, but porky and garlicky variations, and an avalanche of additives that include relish, mustard, ketchup, onions, tomato, cucumber, pickles and peppers. According to Kraig, Chicagoans normally add all of these at once. That's what I did, and was rewarded with a mushy bun, sticky fingers and indigestion.

The most serious of the Chicago hot dog chains is Irving's which has signs outside its stores declaring its products are 'for Red Hot lovers'. The dogs come in paper bags displaying in Olde English lettering Irving's Creed:

'To perpetuate the red hot as the premier American delicacy by serving Vienna, the highest quality pure beef product in a natural casing, tastefully garnished and carefully seasoned, all of which when snugly embedded in a deliciously warm poppy seed bun makes an Irving's dog truly man's best friend. Irving's, the hot dog store with a whole lot more.'

Bruce Kraig is interested in hot dogs because of what they tell him about his countrymen. Hot dogs are the quintessence of how Ameri-

cans want food to be: wet, salty, chewy, mass-produced and able to be eaten fast. They have been so successfully marketed over the years in association with baseball, stars and stripes, democracy, and mother-hood, that nowadays saying you don't like hot dogs amounts to an admission of communism.

Kraig traces the first appearance of the hot dog in America to a German immigrant named Charles Feltman, who in 1871 was selling sausages in milk rolls with sauerkraut from a pushcart in Coney Island, New York. Of course the German sausage, made from minced offcuts of meat, has been around since the 14th century, but Feltman seems to have been the first to turn it into fast food. It's likely he used pork or veal in his sausages, but as the years rolled on, the American preference for beef asserted itself.

At first they were known as 'red hots', probably because of the red colouring of the paprika commonly used in them. The term 'dog' seems to have come from their similarity to dachsunds, another German import that became familiar to Americans in the 20th century.

Hot dogs were standard fare at baseball parks by the late 1890s, and production moved from the homes and shops of German and Polish immigrants to vast factories. Chicago became the hot dog capital because it was the nation's meat packing centre, where scraps and offal were plentiful.

Kraig argues that the hot dog rapidly became more than fast food. The food factories made it part of America's mythology. For millions of immigrants it symbolised egalitarianism – rich and poor alike watched baseball and gulped frankfurts. The big manufacturers played on this in their advertising . . . Eat hot dogs and prove your patriotism.

That's why the hot dog tastes bland, says Kraig. It is industrial food for the masses. There must be no possibility that anyone could dislike it, and maximum opportunity for additions according to individual taste.

In Boston, they serve hot dogs with baked beans in tomato sauce laced with molasses. In the south, hot dogs are dipped in corn batter and fried. People in the southwest smear them with chili. In Kansas they add cheese. New Yorkers prefer them with sauerkraut. And Chicagoans add everything they can get their hands on.

It doesn't do to inquire too closely into the ingredients of the modern American frankfurt, but Kraig offers this list: ground beef or pork (or a mixture); fat (no more than 30 per cent if the maker is obeying the law); sugar or sweet corn syrup; black pepper; paprika; spices like nutmeg, mace, or coriander; and salt (about two per cent of the whole mixture).

I asked Bruce Kraig, whose speciality is early European history, what caused him to study the history and philosophy of the hot dog. He said he'd always been a glutton, and over the past 10 years he'd begun to see how attitudes to food reveal a great deal about a culture, whether ancient or modern. Yes, but why the hot dog? Kraig's answer, now I reflect on it, doesn't quite follow along logically, but this is what he said:

'A couple of years ago, during the Ethiopian food crisis, I wrote an article for a local newspaper on eating dogs to save food. I mean real dogs. I said it was a modest proposal, with all due regard to Jonathan Swift (who wrote a satirical paper in 1729 suggesting that the children of the poor people be used as food for the rich).

'But of course Americans have never read anything, so they took it seriously. They were hysterical. I got phone calls and hate letters from all over the country. You could kill your kid, eat your kid, that would be fine, but say anything about eating dogs and you're in trouble.

'So anyway, then I gave a paper at the Symposium on Food at Oxford in 1985 on western taboos about eating dogs. And when I was planning a paper for the 1987 Oxford Symposium, all this kind of naturally led to research on hot dogs. It turned out to be a real piece of American history, an indicator of American social sensibilities. And I've hardly started yet.'

Raped in demonic lust

Tipper Gore thinks she is the most misunderstood woman in the history of music. She wants it to be known that she LIKES rock and roll. She also likes sex. Goddammit, she has even smoked marijuana. And she is a passionate believer in freedom of speech.

Nevertheless she finds herself constantly portrayed in the US media as a stormtrooper of puritanism, because there's one thing Tipper Gore wants to stop: the exploitation of children by music that promotes rape, violence, drug-taking and suicide. That's why she helped found an organisation called Parents' Music Resource Centre, ran a campaign to persuade record companies to print warnings on the covers of 'rock porn' albums, and has just published a book called *Raising PG Kids in an X-rated Society*.

She says that parents buying albums for their children need to know that the band Kiss is singing 'When I go through her it's just like a hot knife through butter'; that Slayer is singing 'I feel the urge, the growing need, to fuck this sinful corpse. My task's complete, the bitch's soul lies raped in demonic lust'; and that Ozzy Osbourne is singing 'Suicide is the only way out. Don't you know what it's really about?'

Her campaign provoked the rage of many people in the music industry. The singer-composer Frank Zappa labelled her a 'cultural terrorist'. The singer Wendy O. Williams said she was a frustrated housewife. *Hustler* magazine voted her 'Asshole of the month'.

And now she's learning another of the penalties of the activist. Her husband, Senator Albert Gore of Tennessee, was campaigning to become the Democrat Party's candidate for President of the United States. He is a liberal on social issues, but he found great difficulty getting donations from the entertainment industry because his wife is perceived as a puritan.

Mary Elizabeth Gore, better known as Tipper, is 38. As a pretty blonde psychology student at Peabody College, Nashville, back in the 1960s she enjoyed rock music at its most exciting and experimental. She knows it's always been a raunchy medium, associated with adolescent rebellion. In fact, the term 'rock and roll' is a black euphemism for intercourse. When Chuck Berry sang 'We were reeling and rocking, rolling till the break of dawn', he didn't mean dancing. And when he sang about *My Dingaling*, he didn't mean his bicycle bell.

But when Gore bought Prince's album *Purple Rain* at the request of her 11-year-old daughter in 1984, she discovered that rock music has changed a lot. And the more she listened to the new music, particularly the 'heavy metal' style that finds its main audience among 13-year-old boys, the more alarmed she became. It wasn't the sex references that worried her so much, but the sadism that so often seemed to be linked with them.

'Today's teenagers are being told to rebel in a society that doesn't seem to react at all to the outrageous things that are happening, they must push the limits further,' she says. 'It's a quantum leap from the Beatles' *I Want To Hold Your Hand* to Prince singing "If you get tired of masturbating, if you like I'll jack you off." It's a long way from the Rolling Stones' *Let's Spend The Night Together*, which drew protests in its day, to Sheena Easton's *Sugar Walls* and "You can't fight passion when passion is hot, temperatures rise inside my sugar walls."

'Where Elvis sang *Little Sister* about his attraction to his girlfriend's younger sister, Prince now sings *Sister*: "My sister never made love to anyone else but me, incest is everything it's said to be."'

Gore says that parents often buy rock records for young children or give them tickets to concerts without knowing what they will hear and see. She wants to educate parents to think about the possible influence of some lyrics.

She wants to pressure record companies to introduce some sort of rating system similar to what exists in the film industry, and print rock lyrics on the album covers, or at least use stickers saying 'Explicit lyrics – parental guidance advisory'. She wants concert promoters to give warnings about sex and violence on stage in their advertisements for performances by certain bands.

'We are trying to create a mechanism for choice,' she says. 'Many people have tried to characterise that as censorship but we have submitted that it absolutely is not censorship.

'It is trying to create a system by which people can make choices in the marketplace. As consumers, we have that kind of information with movies, television programming, and the only entertainment medium where any kind of guidance is lacking is music.

'That was never necessary before. We've always had some outrageous songs, but we've never had the proliferation of artists selling some songs and video images that include explicit sex and very graphic violence to a younger and younger audience. We've never had a situation before where a band like Judas Priest can sell two million copies of an album with a song about forcing oral sex at gunpoint.

'We're saying the songs can still exist, the artist has a right to speak his mind, but parents have a right to know when a song could contain references that could be inappropriate to younger children.'

One particular concern is a spate of songs apparently promoting suicide. Gore says 13 teenagers commit suicide every day in the US, and there are 400,000 suicide attempts every year.

'All the reasons that a young person will commit suicide are extremely complex,' she says. 'I'm not saying that they will listen to a song and commit suicide. But given the evidence that among the young, suicide increases after publicity and television shows about suicide, should we not ask the same question about rock musicians who use suicide in their imagery, on their album covers, in their lyrics?

'These are disturbing contributing influences, and what I'm trying to say is that most parents, most educators, have not been aware that these subjects are being dealt with in the music.'

In search of failure

Every week in the USA, 100 new products come on the market. And when they do, Robert McMath is there to grab them.

About 20 of those 100 products will be successful. The other 80 will hang around for a while, gather dust on the supermarket shelves, and be forgotten. By everyone but Robert McMath. He will give them immortality, by placing them on the shelves of his Museum of Marketing in the town of Naples, New York. They will join 75,000 other boxes, bottles, cans, jars, and tubes that Robert McMath has chosen to demonstrate the ingenuity and the insanity of American industry.

McMath is the ultimate shopper. He has spent most of his waking hours during the last 18 years sniffing round supermarkets. According to his wife Jean, it's an obsession which gives him no rest . . . 'We go on vacation to Florida and he is out shopping more than he is around enjoying himself and relaxing. And invariably I get stuck labelling, packing – all those fun things.'

But spying out new products isn't just a passion for Robert McMath. It's also his business. He is chairman of an organisation called Marketing Intelligence Service, which numbers among its 1,000 clients some of America's biggest makers of petfoods, detergents, cereals, drinks, shampoos, cosmetics, and snacks.

If one of those clients wants to find out whether a competitor is secretly test-marketing a new product, McMath will know. He'll have found it himself, or he'll have heard about it from one of his 250 field agents across the nation. Or if one of those clients thinks he's made a marketing breakthrough, but wonders if it's been done before, McMath will take a stroll through his museum and pull out four or five packages that might offer a lesson.

The clients also receive an avalanche of printed insights derived from Robert McMath's training in business administration, and 30 years' experience in market research. Marketing Intelligence Service publishes a weekly newsletter called *Product Alert*, which analyses the latest discoveries of McMath's spies within America. It publishes a fortnightly *International Product Alert*, about unusual overseas creations. And it publishes monthly reports on trends within particular sections of the supermarket business.

When he's not shopping, McMath is musing on the psychology of consumers and of manufacturers. Every failure has as much to teach as every success. A stroll through his museum leaves the visitor flabbergasted at the billions that have been wasted by American marketers who seem to have everything but common sense.

What, for example, could have possessed a company called American Kitchen Foods Inc to release a colourful package labelled *I Hate Peas* – 'The new way to get vegetable goodness. Combines pea goodness and potato flavour in nutritious new French fry form. Try also *I Hate Corn*, *I Hate Carrots*, *I Hate Green Beans*, *I Hate Spinach* and *I Hate Beets*.'

McMath explains that the strategy of *I Hate Peas* was to appeal to parents who feared their children's fussy tastes might prevent them from getting a balanced diet. But if kids hate peas (or beans or corn or carrots or beetroot) when they're shaped like peas (or beans or corn or carrots or beetroot), they continue to hate them when they are shaped like chips. The owner of American Kitchen Foods Inc nearly went bankrupt on that great idea, and he has now left the packaged food industry.

Elsewhere in the great failures section of the museum, you find hair shampoos called *A Touch of Yoghurt* and *Gimme Cucumber*. McMath says they were attempts to cash in on the success of herbal shampoos, but they went too far. 'The name is really the problem,' he says. 'People will take all sorts of additives in hair shampoo. We now have tofu shampoo and even placenta shampoo. But you can't confront people with something that sounds ridiculous. Maybe if they had called them *A Touch of Elegance (with yoghurt)* or *A Touch of Elegance (with cucumber)*, they'd have a success.'

So the first rule of successful marketing is: Get your name right. But silly names aren't the only reason products flop. There's also the issue of whether the consumer sees any point to the concept. One shelf displays an array of failed beverages, including *Wallaby Squash*, *Panda Punch*, *Okeechobee Orange Pokem* and '*Afrokola – the Soul drink*' (do blacks feel they are so different from whites that they need their own cola? Apparently not).

The paragon of failed pet products is *Baker Tom's Baked Cat Food* – 'the only cat food that is actually baked in an oven the same way you bake at home'. Apparently Americans will buy tonnes of tins of something called *Catviar*, responding to the temptation to treat their pet luxuriously, but they stop short at the idea that catfood is better if cooked.

McMath says the consumer must be able to perceive a need for a new product, and it must strike a 'chord of familiarity'. That is why, he says *pavlova* and *Vegemite* have never taken off in the US. Americans have no tradition of desserts containing meringue and no tradition of putting savoury spreads on toast. *Vegemite*, despite an advertising campaign using the Men At Work song *Land Down Under*, was 'too foreign tasting'.

But sometimes a 'chord of familiarity' can be misleading, and a product ends up driving consumers into a rage. This was the case with *Wine and Dine Dinners*, in a display pack with their own little bottle of red or white wine. The problem was that the buyers thought the wine was for drinking with the meal. It wasn't. The wine was seasoned and salted, and was supposed to be added to the food as it was being cooked. After they spat out the wine and rinsed their mouths, consumers were left with a lifelong grudge against the food company.

Marketers who misjudge the buyer's psychology can lose millions. One shelf of the McMath museum is devoted to a range of 36 food products sold under the general name *New Cookery*. 'We've heard estimates that Nestlés spent more than $200 million developing the *New Cookery* line,' McMath says. 'It was supposed to be at the leading edge of the healthy trend – less fat, less sugar, less salt.

'Well, *New Cookery* turned out to be the wrong name. It connotes work. And the labels were rather weak looking. And it was too expensive. All the competitors met the challenge by lowering their prices, and people weren't convinced enough of the health benefits to pay more. *New Cookery* was taken off the market after it was tested in three places.'

On the shelf adjoining *New Cookery* is another object lesson in misjudged psychology – a row of glass jars labelled *Singles*. They contain various foods in semi-liquid form, designed to be heated in boiling water and eaten with a teaspoon. They are aimed at busy young adults who don't have time to prepare elaborate meals.

McMath won't talk about *Singles* because the makers, Edgell-Gerber, have complained that he has used them too often as examples of failure (the Edgell-Gerber people are, after all, paying clients). But it's easy to see the problem. What young adult wants to be seen in a supermarket queue with a product that not only advertises his or her unmarried status, but which also looks like babyfood?

Embarrassment in the checkout line is one of the key factors in product failure, and also an occupational hazard for Robert McMath, professional shopper. 'One product category that's always been hard to market is haemorrhoid treatments, because when you're waiting to buy them, everyone on the line, and the clerk, is going to know you've got a problem,' he says.

'When *Preparation H* put out a new treatment in the form of pads, I had to go to a supermarket and buy two dozen packages as samples for clients, and I was as embarrassed as hell. I loudly proclaimed to everybody that I was in market research.'

McMath says one of the great breakthroughs in the haemorrhoid treatment business has been a recent product advertised as being for sunburn and mosquito bites, as well as for haemorrhoids – 'so people can buy it without being typecast as having a problem'.

From all this, Robert McMath has formulated the basic rules of product success – a good name, good packaging, a benefit the consumer can perceive, plausible claims, no potential for embarrassment, and a 'chord of familiarity'. As we strolled through the museum, I asked him to nominate his favourite successes.

'I'd have to start with *Ivory Soap*,' he said. 'It has been around for 100 years, almost unchanged, and still sells on purity and simplicity. Two years ago Procter and Gamble extended into *Ivory Shampoo*, and it became the leading hair shampoo, because they kept it clean and simple. They've also gone into liquid soap with great success.'

Next he nominated *Prego Spaghetti Sauce*, and admitted that he had predicted wrongly when it first came out. 'I said, "Who needs another spaghetti sauce?" and I thought the name confused people. But Campbell's had discovered there were thousands of people making their own spaghetti sauce from scratch. They came out with a much more authentic sauce than any on the market. Now it does $400 million a year.'

But McMath doubts that Campbell's current attempt to extend the *Prego* image into a new line of soups will be as successful. He says giving soup a name like *Pomodoro* causes buyers to worry that they'll get the pronunciation wrong – the embarrassment factor again.

McMath's other favourites are *Clairol Herbal Shampoo*, *Cherry Coke* and *Diet Coke* ('both great ways of extending an already successful line'); *California Cooler*, the pioneer in the wine cooler business; and *Miller Lite*, which started a light beer craze in America.

These products may be triumphs of Yankee know-how, but the shelves of the Museum of Marketing demonstrate that imitation is far more common than innovation in modern America. 'We're seeing a great growth in Me-Too products,' says McMath. 'The *California Wine Cooler* was followed by about 300 imitations and variations – champagne coolers, wine coolers with soft drink, wine coolers with fruit juice, beer coolers, higher alcohol coolers, non-alcohol coolers. Within a year of *Bailey's Irish Cream* working out how to put in fresh cream so you could keep it without refrigeration, you had 50 similar products on the market. With liquid soaps, we stopped counting at 55.'

I asked if McMath was worried about the massive waste involved in all these imitations, many of which will vanish after a few months. 'Well, that's free enterprise,' he said. 'Hope springs eternal. You can't stop companies from copying each other, trying to get a position in the market. I can't fault it. That's America, that's what we built the country on.

'Of course an awful lot of money is wasted. But it keeps people employed. And it keeps bankers happy every time someone with an idea, or even an imitation, borrows money to put it on the market, even if it fails in the end.'

Singing The City

Seated at the grand piano in the Algonquin Hotel, wearing a tuxedo with a high wing collar, Steve Ross is the embodiment of Manhattan. Not Manhattan in 1988, of course. Steve Ross symbolises a time as well as a place – maybe around 1935 – and a style of life that probably always was a fantasy.

His Manhattan is where you drop in on marvellous parties in penthouses every night, where the men wear tuxes and the women wear gowns, where you sip martinis and exchange banter with Elsa and Noel, Tallulah and Cole, Zelda and F, Dorothy, Dash and Lillian.

And there at the piano is Steve Ross, looking a bit like Fred Astaire and singing lines like:

'Get along little elevator, climb once more/To my lone shack on the fourteenth floor/Way out west on West End Avenue/When the sun's a-risin' over Central Park/I pull the blinds and it's nice and dark/Way out west on West End Avenue.

'Redskins may battle/With their tomahawks and axes/I'll join the cattle/In the big corral at Saks's/Oh the wild herd gathers when the moon is full/There's not much buffalo but lots of bull/Way out west on West End Avenue.'

Those words were written in 1937 by Lorenz Hart (part of a show which also contained *My Funny Valentine, Johnny One Note, Lady Is a*

Tramp and *Where or When*). West End Avenue was, and is, a street of fashionable apartment blocks on Manhattan's upper west side. Saks's was, and is, the city's poshest department store. Lorenz Hart was, and Steve Ross is, an obsessive about New York City.

It seems their obsession was shared by thousands of other composers and performers. More songs have been written about New York, or about the New York state of mind, than about any other city in the world. The cleverest of them were written between 1920 and 1940. And Steve Ross knows more of them than any living singer.

When he appears at the Algonquin Hotel (or in one of his annual visits to Australia), Ross won't necessarily play *Way Out West On West End Avenue*. He'll do a lot of Gershwins, Cowards, Berlins, Porters, Novellos, and Arlens that don't even mention Manhattan. But he'll have to do the anthem of the New York obsessive, the 1934 song in which Cole Porter confessed HIS feelings:

'I happen to like New York/I happen to like this town/I like the city air, I like to drink of it/The more I know New York the more I think of it/I like the sight and the sound and even the stink of it/I like to go to Battery Park/And watch those liners booming in/I often ask myself why it should be/That they should come so far from across the sea/I suppose it's because they all agree with me/They happen to like New York.'

And he won't get away without doing *I'll Take Manhattan (the Bronx and Staten Island too)* – 'The city's clamour can never spoil/The dreams of a boy and goil/We'll turn Manhattan into an isle of joy.'

Not all the New York songs Steve Ross knows are happy. There's *Subway to the Country* – 'New York City is a town too big for children/Where there's so much dirt they think the snow is grey/And you have to watch their childhood waste away/Hey, we got to find a subway to the country.' And there's *Another 100 People* – 'It's a city of strangers, some come to work, some come to play/A city of strangers, some come to stare, some want to stay.'

But then again, there's *Autumn in New York* – 'Glittering crowds and shimmering clouds in canyons of steel/They're making me feel I'm home/It's Autumn in New York that brings the promise of new love.'

And there's *Every Street's A Boulevard* – 'It's a thrill to come up from the subway/And see those Broadway lights/I think the uptown bus/Is luxury plus/When you're seeing the sights.'

This New York obsession is terribly contagious. I've started to get it myself. On visits to San Francisco and New Orleans, both wonderful cities, I've found myself missing Manhattan after a couple of days.

It seemed logical to consult Steve Ross about whether the condition is terminal. He said his obsession started at the age of 6, when he used to travel from suburban Westchester into Manhattan for piano lessons. 'I was driven down the Hudson River, and my first views of New York were of the steamships,' he said. 'That was the late '40s, perhaps the salad days of the city.'

His parents moved to Washington, and as a teenager he became a pianist with a dance band. His mother wanted him to become a priest, but music and Manhattan were in his blood. 'I got sick of reading the Arts and Leisure section of *The New York Times*, and yearning to be there, so I moved back,' he said. In New York, Ross found his voice. 'I wasn't really much of a singer, so my style developed from wanting to sing songs that nobody else knew about. Then nobody could say "Well, I like Frank Sinatra's version better". That's how I started on my path into the obscure shadows of musical theatre.'

Ross made his name in the 1970s at a nightclub called Backstage – 'they had a big white piano bar, and everybody went there – stars, producers, actors', – and then at the Algonquin Hotel. In 1984 he decided he could bear to spend some time out of New York, and started performing in other cities – 'anywhere where people care about New York'.

This meant London, Los Angeles, Rio de Janiero, and Sydney, but not Paris ('they don't need New York, they don't yearn to be here, they see themselves as the ultimate city'). 'The sort of songs I do, even if they don't mention New York, contain a New York sensibility,' says Ross. What is a New York sensibility?

'It would be a heightened kind of sophistication, not in a snobbish or effete sense, but just in an evolved sense of urban life. That's what New York represents. It's kind of the pinnacle of what America has put together, even though it's often non-American. I'm an urban person. This is The City.'

It almost sounds as if Steve Ross is taking on the role of roving ambassador for New York. 'Well yes, I don't mind helping to counteract all the negative images,' he says.

'I know a Mexican family with a few bucks who came here about five years ago, and they never left the Waldorf Hotel after 6 pm. They went out during the day, and the mother shopped on Madison Avenue, but they never went out at night, even to a show, because they were so afraid.

'I'm not going to say that you don't have to be alert and watch your purse, but my songs say, I hope, that there is a glamourous beat and a buzz to New York city that makes it worth taking the risk.

'The Amazon sure has bugs and snakes, but it is the Amazon. It's a fantastic primitive river and jungle. Well, this is a primitive river and jungle.'

The fight for unequal rights

Ladies Against Women don't like having to be out all the time campaigning against equal pay, masturbation and female suffrage. They'd rather be ironing. But as family values break down everywhere, and feministic communism stalks America, Ladies Against Women cannot refuse the call to arms.

According to Mrs Theodore William Banks, chairman of Ladies Against Women, nearly 100 chapters of the organisation have been founded across the USA since 1977. Although the Reagan years have been good to them, the ladies feel it's necessary to continue their work on a personal as well as a political level.

These days, LAW's principal weapon against moral decay takes the form of neighbourhood 'consciousness-lowering sessions', designed to recapture the hearts and minds of women who have been tempted to consider themselves the equals of men. I attended one of these sessions in a former church hall in the town of Berkeley, just north of San Francisco. It was an emotional evening. The hall was hung with LAW slogans like 'Procreation Not Recreation', 'Free Ladies From Wage Slavery', 'Make America A Man Again – Invade Abroad', 'Abolish The Environment' and 'Poverty Is SO Tasteless'.

We were frequently asked to stand and deliver chants like: 'Mommies, mommies, don't be commies. Stay at home and fold the jamies'; 'Who me? I'm no queer, I have a baby every year'; and 'What do we want? Nothing. When do we want it? Now'.

Mrs Banks, attired in a black wool frock and a white fur boa that she said came from a baby harp seal, addressed us first on why we needed LAW's help:

'Your relationship with the significant other in your life is based on the respect of two equals. No double standards in your life. You and your partner each have an equal right to initiate or refuse sex . . . and you keep records. You scrupulously ensure that no one person receives more satisfaction than the other. Those of you with children are raising them without the oppression of sexist stereotypes. All your sons play with dolls and all your daughters play with themselves. You make all of your decisions through negotiation. You never resort to hurling insults or collectibles at each other. You own two copies of *Our Bodies, Our Selves*. You have been irrigated. You have been channelled. You have been crystallised. In short, you are fully liberated. But can you leave Berkeley?'

A lady in a pink frock who identified herself as Mrs Chester Cholesterol told us about the rights of the unconceived. In introducing herself, she demonstrated that LAW ladies have a sense of humour. She said her late husband had been 'a margarine rancher – he ran a large spread down in the Imperial Valley'. The audience tittered politely. Then it got heavy. Mrs Cholesterol said unconceived Americans are the most innocent of all.

'You men have just got to learn to refrain from your habits of self-abuse, because millions of unconceived Americans are murdered this way every day,' she said. 'And who knows how many innocents perish every night in those little rubber concentration camps? We have got to abolish these penal colonies.

'And ladies, your hands are not entirely clean in these matters. Your monthly difficulty is the stain of shame that shows you have evaded pregnancy again. You have no right to squander the soul of an innocent microscopic unconceived future soldier of America.

'We are going to get a constitutional amendment against masturbation, menstruation, and other forms of mass murder. Sperms and eggs are people too.'

Mrs Cholesterol presented a slide show of some of LAW's activities during the Reagan years. There was a time when members of the group would crochet themselves to public buildings in protest against moves to have an Equal Rights Amendment incorporated in the US Constitution. After the amendment was defeated, LAW held an 'Iron-in' to celebrate.

LAW set up stalls outside the Republican Party's national convention in 1984, and the slides showed some of the Republican wives eyeing the LAW ladies with astonishment. Phyllis Schlafly, America's foremost crusader against the Equal Rights Amendment, somehow formed the view that the LAW ladies were satirising her, and was quoted in the local media saying, 'They made idiots of themselves. They dressed up foolishly and behaved in a childish way.'

It was a bitter blow for LAW. Members had hoped Mrs Schlafly might take them seriously – unlike their audiences. But they'll survive.

Ladies Against Women started in 1977 as an amateur theatre troupe called the Plutonium Players, based in Berkeley and dedicated to making fun of America's nuclear obsessions. Over the years, the members found that their LAW material attracted bigger audiences, and now that's their focus. The show I saw brought the Plutonium Players back to Berkeley 'to celebrate 10 years of politically correct satire'.

Mrs Chester Cholesterol is actually Gail Williams, who joined the Plutonium Players shortly after their first performance in 1977. 'We've been polishing and updating as we go along,' she says. The group encourages other satirists to emulate it in other cities, so the claim that there are nearly 100 chapters of Ladies Against Women is no joke, although Ms Williams says 'the chapters are ephemeral and a bit fictitious. A lot of them do one-shot events. Some groups have sent us big packages of clippings, and wonderful mementos of their actions.'

The group doesn't restrict itself to theatres. Ladies Against Women has manned stalls outside political events like the Republican national convention, and it organised national 'Amerikon Viewing Parties' to celebrate the showing of the TV series *Amerika*. Ms Williams says they'll appear for free just about anywhere 'if it's a really good idea, and we can get off our day jobs'.

The 10-year survival of Ladies Against Women seems to challenge successfully at least two stereotypes – that feminists are humourless, and that Americans don't understand satire.

7

CITIES

Boston (the Irish conquest) and Atlantic City (a gamble lost).

A fight broke out in my carriage as I was taking the subway to Boston's Saint Patrick's Day Parade. Fights are hardly unusual on St Patrick's Day, especially in Boston, but this one was different. It was between 8 white boys, wearing green scarfs and green plastic trilby hats, and three black boys, wearing grey windjackets and carrying, as it turned out, small revolvers.

I suspect the revolvers were not real. America hasn't quite reached the stage where the average 14-year-old boy casually carries a loaded gun on trains. In any case, the blacks didn't attempt to use the guns, merely taking them out of their pockets when the scuffling got serious, and holding them at their sides while fending off slaps and pushes with their other hands.

The brawl, which began when one of the blacks bumped into one of the whites and spilled his beer, ended suddenly when the whites piled out of the carriage at Broadway station, near where the St Patrick's Day march was to be held. The blacks had another destination.

Seeing that scuffle started me on a line of inquiry about how well Boston's citizens get on together. I had, until then, been content with the usual tourist view that Boston is a quaint-looking city, with an interesting history as the cradle of the American revolution, tasty clam chowder, and infuriating traffic.

Boston, I learn, is much less ethnically diverse than New York. While Manhattan is a fairly even mix of Jews, blacks, Italians, Poles,

Irish, Puerto Ricans and even a few Anglo-Saxons, Boston has two population peaks – Americans of Irish origin and Americans of African origin.

Each group represents about one-fifth of the 600,000 citizens of inner Boston, and each group has its ghetto. The working class Irish concentrate in 'Southie' – South Boston, where the St Patrick's Day march was held. Their numbers are growing rapidly, with large-scale immigration from Ireland.

About 8 kilometres away, the working class blacks concentrate in Roxbury, which was the focus in 1986 of a campaign to establish a separate black city, to be called Mandela. The proponents of Mandela argued that the black areas are so badly serviced by the city council that it would be better to secede from Boston and become a blacks-only city.

'Boston created Mandela already by its discriminatory housing policy, driving blacks into the poorest area,' said Andrew Jones, one of the sponsors of the move. 'Now that we want to incorporate ourselves, they call us racists.' In the referendum, more than 70 per cent of Roxbury's citizens voted against secession, amid arguments about 'self-imposed apartheid'.

Boston's black ghetto and its Irish ghetto are more alike than their inhabitants would care to believe. Both have a mixture of pretty two-storey wooden houses and derelict brick buildings covered with graffiti. The most noticeable difference is that Southie is dotted with pubs with names like 'The Three Shamrocks', while Roxbury has the 'Beau Nubian Brummel Tonsorial Saloon', 'The Second African Meeting House', and 'Teahouse of the Almighty, Psychic Tarot Readings'.

Residents of Southie who know the history of the Irish in Boston must feel some sympathy with the desperation of the blacks who wanted to establish Mandela. From the time when the waves of Irish immigration began, around 1840, until well into the 20th century, the Irish were seen as the dregs of Boston society. The citizens of English origin who controlled the city government were happy for Southie to remain a slum.

In the John F. Kennedy Museum there is a large reproduction of a typical 'Positions Vacant' ad which appeared in Boston newspapers in the late 19th century. The most prominent words are 'Positively NO Irish need apply'.

The Kennedy museum, an edifice of white concrete and black glass on a windswept promontory overlooking Boston Harbour, is as much a monument to the advancement of the Irish as it is to a former president. In its displays, you can trace how the Irish took control of the Democrat party in Boston, and disciplined political allegiances through the union movement and the Catholic Church.

The first triumph was when Kennedy's grandfather, John Fitzgerald, was elected mayor of Boston in 1905. The pinnacle was when John Kennedy became the first Catholic president of the United States, while his brother Bobby became attorney-general and his brother Teddy, aged 30, became senator for Massachusetts.

Then Tip O'Neill, congressman from Boston, became Speaker of the House of Representatives, John Kerry joined Teddy Kennedy as the second senator from Massachusetts, and Joe Kennedy, son of Bobby, got elected as one of Boston's congressmen.

The Irish remain all-powerful in Boston politics. The current mayor, Ray Flynn, grew up in Southie, the son of a wharf labourer and a cleaning lady. A small ruddy-faced man, he was resoundingly cheered as he led the St Patrick's Day Parade through his home streets.

In a speech, Mayor Flynn offered his vision of Boston as 'a family, in which every member of the family is treated with dignity and respect'. He boasts that he has promoted blacks to senior positions in his administration.

The blacks of Roxbury remain sceptical about Ray Flynn's benevolence, because they recall that a few years ago, he rose to prominence by leading a bitter fight to prevent black children from attending schools in South Boston.

A federal court ruled in 1974 that Boston was giving black children inferior education facilities, and ordered that numbers of black children be taken by bus to schools in white areas. The most violent resistance occurred in Southie. A mob pulled a black man from his car, and beat him up. Federal troops had to patrol the corridors of South Boston High School, and students cowered on the floor of school buses as mobs pelted them with rocks and bottles.

The trouble is over now. South Boston High School has about equal numbers of black and white students, and its principal, Jerome Winegar, says, 'South Boston is a better place today because of busing.'

In 1975, when he expelled a white student for beating and kicking a pregnant black girl, Winegar's car was firebombed. For several years he had to travel with bodyguards. But, he says, 'I never doubted for a moment that if you left the kids alone, they'd work things out.'

Bill Miller, a Southie resident who was one of the campaigners against black children entering white schools, now concedes that 'there's been some benefits from busing . . . First, blacks and whites are getting along better in the city because of the exposure to each other. The city's more open. It's not nigger, nigger, nigger anymore. It's just blacks. I think we all realise now that both sides have got niggers.'

It's odd to realise that the blacks were in Boston before the Irish. They first arrived as slaves of the English in the early 18th century. Boston, ever a bastion of liberalism, was one of the first colonies to abolish slavery, and by 1790 all the blacks in the city were free. In the 19th century, Boston became a key station in the 'underground railway', a network of northern towns that helped slaves escape their masters in the south.

But Boston's liberalism has its limits. While the Irish moved in 100 years from underclass to political mastery, most of Boston's blacks remain poor and powerless. It would seem that barriers based on religion and national origin are easier to overcome than barriers based on colour of skin.

Atlantic City: the lost renaissance

On the Boardwalk at Atlantic City, between Bally's Casino and Caesar's Palace, a young black woman with no arms or legs lies on a stretcher, playing an electric piano keyboard with her tongue.

Her repertoire seems to be limited to *Amazing Grace* and *Somewhere Over The Rainbow*, but her money can is overflowing with dollar notes and coins tossed in by gamblers as they shuttle between the gaming houses. This, it would seem, is an example of how the gambling industry contributes to the wider economy of Atlantic City.

It may be the only example. 10 years after gambling was legalised here, for the express purpose of revitalising a town in decline, Atlantic City has changed from a gigantic slum to a gigantic slum with 11 casinos on its edge.

More than 500,000 people visit every week but the average length of stay is 6 hours, and no visitor moves out of the casino belt. That's partly because there's nothing to do outside the casinos and partly because visitors are warned that they risk being mugged if they stray from the Boardwalk.

The local police department says that crime has increased 270 per cent since the first casino opened in 1978 – mostly in the form of theft, prostitution and drugs. There was a spate of bashings in 1986 as a Mafia-controlled organisation tried to take over the city's hot dog stands. But the crime is not all petty. The mayor of Atlantic City, Michael Matthews, was sentenced in 1984 to 15 years' jail for demanding bribes from companies seeking to build there.

The casinos have created jobs for 40,000 people, but most of them come from outside Atlantic City. The population of the central city area has dropped from 40,000 to 30,000 over the past 10 years.

The Boardwalk glitters with high rise hotels attached to the casinos, but behind it the city stretches away in desolate expanses of graffiti-covered tenements and vacant lots where landlords have burned down their houses in hopes of selling the space for new casinos.

Atlantic Avenue and Pacific Avenue – the town's main shopping streets – display drab rows of bars, car parks for the casino overflow, pawn shops offering 'instant cast for silver or gold', and 'adult bookstores' with publications on how to win at gambling.

Forty years ago, they looked very different. Atlantic City was one of America's top seaside resorts. The streets displayed grand hotels, restaurants and department stores. The Boardwalk was lined with amusement parlours, sideshows, aquariums and an attraction unique to America – a diving horse. The horse, carrying a bathing beauty, would be led up a ramp and forced to jump into a tank of water 15 metres below. The tourists loved it, for a while.

Valerie Armstrong, deputy chairman of the New Jersey Casino Control Commission, grew up in Atlantic City, and watched it change as Americans found more exciting holiday spots further away. 'I graduated from Atlantic City High School in 1964 and the decline was obvious at that time. Businesses were failing, shops were closing, people were moving out of the city and by the mid-'70s the area was pretty much down the tubes. When I was a child, we had numerous movie theatres here. They all disappeared. We don't have even one theatre now.'

Valerie Armstrong was one of the people who voted yes in the 1976 referendum to legalise gambling. The big word then was 'Renaissance' – that was what the gambling proponents promised. Now the 11 Atlantic City casinos take in $3,000 million a year (nearly $500 million more than the 60 casinos in Las Vegas), and pay more than $60 million a year in city property taxes and $190 million in state taxes.

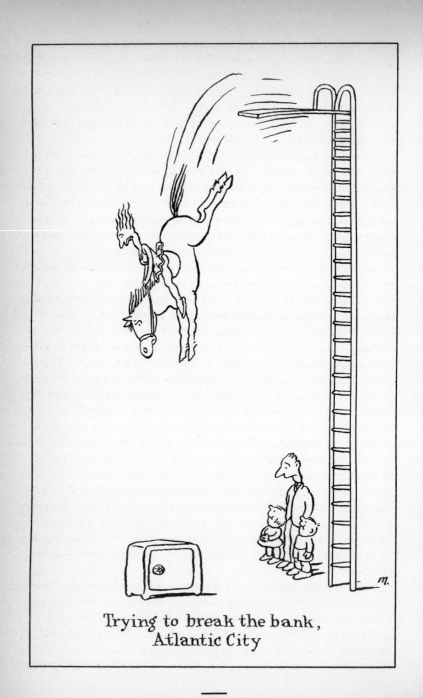

Trying to break the bank,
Atlantic City

The state taxes collected from the casinos go towards subsidising the electricity bills and rental costs of elderly and disabled people throughout New Jersey. But surveys show that the elderly and the disabled of New Jersey are the main customers of the Atlantic City slot machines (as poker machines are known here).

The slot machine players are collected by special casino buses every day from their homes and social centres across New Jersey and in neighbouring states. If they should shuffle off their buses at Caesar's Palace, they are greeted by a huge invitation to 'Come bust our slots'. And, if they spend enough of their social security payments, they might just find their photos and biographies up on the wall in The Slotbusters Hall of Fame – along with such people as Richard Brown, 65, a retired New York subway employee: 'Brownie was just another guy until he won over $185,000 at Caesar's. Now, he's a big man in town – his house is remodelled, his bills are paid and he and his wife are planning their third cruise since fortune smiled on them.'

But, if the state government has found that taxing legal gambling amounts to distributing money from poor to poor, what about the promised 'Renaissance' of Atlantic City? Not even the casino owners have any illusions about that. Alfred Luciani, vice-president of the Golden Nugget says: 'For the city, the experiment has been a dismal failure. The appearance of the city is horrible. The casinos here have been an overwhelming success, but in the city there has been a complete and utter lack of progress.' Valerie Armstrong: 'I have to question whether local government was prepared for this. This was a small town and to have this thing suddenly thrust into the middle of it – this incredible investment, the number of jobs, the number of visitors – they couldn't cope.'

The wheels of bureaucracy grind slowly in Atlantic City. The first effect of the arrival of the casinos was to send property values soaring, so that low and middle income citizens could not afford housing and had to move out. It was not until 1984 that the Casino Investment Development Authority was set up to plan how revenues from casinos might be used to provide moderately priced housing. So far, not one building has been completed as a result of the authority's work.

Sensitive to criticism that they had done nothing for the city, the casino operators in 1985 financed an efficiency audit of the city government by the management company Touche Ross. The auditors found large-scale waste, mismanagement, overstaffing and absenteeism. The worst inefficiency was found in the police department. The new mayor, James Usry, promised improvements.

As Carl Zeitz, a member of the Casino Control Commission, describes it: 'This is a place where it takes you 20 minutes to go four blocks in a car because the city government hasn't been able to synchronise the traffic lights on a computer; a place where once stable, fine neighbourhoods have become scattered, barren, littered lots; a place where public ego takes precedence over public accomplishments; a place, in sum, that is a sorry testament to the supposed advantages of public and private partnership.'

But the history of Atlantic City is that it has always lived on hope. The local tourist development authority is talking about a scheme to turn Atlantic City into the nation's top venue for exhibitions, conferences and conventions. The proposal is that the state and city governments combine to spend some $225 million on building a vast centre to attract hundreds of thousands of conventioneers a year to Atlantic City.

The name of the scheme is 'Renaissance Two'.

On the inside

Harrah's Marina at Atlantic City treats its high rollers well. If Harrah's computerised file on you shows that you're the kind of gambler who regularly spends more than $1,000 an hour at the baccarat, blackjack or craps tables, you need not worry about paying for your accommodation.

You'll find yourself in an individually decorated 'fantasy suite' on the 16th floor of Harrah's atrium tower, with a name like 'The Bombay', 'The Safari', or 'The Versailles Room', and with mirrored ceilings, a jacuzzi and a panoramic view over the bay. If you have a yacht, you'll get free mooring facilities. Or a free limousine if you're coming from the airport.

Meals at any of the five restaurants in the complex, drinks, tickets to see Bill Cosby or Crystal Gayle in the Harrah's theatre? No problem. It's all part of what Harrah's calls 'comps for premium players'. But just make sure you don't spend too long away from the tables, or the computer will show you're not keeping up your averages, and the hospitality might be toned down a little.

Harrah's is good to the low rollers as well. Every few minutes, buses arrive at Harrah's door bearing excited people from New York,

Pennsylvania, New Jersey, Connecticut, Delaware and Maryland. If you paid $25 for your roundtrip ticket from New York, a Harrah's hostess will give you $17 in coins for the poker machines, a $3 meal voucher, and a voucher to be redeemed in coins when you next visit the casino. The bus comes back to take you home 6 hours later.

You walk in to a glittering room the size of a football field, about two-thirds taken up with poker machines, and the rest with 60 black-jack tables, 22 tables for craps (dice), 12 roulette tables, and three tables for Big Six (a kind of chocolate wheel). A discreetly cordoned-off area in one corner contains three baccarat tables.

Only the silliest gamblers play Big Six, where the odds let the house keep about 47 per cent of the money you bet. The next silliest play roulette, where the house keeps 25 per cent, then craps (17 per cent), blackjack (16 per cent), poker machines (12 per cent) and baccarat (9 per cent).

There's a band and singer belting it out on a small stage at one side of the room, but you can't hear a note over the clunk and buzz of the pokies and the shouts of the craps players.

The room has a shiny ceiling, attached to which, every three metres or so, are black hemispheres like soccer balls. The players don't know it, but these contain TV cameras – a total of 200 of them show the casino's security room every action of every dealer on every table. The casino workers call them 'the eye in the sky'.

The dealers move like robots, laying out the cards and the chips in exactly the same way every time a game is played, keeping their hands clearly visible, clapping them together at certain moments, and holding them out for the cameras when they leave to take their 20-minute break every hour. Any unusual move by any dealer or player is noted by three people watching TV screens in the security room, who'll then scurry along catwalks stretching above the casino's shiny ceiling and observe the problem table through the ceiling, which turns out to be made of one-way glass.

Is the dealer trying to cheat the house or the players? Is there a secret arrangement between a dealer and a player? Does the face of one of the players match with one of the photos of undesirable characters arrayed next to the TV screens? Or is one of the changemakers wandering around the room trying to 'short' the rolls of coins?

If the behaviour remains unorthodox, the security room informs one of the in-house agents of the New Jersey Division of Gaming Enforcement, and the suspicious individual is discreetly removed for questioning.

The gamblers at Harrah's Marina lose $600,000 a day – a total earning for the company of $250 million a year from the Atlantic City operation. That makes Harrah's in Atlantic City the most profitable of the company's four casinos in the United States, and helps to make Harrah's the richest gaming company in the country.

Harrah's has come a long way since Wild Bill Harrah first set up a bingo game on Center Street, Reno, in 1937. For one thing, it has become more moral. Bill Harrah's idea of giving 'comps' to premium players was to provide them with free prostitutes along with free booze, accommodation and show tickets. Nowadays Harrah's says the prostitutes are no longer part of the deal. You may find them on the Boardwalk when you step out of the casino for a breath of air, but they're absolutely forbidden inside the casino.

8

CRAZES

Where Americans lead, and we may follow: transcendental vegetation; rap; a philosophy of ethnic jokes; the fadmaster speaks.

There is in the United States a serious businesswoman who rejoices in the name Faith Popcorn. I say 'rejoices' because she chose the name herself. Her real name was Faith Plotkin, but she changed it because she thought Popcorn was more memorable.

In that judgement she is certainly correct. The crucial question is whether any of her other judgements are correct, because Faith Popcorn is in the business of selling predictions. Her company is called Brainreserve, and it gets hired by organisations who want it to identify social trends which can be exploited for financial gain.

Ms Popcorn's major claim to fame in the past was that she warned Coca-Cola company that 'New Coke' would be a failure (but then, her chances of being right in that were 50 per cent). She is also on record as predicting that AIDS will become a major epidemic, that thinness will become unfashionable, that people will go for low-salt foods, and that beef will overtake fish as the favourite food of Yuppies.

But the Popcorn prediction that is getting the most attention is a phenomenon she labels 'cocooning' (the use of pseudotechnical jargon being essential to her image as a marketing genius). Cocooning means a growing tendency on the part of city dwellers to stay home and surround themselves with comforts, rather than go out and confront a complex, AIDS-infested, nuclear-threatened society.

The commercial implications of this have been summarised by Ms Popcorn's greatest fan, the conservative columnist George F. Will. He says cinemas, nightclubs and restaurants will decline in popularity, while takeaway food will boom, because people 'have gone to ground in their dens with their VCRs and compact disc players, snug in their Barcaloungers equipped with stereo headphones, the better to keep at bay the modern world, the discontinuities of which have produced a longing for tradition. The longing is so superficial it is assuaged by '50s "mom food" like macaroni and cheese, and microwave meatloaf.'

People who are cocooning themselves are also known as 'couch potatoes', and in apparent confirmation of Ms Popcorn's prediction, *New York* magazine devoted a cover story to the appearance of the couch potato on Manhattan island. The magazine interviewed a typical example of the species, a 30-year-old stockbroker named Matt Wagner, who says that in the past year he has changed 'from a stud to a spud'.

'You go out and everything's the same and boring and expensive,' Wagner said. 'You can't go bar-hopping without spending a fortune, and all you find are people who are as bored as you are. Frankly, I'd rather stay home, rent *Godzilla vs The Thing*, and eat a chicken.'

There are now couch potato (or sofa spud) clubs, whose main activity is swapping videos and talking on the phone, and shops are offering couch potato dolls, quilts and T-shirts. There's talk of a couch potato convention. One of the hopeful organisers, Robert Armstrong, argues that 'watching TV is an indigenous American form of meditation – we call it Transcendental Vegetation'.

While Manhattan is legendary as the city of bright lights and stimulation, it is actually the easiest place in the world to become a couch potato. You need never leave your apartment, because you can get anything you want delivered.

On nights when I'm tired from overwork, and don't wish to tax my brain, I go home, study my menu collection, get on the phone, and order an Indian, Chinese, Italian, Mexican, Jewish or 'nouvelle American' dinner. Half an hour later a boy with a bicycle and a large paper bag is knocking on my door.

Then I can turn on my television and start pressing the buttons on my remote control. I don't have a VCR, but because I am a subscriber to what is called 'the cable', I have the choice among 35 channels.

There's the 24 hour weather station; the 24 hour sport station; the late night pornography station (including an all-nude talk show); the 24 hour politics station (with live coverage of debates and committee hearings); two Christian stations devoted to financial demands of evangelists; the Chinese channel; two stations devoted to pop music videos and interviews; three 'public broadcasting' stations, showing wildlife documentaries, foreign language discussions, BBC dramas and reruns of Monty Python's Flying Circus; the 'Home Shopping Network' (a permanent kitsch auction by phone and credit card); two stations devoted to Puerto Rican soap operas and musical comedies; the financial news network; the 24 hour news network; three networks showing recent movies; and the four national commercial networks which are almost indistinguishable from Australian commercial channels. Oh yes, there's lots you'd want to watch.

After I'd engaged in this cocooning exercise a few times, I learned an important fact about myself. Not only am I a couch potato, I'm also a flipper, and possibly a zapper and a zipper.

The advertising industry has identified people like me as private enemy number one. I have a short attention span, and I like changing channels more than I like watching programs. Apparently there are millions like me in America.

The ad agency J. Walter Thompson coined the terms 'flipper', 'zapper' and 'zipper' after doing a study of the viewing habits of 1,800 Americans. The study showed that about a third of the sample pressed the remote control button often, just to find out what was on other channels. This group was labelled the flippers. Another 9 per cent changed channel as soon as a commercial came on. These were the zappers. And when looking at programs that had been prerecorded on a VCR, more than 50 per cent fast-forwarded during the commercials. These were the zippers.

The study also showed that compulsive flipping was most common among males. An explanation of the phenomenon comes from Robert W. Kubey, a psychologist in the communications department of the Rutgers University in New York. He says a man likes to play with the remote control because it is one of the few ways he can be dominant in the modern world, and a man may even take an unconscious pleasure in the fact that flipping drives other viewers crazy.

'There are legions of women and children out there who find it hard to watch TV with him,' Kubey says. 'Men in our culture have a lot of difficulty not being in control. I think men also have a lower tolerance for boredom than women.'

But these days every cocooning couch potato, male or female, is a potential flipper, Kubey says. 'People don't watch TV programs as much as they watch TV,' he says. 'You don't care what you're watching. You just want to be relieved of effort.'

Ripe for deconstruction

This is the story of a fad called Rap,
Which you'll need to know so you ain't no sap.
It's a kind of talking and a kind of singing.
In concerts and records, the cash bell's ringing.
Some call it poetry, some call it doggerel.
Sometimes the rhymes are just plain horrible.
Rap is the rhythm of New York City.
If you don't dig it, that ain't no pity.
'Cos the chances are that you ain't black.
And therefore you're unlikely to appreciate it.

I had to give up rapping there because I don't have the natural talents of Darryl McDaniels and Joseph Simmons, who can shout in rhyming couplets for 20 minutes and never run out of inspiration. McDaniels, 22, and Simmons, 23, together with their friend 'Rap Master Jay' (who plays tapes of drumbeats behind their performances), form a group called Run-DMC, and they are the current kings of rap.

Their album, *Raising Hell*, has sold two million copies. The streets of suburbs like The Bronx and Queens are full of kids carrying portable tapedecks (ghetto blasters) and imitating the Run-DMC look – black clothes, gold chains, black Homburgs pulled down low over the eyes, white sandshoes without laces. (Darryl McDaniels describes his look thus: 'I look like I might rob you or something, but I wouldn't. Don't stereotype me by my clothes. I'm a family man.')

If jazz was the sound of urban blacks in the 1920s, and rhythm and blues was the sound of urban blacks in the 1950s, then rap is the sound of urban blacks in the 1980s. And naturally it is now being taken over by whites.

The white reaction so far has been of two types: intellectualisation of rap as the poetry of poverty and condemnation of rap as an incitement to violence. *The Village Voice*, surely the wankiest newspaper in the world, describes rap music as a window into black teen sexuality: 'Ripe for deconstruction, the text of rap reveals itself to be less about sexual performance than about the language of sexual anxiety, repression, exploitation, exaggeration and commodification.'

It's certainly true that the lyrics are 'down and dirty'. Here's a sample from a hit called *Go See The Doctor* by a young rapper called Kool-Mo-Dee, who recounts a sexual adventure and concludes: 'Three days later, woke up fussin', yellin' and cussin', Drip, drip, drippin', and pus, pus, pussin'. I went to the doctor's office and I said "What have I got?" He said "Turn over boy, and take this shot". I looked at him like he was crazy. And I said "What? Ain't nobody sticking nothing in my butt".'

The recordings by male rappers are often criticised as showing contempt for women. But they are now being answered by a small number of female rappers, of whom the queen is a 21-year-old woman (with a five-year-old daughter) who calls herself the Real Roxanne. She sings: 'Bow wow babies, I think you got rabies. You think you're touchin' me, you must be crazy. You got your nerve to wanna be my man. 'Cause they call me the Real Roxanne.'

The big media issue at the moment is the connection between rap and violence. Run-DMC spend a lot of time on TV talk shows denying that they are the cause of the fighting that often breaks out at their concerts. They say that while they do throw microphone stands around on stage, and their lyrics are full of references to 'kickin the asses' of 'dumb motherfuckers', it's all just youthful exuberance.

Run-DMC appeared on Bob Geldof's Live-Aid concert for Africa, and often help to organise concerts against crack (a cheap version of cocaine). They always end their performances by shouting at the audience: 'If you are in school, stay there, don't take drugs, and don't be a dickhead in general.'

Joseph Simmons says Run-DMC have a positive influence: 'Our image is clean, man. Kids beat each other's heads every day. They are fighting because they were fighting before I was born. I'm no sociologist, but we're role models, man, big-time role models.

'They listen to me because I act tough and cool. I got a lot of juice with them. It's like I'm cooler than their teacher, I'm cooler than their mother, I'm cooler than their father. So when we say, don't take drugs and stay in school, they listen.'

Balancing roughness and niceness is giving Run-DMC an image problem. As they have moved towards the white world (particularly since they signed a $2 million contract to endorse Adidas sneakers and collaborated on a record called *Walk This Way* with a white rock group called Aerosmith), they have found themselves being attacked as wimps by their competitors in the rap industry.

Another rapper named Kurtis Blow complained that Run-DMC are 'perpetrating a fraud'. He said: 'They act tough, but they don't know what it's like to be really poor or really street. They've never been hungry or robbed anybody. But I grew up in Harlem, and I know what tough is.'

Their manager, Russell Simmons (Joseph's older brother), is worried they may lose their black audience because their 'preaching' about drugs and school 'gets on people's nerves'. Russell Simmons told *Rolling Stone* magazine: 'I look at them and say "Stop being a pussy". Let's hope a year from now people don't think they're suckers.'

He must have been cheered when Run-DMC were banned from playing in Pittsburgh. John Norton, the Commissioner of Public Safety there, said: 'I would say rap is going to be scrutinised very, very strongly. I feel that when you mix alcohol, youth, provocative and pornographic music, and then super-energise these kids, you're going to have a problem.'

If you listen closely to Run-DMC's *Raising Hell* album, it's hard to understand the fuss. It's just about as anti-social as the rock music I grew up with in the 1960s. Most of Run-DMC's songs are not about sex or violence but about themselves and how well they can rhyme. (Actually 'song' isn't quite the right word for what they do, since the compositions are spoken rather than sung, and the backing isn't music so much as tapping and scratching sounds, but no-one has come up with a better term.)

Run-DMC are even starting to show signs of weariness with success, as their latest hit, *It's Tricky*, demonstrates: 'When I wake up, people take up mostly all of my time. I'm not singing. Phone keeps ringing, could I make up more rhymes? Girl named Carol follows Darryl, every gig we play. Says he kissed her and dismissed her. Now she's jockin' Jay. I'm not bragging, people nagging, 'cause they think I'm a star. Always tearing what I'm wearing. I think they're going too far. In the city it's a pity, 'cause we just can't hide. Tinted windows don't mean nothing. They know who's inside.'

How many WASPS does it take?

Let's get one thing straight right now. The jokes you are about to read are not funny. I'm including them here purely to give you background on American soul-searchings about ethnic humour. If I catch you smiling at any of them, there'll be trouble.

Q. Why does a Jewish American Princess keep her eyes closed when she makes love? **A.** So she can fantasise about shopping.

Q. What do Jewish American Princesses make for dinner? **A.** Reservations.

Q. How can you tell if a Jewish American Princess has had an orgasm? **A.** She drops her nail file.

Q. How do you stop a JAP from being a nymphomaniac? **A.** Marry her.

Jokes like these have been circulating in New York for the past few years, based on the proposition that the daughters of middle-class Jewish parents tend to be vain, greedy, self-centred, shallow, and spoiled. Some of them come from a best seller called *The Jewish American Princess Handbook*. Mostly I've heard them told by Jewish acquaintances, and I've wondered why JAP jokes should be acceptable in a country which is normally so sensitive about racism and sexism.

Well, it turns out they are no longer acceptable. A body called the American Jewish Committee recently held a conference to discuss 'current stereotypes of Jewish women' and told Jews to stop laughing at JAPs. 'There is nothing funny about a putdown of Jewish women that has become a generic term for materialism, self-indulgence, loudness and so on,' Francine Klagsbrun, author of a book called *Married people: Staying Together in an Age of Divorce*, told the conference. 'We are eating away at our community. Why do we women label other women JAPs? It reflects our insecurities and self-doubts. We are setting ourselves apart from the others and that is a form of self-hatred.'

Susan Weidman, editor of a women's magazine called *Lilith*, said the jokes derived from both anti-semitic and anti-female attitudes. 'What had started as humour has escalated into attacks,' she said. 'Imagine for a moment that you are an 18-year-old female Jewish student at a college football game, and when you get up to get a soda you hear someone yell "JAP! JAP! JAP!" Then the cry is picked up by everybody sitting in the stadium.' Weidman said the retelling of JAP jokes by Jews 'gives permission for more direct and classic anti-semitic graffiti, jokes, comments, other kinds of verbal abuse'.

Now consider another joke: A gondolier in Venice was singing *O Sole Mio*. God looked down on him and wondered what would happen if he took away 25 per cent of the gondolier's brain power. The result was that the gondolier started singing 'O Sole, O Sole'. Then God took away half the gondolier's brain, and he sang 'O so, O so'. Finally God took away the whole of the gondolier's brain. He started singing *When Irish Eyes Are Smiling*.

President Ronald Reagan told that joke to journalists when he was at the Economic Summit in Venice. He said it was alright for him to tell it because he was of Irish ancestry. The Jewish critics of JAP jokes would not consider that an acceptable excuse.

But at least it seemed the president had learned something during his years in office. Back in 1980, when Reagan was campaigning for the presidency, he told the following joke during a radio interview:

'How do you tell the Italians at a cockfight? They're the ones who bet on the duck.

'And how do you know if the Mafia's involved? The duck wins.'

There was a flood of complaints. According to Roger Stone, Reagan's campaign manager at the time: 'Italian politicians in our camp were calling to get off the bandwagon. No-one actually resigned, but many of them were mad enough to.'

Reagan survived. And he still likes his ethnic humour. He'll tell the odd Irish joke, but his real passion is Russian jokes. According to a report in *The New York Times*, he has asked CIA officials to pass on to him every Russian joke they can find. He often throws them into speeches. His latest two go like this:

What are the four things wrong with Soviet agriculture? Spring, summer, winter and fall.

A Russian goes to buy a car at the official car lot and is told he can take delivery of his vehicle in exactly 10 years. 'Will that be morning or afternoon?' he asks. 'Ten years from now, what difference does it make?' asks the car salesman. 'Well,' says the buyer, 'the plumber's coming in the morning.'

The New York Times account said collecting and telling Russian jokes had become almost an obsession with the president. 'Visitors sometimes leave sessions with the president feeling frustrated and even a bit alarmed,' it reported. 'Sometimes people who have met with the president report he seems to retreat into his story telling as a way of avoiding tough questions or confrontations.'

The White House spokesman, Marlin Fitzwater, says it's a harmless hobby – 'a way of pointing up the differences between Russian and American society, but without a harsh edge. These stories accurately reflect the president's attitude toward the Soviet Union,' Fitzwater said, 'that the people are exploited by the government. He has a lot of sympathy for the Russian people. That's a very strong Reagan attitude.'

It is often argued that ethnic jokes help people of limited intellect to cope with the complexities of the world. It's easier to lump all Irish together as stupid, all Jews as greedy, all Italians as criminals and all Russians as oppressed, than to confront the reality of individual differences. And if their president does it, who can blame other Americans for emulating him? Besides which, some ethnic jokes are funny.

It seems now that a kind of etiquette is developing in this country about when it's alright to tell an ethnic joke. As articulated by Michael Kinsley, editor of *New Republic* magazine, the code of ethics (what he describes as 'guidelines aimed at providing maximum gaiety with minimum offence') goes something like this . . .

First, it's best to tell jokes on your own ethnic group, so that you may end up challenging the stereotype, rather than endorsing it. (This isn't much fun if you're a White Anglo-Saxon Protestant, since WASP jokes tend to be pretty boring, viz: How many WASPs does it take to change a light bulb? Two – one to mix the martinis and one to call the electrician. What's a WASP's idea of being open-minded? Dating a Canadian. In Australia this might be adapted to 'Dating a New Zealander'.)

Second, if the joke is about another group, consider whether you would be embarrassed to tell it to a member of that group. If you would, don't tell it to anyone.

Third, consider if the joke insults a group which is already suffering rather than a group which can look after itself. On this criterion, you should be less inclined to tell a joke about Aborigines than one about Italians.

Fourth, remember that some traits are more offensive than others. According to Kinsley, jokes about drunkenness, laziness, or greed are more tolerable than jokes about physical characteristics, personal habits or intelligence.

And fifth, Kinsley says, 'if you tell an ethnic joke, make sure it's funny . . . Wittiness is important not only for its own sake – to compensate for any offence – but as a test of motive. An unfunny ethnic joke is merely an expression of contempt. A funny one need not be.'

The search for the Wow factor

A simple question. Where were the following fads invented: the Frisbee, the Pet Rock, Barbie doll, the Hula-Hoop, and Chocca Cacca?

Oh, easy, you say. They were invented in America, the only nation rich enough and silly enough to make millionaires out of people who create useless gimmicks. Well, you're wrong. Only four out of these five gimmicks were invented in America. The other came from Australia.

Mind you, Americans made the money out of it. Two Yankee entrepreneurs named Artur Melin and Richard Knorr, who owned a company called Wham-O Products, discovered the hula-hoop in Australia in 1958. At the time they were promoting their first big success, the Frisbee (originally known as the Pluto Platter), but they noticed Australian schoolkids swirling bamboo hoops around their waists. Wham-O made a version of the hoop in plastic, and within a year was producing 20,000 hula-hoops a day. Melin and Knorr went on to create the Super Ball in 1965, and are now acknowledged as the kings of fadmaking in modern American history.

Perhaps you weren't too familiar with the last of the fads listed in my opening paragraph – Chocca Cacca. This, I must say, has not yet achieved the success of Barbie or the Pet Rock. It's not even in mass production yet. But it was one of the most talked about displays at the Third Annual New York Fadfair, an event where it was possible to preview all the products designed to capture the imagination of Americans in 1988.

Chocca Cacca is, not to put too fine a point on it, a confection in the shape of a turd. A handout from the makers says it is made of caramel and chocolate 'jammed with fresh roasted Georgia peanuts'. It comes wrapped in a disposable nappy, so you can amaze your friends by reaching into the nappy and munching on something they would rather not think about. 'Unique! Whimsical!! Memorable!!! Luscious!!!!', says the handout.

I find it hard to imagine that millions of Americans will be chewing on Chocca Cacca with the same enthusiasm that they brought to past crazes like Slinkies (the spring that flows downstairs, created in 1947), Mickey Mouse phones, Cabbage Patch dolls, and Wacky Wallwalkers. This last item made a millionaire of Ken Hakuta, who calls himself 'Dr Fad' and who runs the Fadfair every year.

Back in 1982, Hakuta was running a hardware export-import

business in Washington. A relative in Japan sent his two children a new little toy: a rubber octopus with sticky feet which, when thrown against a wall or window, would walk down it.

'The children liked them, but I was really fascinated,' Hakuta says. 'I took them to restaurants and threw them against the walls. You should have seen the crowds they drew.

'I decided if I was going to take a gamble in life, it was going to be on this rubber toy. I knew this was the turning point in my life. This would be my contribution to pop culture.'

Hakuta bought the North American rights, and imported 300,000 Wacky Wallwalkers. When they sold out (at $1.69 each), he bought the world rights. Since then, he has sold 150 million in the US alone.

Now Ken Hakuta devotes himself to the search for a fad that will transcend the Wacky Wallwalker. He operates a 24 hour hotline for inventors, getting more than 100 calls a day, and offers his expertise to help in the development of good ideas.

His formula for a successful fad: 'Pick an item that has tremendous uselessness, a great Wow! factor and which is an impulse item. Impulse means inexpensive. Have everybody go berserk about it, like they have to have it yesterday. That means the public, the toy industry, and the media. And, most importantly, be in a position to deliver the goods.'

The Fadfair displays the best of Hakuta's discoveries for toyshops and companies who might want to mass produce them. Here's the range I noticed during a stroll through the fair . . .

The Everbrown: 'a pre-dead plant for people with brown thumbs'.

Tasty Tyrants: squeaking plastic dog chews in the shape of international leaders unpopular with Americans, like Fidel Castro, Colonel Ghaddafi (who is liver-flavoured) and Ayatollah Khomeini (bacon-flavoured).

Masks to put over your pet's head: now you can change your cat into a dog or your dog into a cat.

Galactitags: identification tags to wear around your neck in case you are kidnapped by a UFO and dumped somewhere else in the universe. They are imprinted with a map of the galaxy which pinpoints the earth.

The Dismembear: a cuddly teddy whose extremities are attached by Velcro so they can be pulled apart when you need to vent your frustration. 'Tear his little head off! Rip him limb from limb! Put him back together and then do it all again!'

The portable ulcer: a large red plastic lump which you can squeeze to relieve tension.

The Road Pizza: 'Have you ever been driving along in your car and seen a dark spot in the road in front of you? Then you get close enough to see that at one time it was a small domestic animal, such as a dog or cat or even a wild animal like a squirrel or chipmunk. Now you can own one of these adorable pets. Although Road Pizza is not the real thing, due to health reasons, it is a close lookalike made from safe synthetic materials.'

The Yoodoovoodoo: a 'revenge product . . . each kit comes with an anatomically correct doll, in your choice of male or female gender, which can be hung anywhere from the noose-like rope attached to the neck, and two ornate feather pins, affectionately referred to as "torture implements" '.

The Do-It-Yourself Lobotomy Kit (a plastic hammer and target).

Elegant leather condom pouches, to be clipped to your belt.

The Singles Ring: 'it's the opposite of the wedding ring – wear it if you don't want to be left alone'.

The Date Enhancement Kit: which includes earrings that look like fish hooks, multiple choice cards you can send to people indicating how you feel about them, and matchboxes containing your address which you can casually leave near your target.

'Save The Sewer Gators' products: badges, T-shirts and posters expressing support for this endangered New York species. The kit allegedly includes a freeze-dried baby alligator to flush down your toilet.

Large wooden speech balloons, containing expressions like 'Hi cutie!' and 'Wow!'.

The Landshark: a cap with a fin on top and a double visor in the shape of jaws.

Holovision: sunglasses with three dimensional images in the lenses. You can, at some expense, have a hologram of yourself or your loved one embedded in the lens.

Fridge Raiders: ugly purple and green gremlins designed to startle people who try to steal from your fridge.

The Fruck: a shiny plastic ornament that is a mixture of a duck and a frog.

A toilet seat that glows in the dark: I doubt whether this last item has any future among American fad fanciers. After all, it might actually be useful.

9

CRIMES

*A day with the FBI; a day with the Mafia; ethics for sale;
society scoundrels.*

Special agent David Barth picked up a Heckler-Koch 9 millimetre sub-machine gun and fired a burst of bullets into a target shaped like the silhouette of a man. 'These fire about 13 rounds per second,' he said. 'They're used by our hostage rescue teams and our SWAT teams.' He switched on a light behind the silhouette to demonstrate a neat circle of small holes in the middle of the target's chest.

I asked if FBI agents are trained to kill or only to disable. 'That's not the way it works,' Agent Barth said. 'We're trained to shoot at the centre of the largest mass visible. If that's the whole body, then we shoot at the middle of the chest. We use our guns to protect our own lives or the lives of others.'

In fact, Barth has never fired a gun at a human being, or even drawn his gun to threaten anyone, during his 17 years with the FBI. He says that's the case with most FBI agents. In the 78-year history of the bureau, only 29 agents have been killed by gunfire. Barth says the job is a lot less violent than television would have us believe.

Barth and another agent named Oatess Archey are answering my questions in a small office behind the shooting range in the basement of the J. Edgar Hoover Building, a massive yellow office complex adjoining Washington's porno movie and sex shop district. The 7,000 workers in the J. Edgar Hoover building supervise the labours of 59 FBI field offices and 400 sub-branches throughout the United States, and 13 'liaison posts' in foreign countries (including Australia, where the FBI has an office or two).

Today Special Agents Barth and Archey have been assigned to explain to the visiting reporter how the modern FBI operates. They are polite, friendly and very wary.

I've seen the bureau's laboratories, its museum (including John Dillinger's death mask), its fingerprint files (with records of 170 million people), its firearms reference collection of 2,000 guns and 12,000 bullets, and its crime statistics collection (there's a murder every 28 minutes in the USA, a rape every 6 minutes, an aggravated assault every 46 seconds and a theft every five seconds). I've also been played a phone-tap tape of a Soviet agent trying to get documents from a naval officer, and a tape of a kidnapper demanding a ransom (in which the recipient of the threat says he doesn't have $250,000 and the kidnapper says, 'How about $50,000?').

Now I'm asking about the agents' backgrounds. Oatess Archey is black, a former teacher of social studies and physical education who joined the FBI 13 years ago because he thought it would be 'a challenge'. Nowadays he supervises the bureau's west coast branches in the 'personal crimes' area, which he summarises as 'kidnappings, bank robberies, extortion, threats against the president, that sort of thing'.

David Barth is white, a former Marine who joined the FBI 17 years ago, and now works as an instructor in the bureau's training academy in Virginia. He tells me he spent four years in the New York office working in 'foreign counter-intelligence'. The conversation continues like this:

Dale: 'That sounds interesting. What does that involve?'

Archey: 'Let me say that we're not at liberty to get into that sort of thing. [To Barth] Dave, let me tell you that Division Five have informed us they really don't want to be involved in this interview. That's for your information.'

Barth: 'That's nice.'

Dale: 'I take it Division Five is the counter-intelligence section?'

Archey: 'See, the thing is, they're above us. They tell us we have to talk in generalities, that's it.'

Dale: 'OK, a general question. What would you see as the main priorities of the FBI at the moment, in order of importance?'

Archey: 'I'm not going to put them in any particular order, but the ones we consider our top three right now are foreign counter-intelligence, organised crime, and white collar crime.'

Dale: 'Does foreign counter-intelligence include communists within America? I remember a TV show when I was a kid about an FBI agent who infiltrated the communist party, I think it was called *I Led Three Lives*. Does the FBI do that sort of thing these days?'

Barth: 'That was a true story, but that gentleman was not an FBI agent, he was a citizen who assisted the bureau with its investigations.'

Dale: 'But is that the kind of thing the FBI does, infiltrate political parties and so on?'

Archey: 'You're out of my area. I never worked in foreign counter-intelligence. But not to my knowledge.'

Barth: 'No. You can't do it, it's not legal.'

Dale: 'Are communists within America a threat?'

Barth: 'You mean the CPA, the Communist Party of America? That's a political party. As such, it has a legal right to exist in this country.'

Archey: 'But there's always a concern. We're concerned with any group that might attempt to overthrow the government. We're concerned with security within the continental United States. We look at anyone that might pose a threat.'

I asked Barth what makes a good agent. He said: 'Someone that has a high sense of right and wrong, somewhat tenacious, someone that likes to get involved in a certain degree of detail because there's a lot of detailed work, and I guess an old-fashioned type of person that still has a little bit of patriotism.'

Barth says these qualities should be picked up in the in-depth interview which is a part of the bureau's admission procedure. But first, the applicant must have a university degree, and if the degree is not in law, science, accountancy or languages, the applicant must have three years' work experience after college. The bureau gets 12,000 applications a year from people with these qualifications, and chooses about 500.

The applicant must also pass the bureau's own intelligence and general knowledge test, and satisfy a strict personal background check. The job application form includes the following questions:

'Are you now or have you ever been a member of any foreign or domestic organisation, association, movement, group, or combination of persons which is totalitarian, fascist, or subversive, or which has adopted, or shows a policy of advocating or approving the commission of acts of force or violence to deny other persons their rights under the Constitution of the United States, or which seeks to alter the form of government of the US by unconstitutional means?

'Are you aware of any information about yourself or any person with whom you are or have been closely associated (including relatives or room-mates) which might tend to reflect unfavourably on your reputation, morals, character, ability or loyalty to the United States? If Yes, please attach a separate piece of paper, appropriately numbered, giving your version of this/these incidents.'

Once they're accepted, applicants must pass a 15-week training course, and spend one year on probation before they become qualified agents on a salary of $27,000.

Despite the elaborate selection and training procedures, FBI agents do occasionally go wrong. In 1986 an agent named Dan Mitrione pleaded guilty to taking $850,000 in bribes and to stealing 40 kilograms of cocaine from a shipment seized by the bureau. In 1987 an agent named Richard Miller was sentenced to two life terms in jail for conspiring to pass secret documents to the Soviet Union, and an agent named Robert Freich has been charged with concealing information from the Justice Department about a Teamsters' Union crime figure.

I asked Archey if there was any regular testing of agents once they had joined the FBI. 'Well, we get tested physically twice a year – a one-and-a-half-mile run, push-ups, sit-ups, a step test of endurance. We have a psychiatrist always available if you feel there is a need to be tested psychologically, or if the agency feels there is a need for you to talk to someone. If the agency saw someone acting strangely, or if their behaviour pattern had changed, they would recommend, or insist, that you be given psychological help.'

But that rather informal system is likely to be toughened. There are moves to introduce random urine tests for all agents to check drug use, and lie detector tests for agents working in 'sensitive' areas. Archey observes that these tests are unlikely to turn up many rotten apples. He says the few cases of agents who go bad are hardly significant when you consider that the bureau has 9,000 agents working on many thousands of cases every day.

Certainly urine tests for drugs would be an easy task for the massive laboratories the bureau maintains in the J. Edgar Hoover Building. They're capable of analysing the saliva in a piece of chewing gum or a cigarette found at the scene of a crime and telling the blood type of the chewer or smoker. They can take a chip of paint found at the scene of a hit-and-run accident and determine the make and year of the car involved.

The document analysis section has a computer that can decipher the characteristics of the person who wrote a hold-up note or a threatening letter by the grammar and choice of words. If you use the word 'hold-up', for example, you're in a different file from the kind of person who uses the word 'stick-up'.

The FBI's laboratories are available free to any police force in the United States, and there are hundreds of requests a day. As the assistant showing me around said: 'We won't solve their crime for them, but we will do the tests they want, as long as the evidence is properly wrapped.'

Apart from offering its laboratories to other agencies, the FBI also provides training courses for local police from all over the country at its academy in Virginia. The bureau hopes this will break down an impression sometimes given by the media that local police view the FBI with jealousy and antagonism.

Agents Archey and Barth admit that in the past some local police have imagined that FBI agents look down on them and consider themselves the elite of American crime fighters. 'That's an attitude we're trying to break down, and we have very good co-operation now,' Archey said.

But surely, I said, FBI agents are superior to most local police.

Agents Archey and Barth smiled. Then Barth put on his serious face again and said: 'It depends whose eyes you're looking through. There are many police departments that are extremely competent, extremely well paid, extremely well educated. They've caught up with us.'

'This thing of ours'

When you spend a day watching the Mafia on trial in Federal District Court, Manhattan, one fact strikes you most forcibly: real life criminals talk just like criminals in the movies.

Much of the evidence is in the form of tapes of conversations between Mafia members, secretly recorded by the New York police. Here's a sample of the everyday banter of a gentleman named Joseph Pisani, whose vocation was described in court as 'shylocking' (making loans at heavy interest rates):

'See, I gave the contract out to two guys, make collections for me. "Put them in the fucking hospital, do what the fuck you want with them, they got to come up with the fucking money. They don't want to come up with the money, hit them, do any fucking thing you want to. Let them run to somebody."

'My fucking wife screams like a cocksucker over here, because there's no fucking money to pay the fucking bills over here.'

This last sentence shows the other element which is emerging in the case – how life as a criminal causes personal depression and domestic discord. Two of the defendants, Anthony 'Fat Tony' Salerno, 75, alleged boss of the Genovese family, and Anthony 'Tony Ducks' Corallo, 73, alleged boss of the Lucchese family, were recorded commiserating with each other over the impulsive behaviour of a younger Mob member:

Corallo: 'Did you reason with him?'

Salerno: 'I don't know what to do. I swear I don't.'

Corallo: 'And you have to run downtown when you want something done?'

Salerno: 'No, I'll retire. I don't need that.'

Corallo: 'I know you'll retire, I know you'll retire.'

Salerno: 'Listen, Tony, if it wasn't for me, there wouldn't be no Mob left. I made all the guys. And everybody's a good guy. This guy don't realise that? I worked myself. Jeez, how could a man be like that, huh?'

Corallo: 'No, I know the way he talks. Shoot him, You can't go on, it's disgusting.'

Seen in court, Corallo and Salerno are two chubby grandfathers wearing open neck shirts and cardigans, and chuckling benignly as the tapes crackle over the loudspeaker. Salerno's only 'live' contribution to the proceedings so far has been to pipe up during jury selection with the words: 'What about a hot lunch, judge? Can't we have a hot lunch?'

There are 8 defendants in the case, all alleged to be members of the 'commission' which mediates disputes between various crime families, and plans joint operations for an organisation with a total annual income of more than $15 billion.

There should have been a ninth commission member on trial – Paul 'Big Paul' Castellano, the supposed 'Godfather' over all the families – but unfortunately he had just been shot dead in the doorway of Spark's Steakhouse, after an excellent lunch. The man who allegedly replaced him as 'Godfather', John Gotti, is undergoing a separate trial in Brooklyn.

The Federal District Court is on the third floor of what looks like a massive Greek temple in lower Manhattan. These words are engraved in the grey concrete above the temple pillars:'The True Administration of Justice is the Firmest Pillar of Good Government'.

You pass through two security checks to enter the courtroom, and they're not only looking for guns. The guards confiscated a folder full of newspaper clippings which I was hoping to take inside to help me identify the principal players. The confiscation was to prevent me from showing the clippings to the jury, who are locked up during the trial with a restricted reading list.

Once through the door, your first sight is a multicoloured notice board next to the jury box, headed 'La Cosa Nostra Families of New York'. In blue, you see famous names from the past like Albert Anastasia and Vito Genovese. In green you see family members currently alive but not yet on trial, and in yellow, the names of the 8 defendants.

The front half of the room is taken up with a big L-shaped table where the defendants sit with their lawyers, except for Carmine 'Junior' Persico, who is representing himself. Persico, 53, is the best dressed defendant, in his three piece navy suit and gold watch chain. With his thick red lips, hooked nose, deep set eyes, and tendency to jump up and down with objections, Persico looks just like the star of a Punch and Judy puppet show. It remains to be seen whether he fights with policemen and throws babies out the window.

Persico is spearheading a new approach by the defence team. After years of lawyers in this kind of case denying the existence of the Mafia or la Cosa Nostra, these lawyers now concede that such an organisation exists, but say that membership of it doesn't necessarily make you a criminal.

On the tapes, nobody ever uses the word 'Mafia'. The organisation to which they apparently belong is referred to mostly as 'dis ting of ours'. Members are called 'wise guys'. Joseph Pistone, an FBI under-cover agent who infiltrated the Bonnano crime family for 7 years, testified that he was told by one Mafia boss to get a haircut and 'keep a neat appearance at all times because a wise guy doesn't have a bushy moustache and long hair'.

One witness, Angelo Lonardo,75, described his initiation into the 'thing' as a process which is known as 'being made'. It happened in a hotel room in Cleveland in the 1940s. There was a gun and a dagger on the table, a picture of a saint was burned to ashes, and blood was drawn from his finger.

Lonardo said the leaders shook his hand, kissed him on the cheek, and told him that the organisation's rules included never dealing in drugs or prostitution, and always obeying the orders of his superiors.

Another witness alluded to an irony associated with the earlier policy of denying the Mafia's existence. Joey Cantalupo, a small businessman who is now an FBI informant, said he used to work for Joseph Colombo, the alleged boss of the Columbo crime family. When asked what happened to Columbo, Cantalupo said: 'He was shot dead while attending a rally of the Italian-American Civil Rights League.' The rally was to protest the use of the word Mafia by the media and the FBI. (After the shooting, Columbo's bodyguards killed the assassin, who, it turned out, had been hired by a rival Mafia boss named Joey Gallo.)

In his evidence, Cantalupo revealed that crime is a difficult and often unrewarding business. He said that on one occasion, he and a partner decided to get out of debt to the Mafia by buying a kilogram of cocaine and reselling it. They paid $30,000 for it, and thought they'd probably double their money.

'Did you sell it?' the prosecutor asked.

'No, we couldn't,' Cantalupo said. 'We kept it in my apartment for a week and it went bad.'

The prosecutor seemed puzzled: 'How do you mean it went bad?' he asked.

'Well, you know, it just hardened, turned like a rock, you couldn't do anything with it,' Cantalupo said.

'So did you buy some more?' the prosecutor asked.

Cantalupo: 'Yes, we bought 12 ounces.'

Prosecutor: 'And were you able to sell that?'

Catalupo: 'Yes.'

Prosecutor: 'And who did you sell it to?'

Cantalupo: 'The FBI.'

Prosecutor: 'Oh, I see.'

Postscript: It's not just the Mafia bosses who talk like movie criminals. After this trial ended (with the conviction of all 8 defendants), I had occasion to phone Lieutenant Remo Franceschini, head of the Intelligence Division of the New York Police Department, to ask him what would happen to the crime families now. He proceeded to give me a detailed description of those most likely to take over as the new bosses, and their current activities. At one point, I asked 'Can you tell me how you know all this?' Franceschini replied: 'Because I'm listenin' to duh fuckin' tapes.'

Franceschini comes from the same Brooklyn background that produced some of New York's top criminals, but he went a different way, and became New York's top Mafia hunter. Life for him is a constant challenge to find new ways to plant bugs in Mafia houses, cars, restaurants and social clubs. Having achieved guilty verdicts on the 'commission' members, Franceschini has one target left before he retires: John Gotti, New York's Godfather. The tapes are still rolling.

Workshopping morality

Gary Edwards is in the vanguard of a new American growth industry – he sells ethics to companies that don't have enough of their own. US businesses have become so alarmed by recent scandals involving white-collar corruption, embezzlement, insider trading, and fraud that they are queuing up for the services of 'ethics doctors' like Gary Edwards.

One phone call, the chairman's signature on a contract, and Edwards and his team from the Ethics Resource Center of Washington will move into the company. They will work with the top executives to write a code of ethics that actually means something, devise a system for policing that code, and run training workshops to instil the code into the company's employees. The workshops, Edwards says, will be tough, intensive and 'case study-driven – they don't sit around reading Plato and Aristotle'.

The Ethics Resource Center was established in 1978, funded by annual contributions from many firms and by charging for its services. It grew slowly at first, but its workload has doubled each year for the past three years. It now has an annual budget of $1.5 million, and 12 full-time employees (plus part-time consultants in university business schools and law schools). Capitalism, it seems, has suddenly discovered morality.

'They come to us for a variety of reasons,' says Edwards, who has degrees in law and philosophy. 'Some of them are already on the front page, with serious problems involving improper conduct by employees that need immediate attention. There is partly a public relations aspect to seeking our help, in that they hope the public will be convinced that they're taking the proper remedial actions. But companies in that situation are, in our experience, serious about wanting to understand what went wrong and why.

'Or maybe a company sees other companies in its industry getting into trouble, and doesn't want to follow them into the dock. It wants to bring in internal controls before controls are imposed on it.'

Edwards is presently working with a large company which found out last year that one of its purchasing managers had been demanding kickbacks from suppliers for the past 9 years. The company wants to know why it didn't find out before.

'Apparently everyone in the industry in that part of the country knew about it except that guy's boss,' Edwards says. 'Nobody would tell the people who had to know, because they assumed that kind of conduct was acceptable to the company. Obviously people in the company felt "it's not my responsibility to blow the whistle, my job ends where my job description ends, if I blow the whistle I'll just disappear".'

He says other clients come to the centre because they are about to take over another company and want advice on how to blend their 'corporate ethos' with that of their new partner. And some see the introduction of ethics training for staff as a way of increasing productivity by reducing the 'adversarial' relationship between bosses and workers.

Edwards and his team find that many senior company executives have become worried that the new generation of junior executives graduating from business schools have financial success as their only goal, and are ruthless about achieving it.

'They account for this lack of principle in terms of the decline of religion in everyday life, or the breakdown of family structures, or the lack of discipline in schools, and they don't know if they can trust these new managers to act in a way which won't suddenly put the company on the front page of the *Washington Post*,' Edwards says.

'A lot of companies wrote codes of ethics in the 1970s in the wake of the Watergate scandal and revelations about American companies paying bribes overseas. Now they're finding that's not enough.

'You've got to drive those values into the hearts and minds of the people in the corporation. It's got to be communicated effectively, not just by writing memoranda, but by internal training and development, by taking people off the job, getting them to talk about the risks the company faces, convincing them that senior management does have other values than profit, that they can blow the whistle if they see something wrong.'

One of Edwards's biggest projects has been to reform General Dynamics, the arms manufacturer that was suspended from bidding for government contracts because of evidence of fraud. 'The day after that happened, General Dynamics asked if we could help,' Edwards says, 'In fact they tracked me down while I was on vacation, and the chairman and two executives came out to where I was staying.

'We began by rewriting the corporate code of conduct to make it much stronger. We recommended they should have a board level committee to oversee the ethics program and its implementation.

'We recommended that every one of the divisions of General Dynamics have an ethics ombudsman, a person to whom an employee could go to report apparent misconduct, if that employee felt he or she could not report to a superior. We recommended that between the board level committee and the ombudsman there be a corporate level ethics office, which would have the resources to investigate the ombudsman's report of apparent misconduct. This frees the ombudsman for his other function, which is advisory, to tell people who are contemplating a certain line of conduct that it is covered by the code of ethics and why they can't do it.'

Apart from setting up this elaborate structure to police the ethics code, the centre began a series of 'executive development seminars' within the company to change the attitudes of the managers.

These seminars use a set of dramatised videos showing people in ethical dilemmas, and get the managers attending the session to discuss how they would react. The centre's success with this training method has caused many US companies to develop their own ethical training programs along similar lines.

But Edwards warns that just showing films about ethical dilemmas isn't enough.

'It's very important at these workshops for the commitment of top management to be clear, and for the company to introduce systems to encourage the ethical employee, because if you get people together and they're spilling their guts about their concerns for this company, where things could go wrong, or where pressure for profits is forcing people to meet impossible objectives, and then nothing happens, you're worse off than if you never started.'

The villain's reward

All rich New Yorkers are crooks, but some are more crooked than others. And the more crooked you are, the more you are sought after as the chief attraction at parties given by the less crooked.

Yes, the hottest thing to do in Manhattan these days is build a dinner around a celebrity who has had a brush with the law. The social magnets of the moment are Claus von Bulow, who was accused of trying to murder his wife for her money (she remains in a coma); Steve Rubell, a club owner who served time for tax evasion and cocaine dealing; Sidney Biddle Barrows, a descendant of New York's original pilgrim fathers who got nicknamed 'The Mayflower Madam' when she was convicted of running a prostitution agency; and Ivan Boesky, who was fined $100 million for buying inside information on Wall Street.

I first became aware of this phenomenon when I saw Claus von Bulow and his mistress Andrea Reynolds at a party to celebrate the opening of the musical *Les Miserables*. I was naive enough to be surprised that the show's promoters would invite a man who had been socially disgraced, but others at the event said von Bulow was a highly prized social butterfly.

Von Bulow now jokes about his succession of murder trials. At the *Les Miserables* party, he said he had enjoyed the show 'because I feel so much like Jean Valjean' (the convict hero).

Reinaldo Herrera, an editor at *Vanity Fair* magazine, said he often invites von Bulow to dinner parties to 'create chemistry'. 'Claus is a great catalyst,' Herrera said. 'People instantly loathe him or like him.'

Herrera said his ideal dinner guests would be Jean Harris (currently in jail for killing a diet expert named Herman Tarnower) and Ivan Boesky: 'They would add spice to the evening because she was convicted of murder and he pleaded guilty to robbing nearly the world. But most normal houses don't have these great names at their fingertips.'

Cindy Adams, a society columnist for the *New York Post*, is famous for the clever way she mixes the nice and the naughty at her dinner parties. She is currently planning a birthday dinner for herself, and she already has acceptances from Sidney Biddle Barrows and Steve Rubell. She is sure Claus von Bulow and Andrea Reynolds will accept, 'because they go to the opening of an envelope'.

'All my good friends are indictees or worse,' Ms Adams says gleefully. 'But Ivan Boesky won't come. He won't even answer my phone calls.'

The phenomenon is now the subject of study by the 3,000 academics who make up a group called the Popular Culture Association. 'Never before have Americans been so desirous of brushing up against the notorious and the wealthy,' says Ray Browne, a lecturer at Bowling

Green University of Ohio. (Don't laugh, Bowling Green is just another place name. Americans think Wollongong sounds pretty funny too.)

'These people are a force in television, magazines, books, every medium. We're mad to be in the same room with them, to let a little of the danger they engaged in rub off on us. If they're well born like von Bulow or the Mayflower Madam, well that makes it even more wonderful because we're trading up.'

Neil Postman, professor of communications at New York University, says scoundrels are currently popular because people tend to envy them. 'Today we have white collar characters doing things we can identify with – cheating on taxes, manipulating stocks, prostitution,' Postman says.

'In an age when political interests are dulled, these people are acting in their own self interests. It's a new version of the old entrepreneurial impulse that Ronald Reagan says made this country great.'

10

CITIES

*Chicago (skyscraper and pizza museum); San Francisco
(Venice in decline).*

The city of Chicago has such an inferiority complex that it won't even
admit it has an inferiority complex. But how else do you account for the
fact that each year the Chicago business community chips in money to
fly about 30 foreign correspondents into town for a week, so they can
learn that Chicago is as exciting as New York, and a lot nicer?

The business community decided to take this action in response to
surveys done overseas which showed that the main image of Chicago in
the minds of foreigners involved gangsters, machine guns and organised violence.

In the US everyone knows that big crime shifted from Chicago to
New York at least 30 years ago (this is symbolised by the fact that
2122 North Clark Street, where 4 members of Al Capone's gang
machine-gunned 7 members of Bugs Moran's gang on February 14,
1929, is now an old people's home). But the city fathers and mothers
consider it necessary to demonstrate the untruth of the criminal
stereotype to foreign newspaper readers, so I got a trip to Chicago two
years in a row.

The tour organisers didn't tell us this, but actually there is still crime
in Chicago. Now that the grownup gangsters have moved out (or into
business and politics), it's in the hands of the young. Violence and drug
dealing, by and between teenage gangs in the desolate high rise outer
suburbs, now leads to hundreds of deaths a year.

'We estimate there are 110 street gangs in Chicago with about
10,000 members all told,' says Edward Pleines, commander of the

Police Department's Gang Crimes Unit. 'Arresting kids day after day is not the ultimate answer. We've made so many arrests they can't jail them all.' To find another solution, the city council has established a 'gang intervention network', with a $9 million budget. So if you insist on retaining a criminal image of Chicago, then it should have more to do with *West Side Story* than *The Untouchables*. But my own images of Chicago are quite different.

For me Chicago is America's modern architecture museum, the town that invented and evolved the skyscraper – not the boring boxes we're used to in Australia, but temples to commerce, covered with gargoyles, curlicues of concrete, buttresses, spires and mosaics. (New York has some lovely skyscrapers, too, but they are all bunched in together, while Chicago displays them in vistas from the river and the lake.)

The centre of the skyscraper museum is the point where Michigan Avenue meets the Chicago River, which also happens to be the site of Chicago's first white settlement in 1679. There's the gothic Tribune Tower, which won first prize in 1922 in a contest to design the most beautiful skyscraper in the world. Across from it, 333 North Michigan Avenue, is the soaring marble and stone spire which won second prize in that contest. On the third corner is the baroque Wrigley Building, sheathed in terracotta as white as the chewing gum that paid for it.

Nearby, the State of Illinois building shows that Chicago's architects remain as innovative as ever. Helmut Jahn designed everything in the building to be transparent – even the lifts and the workings of the escalators – as a symbol of 'open government'.

The suburb of Oak Park, about half an hour by elevated railway from Chicago's centre, was the testing ground for Frank Lloyd Wright, the greatest architect of the 20th century. There are about 20 of his mansions within three blocks, some eccentric, some surprisingly traditional, as well as his former home, which he used as a laboratory for new ideas in furniture, windows and interior design.

Chicagoans offer an image of their town as 'a patchwork quilt of neighbourhoods', which is another way of saying Chicago is the most segregated city in America. There are unwritten rules about where you live which you break at great personal risk. This doesn't mean simply black neighbourhoods and white neighbourhoods. There are Italian neighbourhoods, Irish neighbourhoods, Greek, Arab, Hispanic, German, Chinese and Polish neighbourhoods (which in the past were divided between Polish Jewish and Polish Catholic).

Ethnic clashes at the borders of these neighbourhoods are rarer than they were in the 1920s, but they still happen, particularly when one group begins to appear in what is seen as another group's turf. In 1986, two fire bombs were thrown at the home of a black family who moved into the largely Irish area called Gage Park. A few weeks later, black residents of another Gage Park house were attacked as they walked in the street and told 'niggers aren't allowed past Western Avenue'.

There's a funny side to Chicago's determination to be a patchwork quilt rather than a melting pot. Take the street between 42nd and 44th streets. It's not called 43rd Street. It's called Muddy Waters Drive, in honour of a legendary Chicago blues singer. But travel east along Muddy Waters Drive and you suddenly discover that it has changed its name to Pope John Paul The Second Drive. That's because you have moved from a black neighbourhood to a Polish neighbourhood.

Or drive out from the city centre along Pulaski Road. At the point where it crosses 95th street, it suddenly becomes Crawford Road. You have moved into an Irish neighbourhood, and there's no way they are going to have a street that honours a Polish hero.

The ethnic diversity of the city at least ensures a wonderful variety of foods. But what Chicago does best is pizza – not our flat dry pastry smeared with cheese and tomato paste, but 'the deep dish', a crunchy pie crust filled with a 3 cm-depth of eggplant, tomato, cheese, sausage, mushrooms and olives.

When America's *People* magazine did the definitive national search for the best pizza, including what it called the five-second slither test ('Tilt the pizza on its side. If the ingredients slide off the crust like slush off a windshield, it's too greasy.'), the easy winner was Gino's Pizza House in Chicago.

Chicago is the home of the Second City Theatre ('the second city' is one of Chicago's nicknames for itself, in case anybody forgets about the inferiority complex), which has produced 90 per cent of America's great comic actors during its 25-year life.

Most US cities have clubs where comedians do stand-up monologues, but SCT is the only institution in the country that offers training in improvisational group comedy. Its graduates include Alan Alda, Alan Arkin, Dan Aykroyd, John Belushi, John Candy, Elaine May, Paul Mazursky and Harold Ramis.

Chicago is the home of rhythm and blues, the music of the Mississippi blacks who moved to Chicago in the 1950s and electrified their guitars. The Rolling Stones pinched that music and spread it around the world, but in the clubs of Chicago's south side, it's as fresh as ever.

Chicago contains the world's biggest gambling casino, except that it masquerades under the respectable name of the Chicago Mercantile Exchange. The gamblers turn over $4,000 million a day on something called futures. They operate in a huge room at the top of a Chicago skyscraper, where boys and girls in red, blue, yellow or green dustcoats give elaborate hand signals and yell at each other.

I've never understood futures, and three hours in the Chicago Mercantile Exchange didn't help much, especially when the man explaining them to me, Leonard Melamed, chairman of the Exchange's Executive Committee, was able to keep a straight face while uttering lines like, 'Reports about the swine flu virus made the bellies go wild'.

He was referring to the meat on the stomachs of pigs, which is one of the commodities upon which the futures exchange people gamble. In theory, they buy or sell contracts for the future delivery of pork bellies, in the hope that when they actually have to pay for them, the price will have changed to their advantage.

In practice, nobody wants any pork bellies and nobody has any pork bellies to sell. It's just a way of dealing in money, and it gets even more complicated when the futures (and the 'options on futures') are about the value of various world currencies, or the indexes that measure movements in various stock exchanges.

Melamed (handing out an illustrated guide to hand signals) says that the futures market is a wonderful thing because 'we allow a person suffering from uncertainty to transfer that uncertainty'. He says the Chicago Exchange has captured 80 per cent of the world futures business, and he's not above a little gloating: 'New York can't forgive itself that it didn't think of the idea first.'

It is said that most of the young futures traders use a lot of cocaine to keep up their energy levels, that many of them are millionaires by the time they're 30 and most of them are burnt out by the time they're 35. I can't help thinking they'd have had better survival odds making their money under Al Capone.

Never call it Frisco

In the spring, a pink mist settles over San Francisco Bay around 6 pm. It's the best time to fly in. As the plane descends, you can discern a few towers poking unevenly out of the pink, and what might be the two pylons of a red suspension bridge.

You know you're approaching a city with hills, cable cars, great food and wine, and citizens with the reputation of being the most eccentric and self-indulgent on the planet. But even as you touch down, San Francisco is keeping its mystery . . .

Well, enough of that sort of writing. That was how I started a travel article I wrote after my first visit to SF (locals NEVER call it Frisco) in 1981. I went on to rave about the gingerbread houses – wooden mansions built between 1850 and 1900, with turrets, bay windows, tiny balconies and outdoor staircases that lead nowhere. I loved the steep streets and the bay views. I declared the public transport system – a strange mix of buses, trams, subways, and cable cars – the most efficient I'd experienced. I enthused about driving out to the mighty Redwood forest in Marin County, and the pretty vineyards of the Napa Valley (you ain't tasted chardonnay till you've tasted Napa chardonnay).

San Franciscans are used to journalists flying in, having a fine time and gushing away like that. How could anybody be negative about America's most popular city?

But now there's trouble in paradise. San Franciscans are worried that their city is turning into another Venice. What's so terrible about that, you may well ask, Venice is a beautiful place. Indeed it is. But Venice is nothing else. It exists to be looked at. The few people who live there do so only to service the tourist industry. Over the past 500 years, Venice has been transformed from Europe's most powerful financial centre into Europe's biggest open air museum.

The transformation of San Francisco seems to have taken only 10 years. In the 1970s, San Francisco used to thumb its nose at Los Angeles because, despite its small size, it was the commercial and cultural capital of the west. Now The Big Orange has taken over from Baghdad by the Bay.

San Francisco, like Venice in its prime, was always a hedonistic city, but it was also the corporate headquarters of many of America's top companies. With the merger mania that afflicted American business during the 1980s, the SF-based companies started getting swallowed up and shifted elsewhere. That meant a loss of jobs, loss of business donations for civic and artistic activities, and loss of spending money by the citizens.

Loveliness doesn't help. In a survey by the *Wall Street Journal*, the chief executives of America's top 800 companies were asked what city they'd want to live in if they had a free choice. Most said they'd live in SF. But most of them don't. And those who do are leaving.

According to Kevin Starr, SF's former chief librarian who is now writing a social history of California, 'San Francisco is no longer oriented towards power and influence as it is towards connoisseurship and enjoyment. It is elegant and charming, but no longer where the action is.'

Not only is business disappearing, but so is culture. 'In a variety of endeavours,' Starr says, 'art, literature, fine printing, in which San Francisco has so long predominated, a Venetian twilight of decline pervades this city.'

Those who say SF no longer deserves the title 'The City That Knows How' point to the embarrassing disintegration of plans to celebrate the 50th anniversary of the Golden Gate Bridge in May 1987. Events planned for the celebration were cancelled one by one. The promoter, Bill Graham, himself a San Francisco landmark because of the huge rock concerts he staged there in the 1960s, pulled out of the proceedings in disgust at the mismanagement. The Bridge board announced that instead of having the rock group Huey Lewis and the News to play at the celebration, it had invited a high school band from Pottstown, Pennsylvania. The whole thing was pathetic.

Even SF's mayor, Diane Feinstein, grudgingly concedes some cause for concern. 'San Francisco is plagued with narcissism, in my opinion,' she says. 'Unless we recruit new business, we run the risk of problems down the line. We can't sit back on our laurels and commend ourselves for a beautiful bridge and cable cars.'

But she won't admit that Los Angeles has taken over anything worth having from San Francisco. She wrote a long letter to *The Los Angeles Times* complaining of a 'rash of San Francisco bashing'.

'For those of us who live in San Francisco – and believe it to be the world's most civilised city – recent articles in national publications raise our hackles. The message is: What's happened to San Francisco? It used to be a thriving metropolis. Like reports of Mark Twain's death, the stories of San Francisco's economic decline are greatly exaggerated.'

She pointed out that San Francisco has a lower unemployment rate than Los Angeles and a higher growth rate in 'total taxable retail sales', and that 'school enrolment is up, voter registration is up, the number of drivers' licences is up, all indicators are up – does that sound like a has-been city?'

No it doesn't, I suppose. But I wonder if the mayor of Venice was producing statistics like that some time around the year 1687.

The words of The Prophet

If anyone would know whether San Francisco is in decline, it should be Herb Caen. He has been writing a daily column for the *San Francisco Chronicle* for 50 years. There are those who say he made SF what it is today. That may not be entirely a compliment.

In a lifetime as one of America's most influential journalists in America's most open city, Herb Caen has seen the fads come and go, first in San Francisco, then across the nation, and then around the world . . . the beatniks (he invented the word in 1958), the hippies, the gays, and now, in the late 1980s, the humourless conservatives.

Caen has come to be known as 'The Prophet of The City' (and 'The City' is what he always calls it). He led the campaigns to keep The City livable – against high rise, against freeways, for public transport, for preservation of natural and historic areas. He attacked capital punishment, America's participation in the Vietnam War, and the nuclear build-up. But mainly, he says, he made a lot of jokes.

With the help of one assistant, he has written six 1,000-word columns a week since 1937. He is paid more than $120,000 a year (but no expenses). Caen, who is his own toughest critic, describes what he does as 'old-fashioned, three-dot journalism: short items, one liners, so-called insider stuff now and then, anecdotes, funny licence plates, bright sayings of stupid children and stupid sayings of bright children. It's a formula that was very much in vogue in the 30s and 40s, and that's where I'm from.'

But he does concede that the column is not wholly entertainment. 'You have to have some backbone, some point of view,' he says. 'The readers know where I stand.' His hate mail is heavy. 'It's not a good time to be a liberal,' he says. 'Eight years of Reaganism has made a great difference in this country; it's depressing to watch.

'The public has been brainwashed into being either middle of the road or conservative. I'm going the other way, to the left, right down to the end, a fighting limousine liberal.'

I ask what issues he is currently fighting. Suddenly Caen, sitting with rolled up sleeves and tie unknotted in his dingy office in the *Chronicle* building, starts to talk more slowly and quietly. He says that at the age of 71, he is suffering a crisis of confidence.

'I'm sort of in a little valley right now, waiting for another crisis to come along,' he says. 'It's harder than it used to be. I'm wondering if I might not be a bit dated, been on the job maybe a bit too long.'

This feeling started when he made a mistake a couple of years ago. 'I was stupid enough to make a few AIDS jokes right at the beginning. I don't think I realised how serious it was. Now I'm very careful about what I write.'

Caen worries that he's losing touch with The City. He eats lunch and dinner in restaurants every day, keeping up with the gossip – but his best contacts keep dying. He feels the city has grown beyond his control.

'I remember the small, beautiful town that was sort of a magical place at the end of the world, where we all thought we were members of the club,' he says. When the 'quick-buck artists' started to arrive in San Francisco in the 1940s, Caen had his finger on The City's pulse. The column could crusade against the scoundrels as well as gossiping about the elite. Caen recalls the slogan of another columnist, Walter Winchell: 'When people wants their names in the paper, it's publicity. When they don't it's news.'

A columnist was particularly lucky to have San Francisco as a source of material in the 1960s. 'It seems like there was more creativity here in the old days, starting with the bohemians,' Caen says. 'I don't know where they went.'

In the 1980s, the city has changed too much for Caen's tastes. He's been horrified at the number of beggars on the streets of a town that used to pride itself on taking care of all its citizens. He's been depressed by gimmicks designed to attract tourists. He says he got a letter recently from a girl who was travelling to California and couldn't decide if she should see San Francisco or Disneyland.

And the readers of the *Chronicle* are different. 'There are so many new people, so many neighbourhoods that I can't get to the heart of, mainly Asian, and lots of refugees. The new communities are not really fodder for a column like mine. I wander round the streets and feel like a stranger in my own home town.'

For his 50th anniversary, Caen wrote a particularly sad column about how San Francisco was 'in the December of its years, a restless city that lost its way – the old town lives on in bits and pieces, no longer connected into the congenial whole'. He wrote about meeting 'the guy that used to be me' in one of his favourite restaurants.

'You won't like to hear this, but you've got to stop living in the past,' Caen told his alter ego. 'You meet a better class of people there,' the nostalgist replied.

So is this living legend of journalism thinking of retirement? Definitely not. 'I think I'll stay here and just go on writing till I hit the end of the line,' Caen says.

'The last column is going to run with a black border on it, headed "The Kid's Last Column". I can see it. And they'll run a picture of me face down on my typewriter.'

11

EXCURSIONS

*Adventures by bus and subway: Harlem; the collective
farms of the Hudson; Catskill comics; Niagara Falls;
Coney Island and the red menace.*

Harlem has two faces. If you travel through it by bus, which is the only
way most white New Yorkers ever see it, Harlem looks like a war
zone . . . burnt out buildings with bricked up doorways, shops with
broken windows, vacant lots overgrown with weeds, groups of young
men lounging on front steps, staring at nothing.

But if you get off the bus and walk off the avenues into the side
streets, you're in a different world. Parts of it could be Paddington or
Carlton, except that the renovated brownstones are much more elegant
than most inner city terraces in Australia.

People are lounging on front steps here too, but they are families,
chatting to each other. When a white person strolls past, they watch
with curiosity but no apparent resentment, smile and ask how you like
the area.

I like it a lot. I've done a couple of long Sunday walks around
Harlem, and I've kept finding surprise. Like a street artist named
Franco. He has spent 8 years in a one-man project to beautify a street
called Martin Luther King Boulevard (known to white New Yorkers as
West 125th Street).

Franco – ask his last name and he replies 'The Great' – paints giant
murals on the aluminium shutters of the shops along the street, which
means his art is visible only when the shops are shut. Sphinxes,
mountain ranges, mermaids, grazing cows, waterfalls, dogs playing

snooker . . . the shutters in the 2 blocks Franco has finished so far prove that his imagination is well up to the task of decorating the 8 blocks ahead of him.

He says painting one shutter takes about three Sundays. He has to spend a lot more time persuading the shopkeepers to let him do it. 'They don't have to pay anything, but they are still cautious,' he says. 'Some of them say they'd rather have them left plain, can you believe it?'

Franco sold me a poster containing his manifesto, which says: 'The gates of Harlem are known to most people as the "Riot Gates" of the 1960s. They were once shrouded in grey despair, now illuminated with optimism. In 1980, the effect they have on viewers reflect a New Life Style. Hundreds of people asked Franco how he is able to achieve such a high degree of harmony and uniformity on corrugated steel. "I have the faith it takes," he replies.'

My first visit to Harlem was to see the street festival that marked the end of Harlem Week, 13 days of concerts, sporting contests and lectures celebrating black culture.

I went with considerable trepidation. Guidebooks to New York are almost unanimous in recommending against Harlem. The bravest of them is the *Michelin Guide*, which rates Harlem as a one-star sight and lists several historic buildings like the 1765 Morris Jumel Mansion and the 1801 home of Alexander Hamilton, a US treasury secretary who was killed in a duel. The *Michelin's* description concludes: 'It is advisable to travel through these areas during the day.'

The street festival was a small affair, with the sightseers almost outnumbered by police. Judging by the big signs everywhere and the free samples being handed out, the main sponsor of the festival was Salem cigarettes, but several of the stalls proclaimed their interest in personal hygiene.

The big fad for the health conscious in Harlem would seem to be 'colonic irrigation'. One of the many pamphlets I was handed on this subject offered a free initial treatment and contained testimonials from satisfied customers, including someone called 'CD', who boasts:

'I always felt that this cleansing program made more sense to me than running to the average doctor for drugs, surgery or chemotherapy etc, but when I looked in my toilet bowl after the cleanse I stayed there for 20 minutes just looking at what I'd been walking around with for years.'

I decided that my health needs would be best served at other stalls, which offered sweet potato pie, fried beef and peppers, and curry puffs.

Later I went back to Harlem to join a walking tour organised by a local schoolteacher named Larcelia Kebe (pronounced Keebee). The slogan of the tour company she runs from her home (an 1882 brownstone), is 'Harlem – it's nicer than you think'. I asked her if that didn't sound a bit defensive.

'Well, the press has not been kind to Harlem in the past 30 to 40 years,' she said. 'The guidebooks all say stay away. The first question people ask before they take my tours is "How safe is it?" I tell them the only time I ever had my purse stolen in New York was down on Fifth Avenue near Bloomingdale's.'

Kebe says the main customers for her tours are Europeans and Australians. Americans from outside New York, white or black, are too scared to walk through Harlem, even escorted.

My escort for the day was Darryl Outlaw, a young man who works as a tour guide in his spare time, and drives a hire car during the week (he says the most famous person he has ever driven was Diana Ross). He grew up in The Bronx (an outer suburb), but moved to Harlem because it's close to the excitement of Manhattan.

He summarised Harlem's history: discovered by Peter Stuyvesant in 1700; first a Dutch colony, then English; the fashionable spot for rich New Yorkers to build their country retreats in the mid-19th century; subject to a building boom around 1900; occupied by southern blacks seeking cheap accommodation after the First World War; now an area of massive unemployment.

Outlaw pointed out the site of the old Cotton Club, one of Harlem's hot nightspots when it became a jazz centre in the 1920s. Only whites were allowed to be customers of the Cotton Club, and only whites were allowed to work in the shops in Harlem until the late 1950s.

'It used to be that whites owned all the shops, so none of the money stayed in Harlem,' Outlaw said. 'Now most of the shops are owned by Koreans, so the money still leaves. This place is not going to get anywhere until blacks own the property themselves.'

I asked why so many old apartment buildings were derelict. 'The landlords say they can't afford to make the repairs, so the city condemns them, and then they stay empty, or squatters move in, until some developer thinks he can turn them into condominiums for rich people,' Outlaw said. 'It used to be that the city could save some of the buildings, but Reagan cut the funds for inner-city renewal.'

We went to a service at the Abyssinian Baptist Church and listened to some fiery gospel singing and some even more fiery talking from the Reverend Derrick Harkins. His theme was 'the power in the blood'. He said that while the men on Wall Street and the men in Washington might boast about their power, the true strength lay with those who had the spirit within them.

'Rise up young black people suffering without work,' he said. 'Rise up people in South Africa and know that your time is at hand. Rise up all the disenfranchised and know your power.'

'Amen,' said the two old women next to me.

An offer from Moscow

There were three Russians on our bus – Edgard and Yuri, who were journalists, and Boris, who was the driver. That made Russian the majority language, so it was spoken most of the time.

There was also a Bulgarian (who spoke Russian), an Italian, a Venezuelan, a Finn, an Australian and an American. We were on a two-day tour of the farms and agriculture laboratories of the Hudson River Valley, near New York, organised for foreign correspondents by the United States Information Agency. This could have been one of the most boring experiences of my life, but the presence of Edgard, Yuri and Boris The Driver ensured that it was not.

Edgard and Yuri got a shock when they boarded the bus and found that the driver was a Russian Jewish emigré, and initially treated Boris with a degree of caution. You don't have to be particularly paranoid to suspect that the US State Department could have placed Boris on board to report on what the Russians were saying to each other.

Soviet journalists in America are subject to considerable surveillance. Edgard, who works for Novosti Press, and Yuri, who works for Tass News Agency, have to get written permission from the State Department if they want to go more than 40 kilometres from New York. They can't pay for their own accommodation – the State Department pays for their hotel rooms, and sends a bill to the Soviet Embassy. Similar rules apply to American correspondents in Moscow.

But it quickly transpired that if Boris The Driver was an American spy, he was a most peculiar one. He never let anyone else get a word in. In English and Russian he complained about how the universe had treated him. He had escaped from Russia in 1979, got thrown out of an assortment of European countries, landed in America and decided he didn't like it. When he found out I was Australian, he asked 'What kind buses you got there?' I didn't know. I was therefore unable to comment helpfully on the prospects for Boris in moving to Australia and starting a tour bus company.

I asked him what he had been discussing with Yuri and Edgard. 'They nice guys, you know, but they don't want to open up to me,' he said. 'They asking me what I'm doing here.'

As we moved from fruit farm to vegetable farm to chicken farm, Edgard and Yuri asked the farmers more questions than the rest of us put together. They got a good story, too.

The farmers kept referring to 'the crisis in American agriculture'. There is massive overproduction, the farmers said, and too much competition, which makes prices too low. All the farmers, without exception, favoured the introduction of a co-operative system between farms so the prices could be set at an economic level. They were preaching socialism in the bastion of capitalism.

I recorded the following exchange when we were visiting an orchard called Montgomery Place. Doug, the farm manager, had been talking about the low prices he receives for his pears, supported by Jeff, his boss.

Yuri: 'You told about the crisis of agriculture. Can you tell more of your ideas about the crisis?'

Doug: 'We're growing too much, that's what it is.'

Edgard: 'How much are you paid?'

Doug: 'What me? I don't know if I should say. Or do you mean the pickers? The pickers get $16 a box and a good picker can do five boxes a day.'

Jeff: 'You realise you're going to be written up all over Russia as the oppressor of the masses?'

Edgard: 'What is wrong to tell what you are paid?'

Doug: 'Alright, I don't care, this has been boiling up inside me. I get $22,000 a year and a free house. That's it. I have a degree in agriculture. No-one's in this business for the money.'

Yuri: 'What do you see for the future?'

Doug: 'All this farming land around here is being sold off for housing. Soon California will be the only real farm state. The last farms around here will turn into visitors' pick-your-own, some kind of Disneyland – selling city people "The Farm Experience". They'll pay farmers for entertainment, not for food.'

Later I asked Yuri, who is very tall and in his mid 20s, what kind of stories he usually writes for Tass. He said he has written a lot about 'native Americans'. What, I asked, like Clayton Lonetree, the Marine accused of helping the Russians to spy on the US embassy in Moscow? 'No, we don't write about him,' Yuri said. He said he had done a detailed coverage of the case of an Indian activist named Leonard Peltier, who is accused of shooting two FBI agents. I had not seen a word about this in the American press. I asked if Yuri considered Peltier to be a kind of political prisoner or dissident, and he said 'Perhaps'.

I asked what sort of story he would do on the farm trip. He said, 'I think I will write about the management of the farms. You know, our agriculture is at kind of a crossroads, so we are interested in methods of agriculture.

'But I will not write the technical information in case I get into trouble. One time when I wrote about the Peltier case, I wrote about his eye disorder. The editor didn't check it, and they received many letters from ophthalmologists in the Soviet Union saying I didn't know what I was talking about.'

Journalists' troubles are the same the world over.

Edgard, from Novosti Press, is a craggy faced veteran in his mid 50s. He's a lot quieter than Yuri. He said he concentrates on features about the American way of life, rather than news stories. I asked where his articles appeared, and he said they were sometimes translated into English for *Moscow News Information*, a weekly paper which circulates in the West. I said I used to read it, and often wrote about its unusual stories when I was editing a newspaper column back in Australia. Edgard was delighted.

'Would you like to write for *Moscow News?*' he asked suddenly. 'What would I write about?' I said. 'Your views about our new policy of glasnost,' said Edgard. I said I couldn't do that because I didn't know much about glasnost, and anything I would write would be very superficial. 'No, no, no,' said Edgard. 'Just write the first few paragraphs about glasnost and then write about anything else you like.' He handed me his card.

It's a handsome offer. A chance to reach hundreds of thousands of new readers. I'll think about it. Perhaps I'll just send him a copy of this chapter, and see if they'd like to reprint it in *Moscow News*.

Kosher comedy

The Catskill Mountains, about two hours' drive north of New York City, are famous for many things. Rip Van Winkle slept here. So did George Washington – again and again and again, if we are to believe the signs in mansions and inns dotted all round the foothills.

But Americans who have stayed awake in the Catskill Mountains are most familiar with them as the training ground for generations of great Jewish comedians. For the past 40 years, a group of gigantic resort hotels in a part of the mountains known as the Borscht Belt have been home away from home for the Jewish families of New York. They have gone to the Catskills to breathe fresh air, eat kosher food, play shuffleboard or indoor tennis, and laugh. The laughter has been provided by young standup comics with names like Woody Allen, Lenny Bruce, Jerry Lewis, Don Rickles, Jackie Mason, and Joey Bishop, who, if they survived the Borscht Belt audiences, went on to become TV scriptwriters or variety show hosts or film-makers or just Living Legends.

In recent years, the Borscht Belt has fallen on hard times, as many of the traditional clientele decided they preferred Florida or Europe for their holidays. In 1986 the oldest Catskill resort hotel, Grossinger's, closed down, leaving dominance of the business to a more modern establishment called the Concord at Kiamesha Lake. A weekend there is an experience I commend to every student of anthropology.

Everything about the Concord is BIG. It has 1250 bedrooms, stacked in concrete high rise slabs built around a central entertainment area. It has two swimming pools, both much longer than Olympic size, three golf courses with a total of 45 holes, and 16 indoor tennis courts, which, on my weekend, had been converted into an exhibition area for the latest in ladders and nozzles, because the Concord was hosting a fire chiefs' convention.

The dining room seats 2,800 people, and it was full when I walked in at 7 pm. A brochure informed me that the dining room consumes 100,000 pounds (46,000 kilograms) of butter, and 10,000 pounds (4,600 kilograms) of cream cheese per year. This may explain why the biggest thing about the Concord is its customers. I looked in vain among the array of elderly men and women in the dining room for a thin body, or even a normal size body. I realised then why each Concord bedroom contains two double beds. Two of these people could not fit into one double bed.

Throughout dinner, there was a series of announcements over the loudspeaker system, previewing the pleasures to come for tonight and tomorrow . . . an art auction; 'the joy of floral arranging' with Isabelle; 'Cosmetics, Colours and You' – a demonstration courtesy of Lejeune Cosmetics; a 'co-ed touch football game' in the outdoor sports area; aerobics with Amy; yoga with Geri; a 'co-ed sauna and splash party' in the men's health club; and for the less energetic, a backgammon tournament in the lobby nearest the dining room.

And if you get an idle moment, you can always visit the Concord's resident rabbi or resident stockbroker. Or settle into one of the three bars, with barmen who, as the brochure puts it, 'know a thing or three about making your average drinking man glad to be alive', whether he is 'doing some serious drinking or some pre-dinner sipping'.

I've been putting off talking about the food, but now I must. A Jewish friend had said to me that although the Concord is supposed to be kosher, 'their cash route is suspect'. I pricked up my journalistic ears at this, thinking she meant they laundered money for the Mafia, but she explained that she was not saying 'cash route' but 'kashrut', a Hebrew term for the strictness with which the kosher rules are observed.

Perhaps if they were stricter, the food would be better. The absence of pork and shellfish is not a problem. The absence of any cooking ability in the kitchen is. I'm sure that kosherness doesn't have to mean dried-out chicken, soggy fish, stale bread, tinned vegetables and limp salad.

The service was constant, mainly involving repetition of the question 'howya doin, okay?' by a busboy who identified himself as Peter, a waiter who identified himself as Frank, and a Maitre D who identified himself as Lucio.

But there was the entertainment to look forward to. Another Concord brochure observes that 'the Concord is to popular entertainment what La Strada is to opera and what The Palace was to vaudeville. For an entertainer, a booking at Kiamesha Lake, NY, is just about as important as a command performance at the White House (when the Republicans are in office).'

On this night, the entertainment was a singing quartet called Four On The Town, who wore shiny outfits and did medleys from Broadway musicals, and a very thin comedian in his mid 30s named Lenny Rush.

In America today there's a new generation of standup comics, who explore issues like urban alienation, political hypocrisy, and difficult relationships in the AIDS era. Lenny Rush is not one of these. His act could have been performed as easily in 1950 as in 1987. Indeed, it probably was, though not by him.

Here are some highlights from the tape recording I made of Lenny Rush in the Concord Imperial Room (seats 3,500) at 10.30 on Friday night:

'I'm so thrilled to be here. I was here five years ago. Tonight I'm back by popular demand.

'What a beautiful audience this is. I was reading in the paper the other day that one in every three people is ugly. Take a look on either side of you. If they look good, you're the one.

'My father was a great guy. He used to take me swimming when I was a kid. All the other kids were ice skating. He'd take me out in a rowboat and throw me overboard, said that was the best way to learn to swim. Swimming wasn't hard. Getting out of the bag was hard.

'How many of you go down to Florida? (Loud applause). Yeah, I play there a lot. I do the Medicare convention, and I lead the Prostate Day Parade. It's a good place to die, Florida.

'Hello honey, you're a pretty girl. What's your name? Loretta. Is this guy your husband, Loretta? How many years you been married? 18 years? God bless you. You know if you'da murdered him on your honeymoon you coulda been out of jail 9 years?

'Do you believe in sex before marriage? You do? Even if it holds up the ceremony?

'And what qualities do you look for in a man, Loretta? Good looking? Tall? Loretta, how about honesty and intelligence and sincerity and respect? Those are the things I look for in a woman. Unless she has a big pair of tits.

'I was engaged once, you know. Lovely girl, Ramona Lipschitz, from the very famous Lipschitz family, of Alabama, makers of Lipschitz Grits. I met her through a computer dating service. She's a lovely girl, got a glass eye with a crack in it. On a cloudy day she can see rainbows.

'I just got a police dog, for protection. But he howls all the time. I think maybe the badge is hurting. He's a German shepherd. He knows I'm Jewish, too. Goes in the closet and pees on my shoes. Goes round with his front leg up like this.'

And so it continued. Lenny Rush was a smash hit. The audience screamed. They demanded three encores. It is good to know that, at least in the Catskills, some things in life never change.

The honeymoon is over

Driving into Niagara Falls, I got stuck behind a battered Land Rover. The back of it was covered with stickers bearing messages like 'Stop crime – shoot first', 'Reagan-Bush 84', 'Good fishermen know how to use their rods'; and 'I am the National Rifle Association and I vote'.

That Land Rover, I decided, would have to be the worst car in America to run into the back of, so I drove very carefully. I wondered whether its driver worked for one of the Niagara Falls tourist agencies. These days, knowledge of firearms is an essential career skill for anyone in the Niagara hospitality industry, because big trouble has come to the world's most famous honeymoon resort.

Late in 1986 two privately run tourist information offices in Niagara Falls were firebombed, and for several nights in a row shots were fired at the home of the man who owns the town's main tour agency. At the same time, all the signs erected by the town council to direct visitors to the falls were stolen or made illegible.

Competition for tourist dollars has always been fierce in Niagara Falls, but shooting, bombing, and stealing go beyond what are considered the normal activities of a free-market economy. David Fleck, president of the local Hotel and Motel Association, felt compelled to speak out about it. 'When tourist information booths are getting bombed, people don't get a very good impression of Niagara Falls,' he said. 'This isn't Beirut. It's America.'

The problem is that Americans aren't flocking to the falls in the numbers they once did, and some locals whose livelihoods depend on tourism are getting desperate. On the roads leading into Niagara Falls they've set up booths which pretend to be official tourist information offices but which actually try to sign up visitors for their own package tours and affiliated motels. They steal the official direction signs so visitors will be forced to drive around aimlessly and finally come to their shops or booths for help. And they use bombs and guns on each other to reduce competition.

After spending two days in Niagara Falls, I can understand why tourism is declining. I wonder how tourism ever got started there. The highways leading into the town make Parramatta Road look like the Champs Elysees. First you pass chains of chugging factories, then used-car yards, then hundreds and hundreds of red brick motels with names like 'Lovers Rest', 'Two Hearts', 'Wedding Bells', 'Cascades

(Free TV)', 'Bit-o-Paris (Waterbeds)', and every permutation on the word 'honeymoon'.

The middle of town is neat and modern, mainly consisting of a big shopping mall and a convention centre. Behind the buildings you can see a heavy mist rising, and you get excited that you're about to see the falls. Then you discover the biggest fraud of all: YOU CAN'T SEE THE NIAGARA FALLS FROM AMERICA.

The river that becomes the waterfalls is the border between Canada and the United States. America is above the falls. So you have to go over a bridge into Canada to get a reasonable view of them. Not knowing this, I hadn't thought to bring my passport. Now I realise that the line from the old song *Thanks For the Memory*, which refers to 'that weekend at Niagara when we never saw the falls', is not a joke about busy lovers. It's just a description of the usual fate of American visitors.

But, finally, the consumers are waking up. In 1986, 5 million tourists visited the American town of Niagara Falls. By comparison, 15 million tourists visited the Canadian town of Niagara Falls. Most of the visitors to the Canadian side were Americans. They drove through their own side so fast they didn't register as statistics.

According to Eugene Guido, who runs Gray Line, the town's biggest tour agency, the first question most visitors now ask is 'Where's Canada?' He summarises the job of the tour agencies on the American side: 'Number one, we have to talk people out of Canada. Number two, we have to book them a room. And number three, we have to sell them a tour if we can.'

He admits he sympathises with the person who keeps stealing the direction signs, since tourists should not be given too much free assistance. 'I feel very strongly that tourists should be left alone once they get to the city limits,' he says. 'They'll find the waterfalls sooner or later. But first, we want them to filter through our business community.'

For those visitors who find themselves stuck on the American side, filtering through the business community and looking enviously over at the Canadian side don't really make a holiday. Niagara Falls USA isn't exactly flush with commercial entertainment. The only cinema in town shows porno movies.

But you can always take in the latest production of the Niagara Falls Little Theatre Company. They were doing *Annie* while I was there. Just about every schoolkid in town had been recruited to be an orphan.

Another instructive way to pass the time in Niagara Falls is to visit Love Canal. This is not a scenic experience. It's more like being in an episode of *Twilight Zone*. Love Canal is a suburb of substantial middle-class houses about three kilometres from the centre of town. Within an area about 6 blocks square, all the houses are empty, with their windows boarded up. As I drove into the neighbourhood, the streets were thick with snow, without a single tyre mark. The air had a smell reminiscent of Brasso.

Love Canal has been this way since 1980, when the New York state government ordered the evacuation of the area. The rate of serious illness and birth deformities among the residents had led to the discovery that several chemical companies in Niagara Falls had been dumping toxic wastes into Love Canal for nearly 40 years. A spate of lawsuits concluded in 1985 with the Occidental Petroleum Company and the City of Niagara Falls paying $20 million as compensation to 1,300 former residents of the Love Canal area. Now there is talk of trying to clean up and repopulate the area.

On the edge of the ghost suburb is a building labelled 'New York State Department of Environmental Conservation. Love Canal Revitalisation Agency'. It was empty when I drove past.

Russia invades the funfair

Winter is the worst time to go to Coney Island, they told me. It's depressing enough in the summer, but at this time of year, it's suicidal.

You may think of it as the big daddy of funfairs, they said, but you need to know that it isn't a carnival, it's a suburb. And what's left of the funfair only symbolises how far the world has moved from innocent amusements. All you'll see are muggers and old Russians.

New Yorkers worry about Coney Island, the sandy tip of the borough of Brooklyn, about an hour by subway from Manhattan. They know that for foreigners, it is a legendary name. In the 18th century, it was just a place where people hunted rabbits ('coney' is the old Dutch word for rabbit). But people started building holiday homes there. The world's first hot dogs were sold on Coney Island in 1871. The world's first roller coaster was built there in 1884.

Ocean bathing as a mass amusement happened first at Coney Island's Brighton Beach (in 1890 you could rent a bathing costume – full length, of course – for 25 cents, with a dish of clams thrown in free). New York's evangelists called it 'Sodom By The Sea'. There were gambling casinos, brothels, gin joints, grand hotels and three racetracks.

In the 1930s, immigrants sailing into New York Harbour at night found that their first view of America was not the Statue of Liberty, but Coney Island's brightly lit Parachute Jump and Wonder Wheel (built by George W. Ferris in 1890). Woody Allen claims to have spent his childhood in a house right under the Big Dipper (watch him trying to eat his shaking soup in *Annie Hall*). Neil Simon grew up within sight of the Dreamland Tower and devoted not one, but three plays to the area (starting with *Brighton Beach Memoirs*).

And now? The temperature is just above freezing and the wind squeals through the rusty iron and splintered wood of the two remaining roller coasters. The Wonder Wheel has no seats and the Dreamland Tower Parachute Jump has no parachutes. The sideshows, with signs like 'The Human Cigarette Factory: See him roll them in his mouth', are surrounded with barbed wire. Lime green paint is peeling off the walls of the Aquarium. The cafes, advertising hot dogs and knishes, have their aluminium shutters down.

But the sun is shining, the sea is glistening, and old people are sitting in portable chairs all along the boardwalk. They are so bundled up in colourful scarves and coats, and they sit so stiffly, that they look like those Russian dolls that open up to endless smaller dolls within.

Nowadays Coney Island has the nickname 'Little Odessa', not just because of its physical similarity to that resort on the Black Sea, but because 100,000 Russian immigrants have settled there since the mid-1970s. One block back from the boardwalk, underneath the elevated railway which runs along Brighton Beach Avenue, it is hard to find a shop sign in English, and harder to hear anyone speaking the language.

Step into M&I International Foods, 249 Brighton Beach Avenue, and you almost bang your head on rows of salamis hanging from the ceiling. The owners claim they sell more than 100 types of sausage. Each one is labelled in Cyrillic characters. And of course there are bottles of preserved apricots and sour cherries, jars of caviar, cream cakes, chicken croquettes covered with paprika, and giant loaves of bread.

In the New York tabloids, Coney Island is currently notorious as the home of a group called 'the red mafia'. The name couldn't be more inaccurate, since the people concerned are definitely not Italian and are the opposite of communists. In fact the red mafia members are at the cutting edge of capitalism, engaging in credit card frauds, tax evasion schemes, extortion of shopkeepers, and diamond thefts.

The New York Police Department has set up a Russian Desk, staffed by 5 detectives, to track these characters, who have allegedly been responsible for 7 murders in the Coney Island area. In one case a mother and son were found dead in their apartment with their eyes gouged out, apparently as a lesson to others who were refusing to co-operate. The police theorise that the Soviet government played a mean trick on America, by issuing exit visas to about 400 jailed criminals amongst the thousands of genuine cases who wanted to join relatives in the United States. These criminals have found a whole new range of moneymaking ventures in the land of the free.

The police have a hard time getting anyone to talk. Sergeant Vincent Ferrara, squad commander of the 60th Precinct, which covers the Coney Island area, describes one Russian emigré they'd brought in for questioning: 'His leg looked like a pretzel. It was broken in a dozen places in a Soviet prison. He showed it off and said, "You're going to do worse to me?"'

The most spectacular recent murder happened outside Coney Island's most popular Russian restaurant, Odessa. A 44-year-old businessman named Vladimir Reznikov was getting into his car after dinner, when a man rushed up and pumped 6 bullets into him. Reznikov was widely believed to be an 'enforcer' for the 'red mafia'. The killing remains unsolved.

So it seemed logical to end a day's excursion to Coney Island with dinner at Odessa. Downstairs it looks like a pinball parlour. Upstairs you enter a huge red-wallpapered room crammed with tables. The women are short and round and wear spangly dresses and stiletto heels. The men wear leather jackets or sweaters, and have big sad faces. All of them seem to be smoking. Most are drinking vodka. Children in suits run around at random.

There is no menu. The minute you sit down, the food starts arriving. 'Yis colt eppitisers,' says the waiter, setting plates over every square centimetre of the tablecloth and then, having run out of space, stacking more plates on top of the first layer. A bottle of French wine arrives. The waiter has divined telepathically that we four Westerners are too wimpy for vodka.

Barely have we begun to taste the stewed eggplant, devilled eggs, caviar, herrings, tarama, mushrooms and rolled veal, when the waiter returns with another tray. 'Yis hyot eppitisers,' he says, making a third layer with fried potatoes, stuffed cabbage, stuffed chicken, stuffed intestines, unidentifiable crumbed things that may be fish. Jugs of Coca-Cola and ice keep arriving. When we ask for another bottle of wine, the waiter says, 'Yis extra, right? You know dyat, right? I tole you dyat, right?'

Then there's an amazing moment. A tall black woman in a black leather mini skirt and thigh length black boots walks through the door. 'Boy, is she ever in the wrong place,' we think. But she comes over to the table next to ours and effusively greets a man there, then pushes through the crowd to the back of the room, where a band is setting up.

It turns out she is the floor show. As the waiter brings 'myen cyourses' – skewers of tough meat, with tinned peas – she starts belting out pop songs in apparently fluent Russian. One of the people at the next table, who has earlier established that the reason I am taking notes is that I am a journalist, leans over and whispers to me: 'Point of interest. That guy she spoke to. He's her gynaecologist.' The gentleman in question beams proudly.

The meal (dessert was chocolate-covered meringues and cream cakes) has made it imperative that we dance. The band blends Russian, Hebrew, Spanish, Italian and '60s American rock. My most vivid image of the occasion is around midnight, when the band strikes up the old Beatles song *Back in the USSR*. The crowd cheers wildly at the line: 'Back in the USSR, you don't know how lucky you are, boys'. As they say in these parts: go figure that.

12

TASTES

*The outer edges of American eating: the best in breakfast
(and probably dinner); hunting the wild chili; the
birthplace of fast food; LA luscious; new nationalism in
New York.*

The best breakfast in America is to be had in Berkeley, California. I
suspect that the best dinner in America is also to be had in Berkeley,
California, but I'm reluctant to be so dogmatic on that subject, because
there's a lot more competition in the dinner business than there is in the
breakfast business.

It should not be too surprising that this town of 100,000 citizens,
about half an hour by train from San Francisco, has a restaurant
offering the best breakfast in America and another restaurant offering
probably the best dinner in America, since Berkeley has been a
pioneer of exciting ideas ever since the 1960s.

The Free Speech Movement started at the University of California at
Berkeley in 1964, spread to other campuses, and turned into the
anti-Vietnam War movement. Berkeley elected the first town council in
America to call itself 'socialist'. Since 1971, the council members have
refused to say the American Pledge of Allegiance which all other
councils say before meetings, because they don't believe the United
States is 'one nation, under God, indivisible, with liberty and justice for
all'.

The Berkeley Board of Education has rewritten the Pledge of
Allegiance for schoolchildren to include a call for world peace.

Berkeley schools do not fly the American flag, in defiance of a State law that requires it.

In 1982, Berkeley voters passed a referendum that made the use of electroshock therapy by psychiatrists illegal. In 1983, the council declared Berkeley to be a sanctuary for refugees from right-wing regimes in Central America, and sent food parcels to the left-wing rebels in El Salvador. In 1985, students at Berkeley's university started a series of sit-ins to protest the university's investments in companies doing business in South Africa, and 650 people were arrested in a month. The anti-investment movement quickly spread to other American campuses.

But these days Berkeley is becoming better known for its hedonism than for its radicalism. Restaurants are replacing revolutionary bookshops. Gourmets from all over America now make the pilgrimage to Berkeley to visit two shrines – Chez Panisse for dinner, and Bridge Creek for breakfast. This is not simply because they offer fine food. Chez Panisse and Bridge Creek have sociological significance far beyond their menus. They symbolise the return of American values to eating.

Alice Waters, who founded Chez Panisse in 1972, is acknowledged as the creator of the style that has come to be called 'California cuisine'. When she started, her plan was simply to recreate some of the tasty dishes she had sampled in provincial France. But over the years she and her partner Jeremiah Tower moved away from French recipes. They abolished heavy sauces which mask flavour, introduced fresh local ingredients – leaves, root vegetables, herbs, black beans, mutant mushrooms, as remarkable for their colour contrasts as for their tastes – and used simple cooking methods, especially grilling, to keep every element sharp and distinct. Jeremiah Tower eventually split from Alice Waters, and now runs his own excellent restaurant called Stars in San Francisco, but Chez Panisse retains its reputation as California's most innovative dining place.

Bridge Creek is much newer – it opened in 1985 – and it serves only breakfasts, but already it has been written up in *The New York Times* as 'the new wave in American cuisine'. *The Times* said it recreates the great midwestern breakfasts that many Americans imagine they ate in their childhood.

So of course I had to make the pilgrimage to Berkeley. I had learned that serious hedonists stay in a small modern inn called The French Hotel, number 1538 Shattuck Avenue. Look across the road and you see a sign saying Jungian Dreamwork Institute. This is an important landmark, because it is next door to Chez Panisse, which has a tiny sign that is easy to miss. Bridge Creek is in a two-storey wooden mansion half a block down the street.

I'd eaten at Chez Panisse once before, and had one of the most glorious experiences of my life. This time it was even better – a set dinner for $45 consisting of wild mushroom tart, a soup of celery root, parsnips and turnips, plump pigeon pieces with truffle sauce, a salad of multicoloured leaves and lettuces, and a tangerine sorbet.

I wondered how I'd face breakfast the next day, but an early morning walk through the Berkeley campus brought back my appetite. The walk also proved that, unlike me, Berkeley hasn't become completely bourgeois – there were signs advertising a workshop on The Oppression and Empowerment of Women, Tai-Chi classes, and a rally to Stop Trident Two Testing. I passed the Women For Peace Shop, selling posters that said 'Jobs Not Bombs: You Can't Hug a Child with Nuclear Arms.'

Bridge Creek has strict rules: no credit cards, no cheques, no alcohol, no smoking and no reservations. The last of these meant we had to wait 45 minutes for a table (but then, breakfast hours are from 8 am to 2.30 pm, so there's no hurry). Behind us a queue stretched down the stairs, looking too Berkeleyan to be real – long-haired women, bearded men, intelligent children, carrying books and magazines and wearing wool, cotton and leather (the house rules don't need to include 'no polyester').

Breakfast starts with muffins – one flavoured with mixed fruit, cinnamon and nuts, and the other with ginger. There's a pot of home-made strawberry jam on the table, and to have something to put it on, we order 'biscuits', which turn out to be what Australians call scones – crunchy on the outside, soft and moist on the inside.

Then we have sour cream hot cakes, which are the lightest pikelets in the universe (with real maple syrup), and scrambled eggs with minced ham, chives and cream cheese (accompanied by thin chips that would make McDonald's envious).

Tragically, there's no room for the waffles with fresh fruit, or the four-grain toasted cereal with pecans and red banana, or the cornmeal Johnnie cake, or the cheddar omelette with apple-smoked ham, or the gingerbread pancakes with herb sausage. The Bridge Creek breakfast costs $20 for two and leaves a determination to come back and spend a month in Berkeley.

Talking to some locals later, I learned that all is not idyllic in what is known in the town as Gourmet Gulch. A catering industry union was trying to persuade the local restaurants to employ union members, or to let their existing workers join the union, but some restaurants refused. The union urged Berkeleyans to boycott non-union restaurants, but most of the citizens, including some with anti-apartheid stickers on their cars, crossed the picket lines and entered the restaurants without a second glance. The attempt to unionise failed.

The vice-mayor of Berkeley, Veronica Fukson, who is a member of the ruling socialist faction, finds this pretty depressing. 'I think, to a certain extent the population of Berkeley is changing,' she said. 'Property values are rising and I think we're seeing more professionals come in who don't necessarily have the pro-worker, pro-union attitudes that people used to have. To a certain extent, Berkeley is becoming very Yuppified.'

Hot town, chili in the city

The rendezvous: Mike's Bar and Grill, 650 Tenth Avenue, New York City, in an area known as Hell's Kitchen. Hell's Kitchen has been a notorious crime zone for decades, and is the home of a gang called The Westies, 9 of whom are currently on trial for multiple murders. We are not seeking them tonight.

The mission: to begin a chili crawl through Manhattan, to boldly taste the spiciest creations of three cafes famed for their pepperific potpourris.

The motivation: The US Congress is currently considering a bill to declare chili the national food of America. Now is the time to learn more about a dish which the world wrongly imagines was invented in Mexico.

The guide: Jonathan Levine, Chairman of the New York chapter of the International Chili Society, a man whose telephone answering machine advises callers to 'remember, there are only three important things in life: good chili, good wine and Nero Wolfe novels.' Tonight we will test the first of those assertions, and a bit of the second.

Encountered just inside the door of Mike's, Levine proves to be a large man in a safari suit. He introduces his friend Ed McGarigle, a slightly less large man in a safari suit, who has just become chairman of the New Jersey chapter of the International Chili Society. They have kindly given up their Saturday night to assist the researches of a curious Australian, and because they will eat chili at the slightest provocation.

Levine is not optimistic that the bill to honour chili as the national food will ever be passed in congress, because certain states are trying to sabotage it with competing claims for dishes like apple pie and barbecued ribs. But he has no doubt that chili deserves it.

He says it was invented last century during a cattle drive in Texas. The cooks often threw in hot peppers to vary the flavour of the beef stew that was standard diet on the trail. One time, a stampede distracted everyone's attention and the stew stayed on the fire too long. The water evaporated, and the peppers and the meat dissolved together. The cowboys came back from subduing the cattle and discovered a wondrously concentrated new taste sensation.

Some Mexican restaurants, trying to lay claim to the dish, add beans to it and describe it on their menus as 'chili con carne', which Levine dismisses as a fake name. Americans just call it chili.

From Texas, it has spread across the nation. Almost every state now has its own 'chili cookoff' each year, sending the winners to a national cookoff held in California in October. Levine, who travels the country as a judge for these events, has to put up with extraordinary regional variations.

'In Cincinnati they like to add chocolate and cinnamon to their chili,' he says. 'In North Dakota they add honey, celery, it's like a sweet vegetable stew. Sometimes it looks like vomit.

'In Maryland one time I tasted the winner of a cookoff and it was like Campbell's tomato soup with pieces of uncooked pork. I was gagging. They like their tomatoes in Maryland.'

(As Levine tells it, cookoffs tend to be chaotic affairs. In addition to mass tastings, the New York cookoff includes a tortilla throwing contest, a hat stomping contest and a 'shoot and holler' contest, in which the entrant must swallow a stiff drink and yell. One sideshow got so popular that Levine has broken it off into a whole day's event of its own – 'the Bloody Mary Mixoff'.)

The chili in Mike's Bar and Grill gets high marks from Levine and McGarigle. Levine is even prepared to tolerate the presence of 'garbonzo beans' (chickpeas), although they would be frowned on by most judges. We agree that Mike has clearly been stewing his chili long enough to blend the flavours, and it's not so hot as to destroy the palate.

Mike's also has the wonderful sounds of the Animals, the Dave Clark

Five and Dusty Springfield blaring from the juke box, and the following message on the bottom of the menu: 'Mike feels the loud music is important to the atmosphere – don't even ask!'

We take a cab to our next test site, a diner called Exterminator Chili in an area called Soho (for SOuth of HOuston Street). Soho is an artists' quarter, where the prevailing fashion colour is black, and the prevailing hairstyle is neo-punk. These are on full display among Exterminator's staff and customers, who sit in 'theme' booths decorated with objets de kitsch. The best booth is a shrine to Elvis Presley, surrounded with dolls, posters, busts of The King and electric candles to keep his memory alight. The crowd is so loud the music is inaudible.

Exterminator offers unorthodox ingredients in its chilis, and you can choose among three strengths: residential, commercial and industrial. We sample a residential strength turkey chili (with a dash of cinnamon), a commercial strength beef chili, and an industrial strength creation made with salamis and kidney beans.

They are all oddly weak, suggesting to the experts that longer stewing is desirable. Levine confides that Exterminator's owners got into 'a bit of a snit' because they didn't win the commercial section of last year's New York Chili Cookoff, and have refused to enter this year. The consolation is that Mike's Bar and Grill is entering for the first time.

We are glad to move on to our third destination, the Manhattan Chili Company in Greenwich Village. This is the most serious chili establishment in town. The owner has written a cookbook, and proudly displays a bronze plaque indicating the Manhattan Chili Company was the winner of last year's commercial cookoff.

The chilis have cute names ... Texas Chain Gang, High Plains Buffalo, Abilene Choral Society and Music Guild (that's mild, or, more euphemistically, 'gourmet'). Lamb, pork, chicken, even seafood feature among the ingredients. They're pretty good, but we all have a hankering for the full-flavoured simplicity of Mike's.

I've been keeping pretty quiet during our chili crawl, just eating, drinking, and observing. But I must had been doing something right. As the night ends, Levine bestows upon me a singular honour – he asks if I'd like to be a judge in the New York State Chili Cookoff on 13 September. I cannot decline.

Postscript: The superiority of Mike's was never definitively tested. So few restaurant representatives attended the New York State Chili Cookoff, owing to constant rain on the day, that the professional part of the proceedings was cancelled.

But that left the amateur chili cooks, of whom about 50 appeared in the playground of a primary school on Manhattan's Upper East Side, laden with pots and packets of secret spices. As one of 10 judges, I had to taste 22 chilis and 16 chili pies.

It rapidly became apparent that I lacked the necessary subtlety of palate for the task. Most of the chilis tasted identical to me, and my choice of the best three chilis and the best three pies had nothing in common with the ultimate majority verdict of the judges.

Where the fast tests first

Columbus, Ohio, is the fast food capital of America, which means, of course, that it's the fast food capital of the world.

Eight major fast food chains have their world headquarters in Columbus. Every Big New Idea in the fast food industry gets tried out first in Columbus.

Drive along its main roads and you'll pass 57 Wendy's Old Fashioned Hamburger stores, 56 McDonald's, 38 Dairy Queens, 30 Kentucky Fried Chickens, 28 Pizza Huts, 15 Taco Bells and hundreds of shiny outlets bearing company names which you've never heard of in Australia but which you soon will. (Except perhaps for a new 'gourmet burger' group called Fuddrucker's, which somehow doesn't have the sound of success about it.)

There are also the ghost stores – peeling remnants of fast food ideas whose time hadn't come, like Wuv's, Burger Boy Food-A-Rama, Big Bite Pita Bread Sandwich and, probably the most idiotic concept in the history of the industry, Prusutti and Chin, an attempt to combine fast Italian and fast Chinese.

The world's first fast food chain, White Castle, started in Columbus in the mid-1920s (30 years before the first McDonald's Speedee Service Drive-In opened its doors). White Castle still has 220 stores across the US, making miniature hamburgers (about a third the diameter of a Big Mac) at 40 cents each.

Their unique feature is that the beef pattie has holes in it and is cooked in a bed of onions, which get sucked up into the holes and suffuse the beef. White Castle burgers are known affectionately in

Columbus as 'sliders' or 'rectum rockets'. The locals tend to prefer the more elaborate Wendy's burgers, which were also founded in Columbus, and have now spread as far afield as Switzerland, Singapore and New Zealand.

Fast food is not the only claim to fame of Columbus, Ohio. The city was also the birthplace of the disposable vacuum cleaner bag, the automatic teller machine for banks, the ice cube tray and James Thurber, the comic writer and cartoonist. Thurber's pretty gingerbread house is on display in a Columbus suburb.

After that, there's not a hell of a lot to say about Columbus, Ohio. So why am I visiting it? I'm here for the opening of a new branch of Westpac (the Australian bank).

In its restless search for powerful American dollars to prop up its Australian profits, Westpac discovered that the state of Ohio exports more goods to Australia than to any other country, and that Ohio is the home of 68 companies with affiliates or subsidiaries in Australia. Westpac pinpointed Columbus because it is Ohio's biggest town, and the brightest spot in the declining industrial area known as 'the rust belt'.

Judging by the reception turned on by Columbus, the arrival of the Westpac branch is the biggest thing to happen to the town for years. Reporters and camera crews from all the local papers and TV stations turned up for the opening ceremony, and the governor of Ohio, Richard Celeste, took time off from his re-election campaign to cut the ribbon.

In the election, Governor Celeste, who is in his 50s, faces a Republican opponent named James Rhodes, who is 77. Mr Rhodes's age is generally seen as a big election liability, except that Governor Celeste has a liability too – several members of his Cabinet are on trial for taking bribes and there are allegations that the companies that got the most business with the state government were those that contributed most to Celeste's campaign funds. (The battle between Celeste and Rhodes is summarised in Columbus as 'sleeze versus geeze'.)

Westpac is too new and innocent yet to know the unwritten rules of Ohio's corporate culture, so we should not see any sinister significance in the fact that Westpac's chief executive, Bob White, presented Governor Celeste with a large boomerang. Westpac doesn't expect to be doing much business with the government anyway.

I asked Westpac's Columbus branch manager, Mike d'Silva, whether any fast food companies were among the bank's customers.

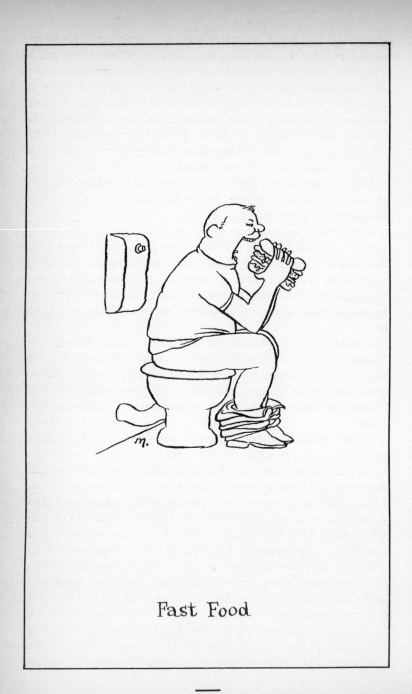

Fast Food

Not so far, he said, and added: 'Wendy's did have a small operation in Australia, but I believe they are now closed. It wasn't the greatest success with Australians.'

The fact that Australians prefer McDonald's to Wendy's suggests that we are still at a primitive stage of development in our fast food tastes, because Wendy's is a superior burger in every way. But even Wendy's is not the leader in the fast food field. That honour belongs to another Columbus company called Rax.

It is unanimously agreed that Rax, though relatively small (it has 500 outlets, compared to Wendy's 3,500), is the most influential company in America's mass consumption industry. Rax is known as the innovator. It pioneers the ideas, and if they work, the other companies steal them.

Look at Rax and you see the future of fast food in America (and eventually in Australia). Rax introduced the salad bar, to let people choose extra ingredients that gave them a feeling of health with their beef. It introduced the takeaway baked potato, with a choice of fillings like cheese, broccoli or chili. It added little solariums with hanging plants to all its stores. It introduced do-it-yourself taco filling counters.

So naturally, while I was in Columbus, I went to see the most admired man in the US fast food business, the chairman of Rax, Pat Ross. He's a wiry and fidgety character who gives the impression of juggling a thousand thoughts in his head at every moment.

He started in the business by running some stores for Burger Chef and Wendy's in the 1960s and then took over a roast beef sandwich company which was originally called Jax, then Rix, and finally Rax, in 1976.

'We did a couple of things that nobody had ever done before,' he recalls. 'We put a big salad bowl with lettuce in it and a couple of kinds of dressing out in the dining room. That has resulted today in a salad bar which is the premier in the industry and is 22 per cent of our sales and has 50 items on it.'

The next major change was to move away from roast beef. First came the stuffed baked potato. Then, when research indicated Rax was appealing more to women than to men, the Mexican Bar was added, where you can 'build your own taco or burrito'. Finally, Rax made the big move – to hamburgers.

'It was getting to where the roast beef was the reason for not coming to Rax,' Ross says. 'America eats hamburgers, you know, 11 times more than the most ordered sandwich on our menu. If you have four people in a car and someone says "Let's go to Rax" and one person says "I don't want to go there, they don't have hamburgers" then we lose out. That's how we got started down the hamburger trail.'

The Rax hamburger took two years to research, and another year of trials in selected stores. The final, perfect form appeared in 1985. It has an uneven, wheaty tasting bun, dusted with powdered corn, and a vast variety of optional additions. Ross observes that Wendy's has now introduced a new burger called 'The Big Classic' which is identical to the Rax 'Worksburger'.

I asked him why Americans eat so much fast food. 'We like to do things in a hurry in America, and I think eating is less of a vocation with us, in the sense of setting aside time for a leisurely meal, than it is in other countries. Then there are a lot of families where both parents work, and the fast food experience may be the only time when the family eats together.'

The current problem facing the fast food industry is the age pattern of the US population. In the years to come, there will be fewer teenagers available to work cheaply, and fast food stores will have to pay higher wages and employ more old people and handicapped people.

But Ross envisages continuing steady growth, and his ultimate goal is 2,500 Rax stores across America. He has no plans to tackle Australia. We're just not ready for Rax yet.

Puck's picks

In Los Angeles, there are those who become celebrities and then go into the restaurant business, and there are those who go into the restaurant business and then become celebrities.

Dudley Moore is in the first category. Wolfgang Puck is in the second. Mr Puck's future in food is bright. I'm not so sure about Mr Moore's.

Dudley Moore's restaurant is called 72 Market, which is also its address in Venice Beach, a bohemian area of the city. He opened it in 1986, after making five flop movies in a row. His partners include Liza Minelli and Bruce Paltrow, executive producer of the TV show *St Elsewhere*. It is currently one of the hottest spots to be seen in LA.

Like most restaurants opened in America lately, 72 Market has stark white walls and high ceilings. A lovely lady in black plays a grand piano at the back of the room. The menu is an attempt to combine

America's two current eating fads – 'nouvelle Californian' and back-to-basics motherhood food. Thus there are lots of exotic salads, grilled meats and fish with spicy sauces, and meat loaf with spinach and mashed potato.

But what Dudley Moore's menu lacks is imagination, which is supposed to be the most important ingredient in California cuisine. It's not enough to barbecue a piece of fish over wood and stick some chopped tomato and coriander on the side. Every second restaurant in California is doing that now.

Imagination is where Wolfgang Puck has the advantage. In his two restaurants, Spago and Chinois, you can spot just as many celebrities as in 72 Market, but you can also have your taste horizons dramatically broadened. Puck defines what the food critics mean when they rave about 'Nouvelle Californian cuisine'.

Puck made his name as chef at a Los Angeles landmark called Ma Maison, but left it because he felt that traditional French cuisine was too limiting. When he opened Spago five years ago, he put himself on show by building an open kitchen (now a standard feature in California cuisine restaurants) and he got a pile of publicity by reinventing the pizza. He developed a light crunchy crust to be cooked in a wood fired oven, and a range of toppings that managed to be both healthy and tasty. And he abolished tomato sauce.

When I visited Spago, the pizza toppings included artichokes, shiitake mushrooms, leeks, red peppers and sliced parmesan; or lamb sausage, coriander and sliced onions; or goat cheese, grilled eggplant, sun dried tomatoes, summer squash and garlic. They cost $11 each.

But the pizzas are only the beginning. Puck also offers magnificent creations like grilled pigeon with parsnip pancakes and blackberry sauce; roast lamb with artichoke mousse and rosemary butter; duck ravioli with smoked chili sauce; and wild rice and corn risotto with grilled quail.

In 1987, Spago served 126,500 customers and took in $5 million. Inspiring food and a flair for self-publicising have made Wolfgang Puck a superstar and a millionaire.

Bruce Colen, the food critic for *Los Angeles* magazine, says of Spago: 'I can't think of any other place in the nation, unless it's Paul Prudhomme's (in New Orleans), where one of the featured attractions is seeing the chef himself. The food can still be splendid, but when the genial, gentle Wolfgang Puck is not at Spago, the experience is not as fulfilling.'

Puck was not at Spago on the night of my visit, but I saw him later that week when I had dinner at his other place, Chinois (which has a slightly Asian slant to the same extent that Spago is Italian-influenced).

Unless you want an intimate tete-a-tete with your companion, the best place to sit in Chinois is at the counter overlooking the kitchen. This gives you a floorshow of flames shooting from the grill, live lobsters being cut in half and dropped straight into frying pans, and Puck wandering around nibbling at food in bowls. I overheard him telling one of his junior chefs that he'd been up to San Francisco that day and had a great lunch at Stars, the restaurant run by Jeremiah Tower, Puck's northern counterpart in Cal-cuisine.

For all my joy in Spago and Chinois, the meals I ate there were not my peak eating experience in Los Angeles. That happened in a place called St Estephe, unprepossessingly set in a shopping centre near LA International Airport. Here a chef named John Sedlar has created yet another new wave – a combination of classical French and the spicy desert fare of Santa Fe. He calls it 'modern southwestern cuisine', although he can trace the origins of many of his dishes to the ancient Mayans and Aztecs.

Sedlar does strange and wonderful things with chilis, peppers and seaweed, and was the first chef to bring blue corn from New Mexico to California (where it's now something of a cliche in tortillas and pancakes). As a joke, the menu is written in French, a language not designed to cope with southern American food concepts. So you find hilarious titles like 'Huevos rancheros au chevre, jalapenos poivron doux et fleches de mais bleu', which is eggs in a hot chili sauce with goat cheese, jalapeno peppers, sweet peppers and blue corn pastries.

My favourite dishes were ravioli stuffed with pork chili in a garlic cream sauce; 'tacos' of radicchio leaves stuffed with smoked chicken; a long green relleno chili pepper stuffed with mushroom puree, and a dessert of blue corn pancakes stuffed with pumpkin icecream.

You may have gathered by now that it's possible to spend a fortnight in Los Angeles and eat well on nothing but American food. After Spago, Chinois and St Estephe, you'd have to try Citrus, in Hollywood, where the specialty is 'tuna burger' (chopped tuna briefly seared on either side and served on a brioche with mayonnaise and asparagus); and Le Dome, also in Hollywood, where the movie moguls and agents go for a power lunch and consume a salad described as 'baby California-grown fifteen different mixed greens with vine ripe tomatoes and feta cheese served with walnut oil dressing'.

Designer patriotism

Ronald Reagan's star may be fading, but he has left an important legacy in a surprising place – the kitchens of New York. The president's New Nationalism has inspired a new generation of chefs to create a local cuisine that leaves hot dogs and hamburgers far behind. The more pretentious call the style 'nouvelle American'.

In their passion to prove their patriotism, the chefs have ranged geographically (through the regional specialities of America's outback) and historically (through the chronicles of the early settlers) to develop menus that persuade New Yorkers they are still part of a nation of pioneers, living on what's fresh from field, forest or foam.

Over the 1980s, New York has seen the opening of a horde of restaurants with names like An American Place, American Harvest, Arizona, Carolina, Memphis, the Southern Funk Cafe, Gotham, Texarkana, the Cadillac Grill, and Uncle Sam's. The self-consciousness in the names extends to the menus. You'll find dishes like Maine mussels, Virginia ham with sweet potato salad, Pennsylvania Dutch vanilla crumb pie, marinated Oregon salmon with sweet mustard sauce and Cajun popcorn (crawfish tails in peppery batter). Even the dreaded chicken Maryland has made a comeback, but the chicken is free range and the batter is low calorie, with a pot of corn and capsicum custard on the side for colour.

The appeal of this food is partly nostalgia, partly the illusion of health (because if it's grown nearby it must be better for you – and don't mention the chemical fertilisers, ripeners and preservatives) and partly novelty, for diners jaded with Manhattan's cornucopia of Italian and French restaurants (because, of course, Boston crabcakes are totally different from what used to be called quenelles de crabe).

The main elements of nouvelle American cuisine seem to be:

1. Mesquite-barbecued meat or fish. Mesquite is a fragrant wood supposed to impart an exquisite flavour to raw flesh. Not all restaurants go as far as The Red Cadillac in Greenwich Village, which offers a speciality of mesquite-grilled rattlesnake, tasting like old sock.

2. Meatloaf and mashed potato. This celebrates the family values of America in the 1950s, the formative years of the kind of people who can now afford to eat out. Fortunately today's meatloaf is often seasoned with ingredients their mothers never knew about, like chili and basil.

3. Blackened redfish. This recipe, invented by a New Orleans chef called Paul Prudhomme, has become so popular that the redfish, which is caught in the Gulf of Mexico, is likely to become an endangered species. The fish is smeared with a paste made of peppers, herbs and spices, and briefly seared on a very hot griddle, so it ends up with a burnt crunchy crust and a moist interior. Some restaurants unable to find the original ingredient are offering 'blackened bluefish', which sounds violent.

4. Warm goat cheese, usually sitting on red or purple lettuces.

5. Soft shell crabs, often sauteed in butter with pecan nuts. This is a species that sheds its shell and takes a long time growing a new one. Clever fishermen grab the crabs before the new shell has hardened. You eat the lot, including the claws.

6. Charcoal grilled slices of eggplant and zucchini, with noticeable burn marks.

7. Multicoloured mushrooms, leaves and roots with exotic names and sharp flavours, chosen to provide textural and visual balance on the plate. Remember that nouvelle American is designer food as well as patriotic food, and must look as if it was just photographed for *Gourmet* magazine.

Nationalism doesn't come cheap. You're lucky to leave places like Jam's, Melrose and The River Cafe for less than $100 a couple (including your Californian chardonnay, your tax of 8 per cent, and your tip of 15 per cent). But I'm inclined to think they're almost worth it, particularly The River Cafe in Brooklyn, offering a spectacular view of the East River and lower Manhattan.

My favourites among the more reasonably priced American places are Arizona and the Union Square Café, which achieves the astonishing feat of making mashed turnips into a delicacy.

One joyful side effect of the nouvelle American fad has been the rediscovery of two old American establishments which had been plugging away unrecognised for years. They are run by blacks and offer the gutsy food of the south.

The classier is Jezebel's, with mirrors and lace decor designed to give it the look of a New Orleans whorehouse. It serves classics like ham-hocks with black-eyed peas, garlic shrimp, and baked hen stuffed with fruit and pecan nuts. The other is Sylvia's, in deepest Harlem, where you find the best fried chicken and barbecued ribs in New York, and a welcome warm enough to demolish all stereotypes about its location.

Postscript: It occurs to me that some readers may not share my fascination with American food, and may be curious about the standard of French and Italian dining places in New York.

Most of New York's Italian restaurants seem to be locked in the 1950s in their devotion to tough veal and pasta with salty red sauce. But a few newcomers demonstrate the diversity of Italy's regions, for example Marcello, Arqua and Remi, plus Orso for celebrity watching.

French remains the snob cuisine, and most guidebooks rave about Lutece and Le Bernadin. But my nomination for best cheap French would be Provence in Soho, and for the best posh French restaurant in New York (possibly the world), I'd have no doubt about Le Cirque. Not only is the food delightful, but the service is unfailingly charming, whether you're Henry Kissinger (a regular customer), or a first time visitor. And the chances are high that you'll recognise at nearby tables several luminaries of American theatre, business or politics. You'd better, because at Le Cirque you'll be paying at least $60 a head.

13

CITIES

*Salt Lake City (trapped by the Mormons); New Orleans
(hard times and easy eating).*

Laundry is the curse of the long distance traveller. Smelly shirts and socks accumulate in the corner of your suitcase. Hotels charge a fortune to wash them. The Algonquin Hotel in New York, in most respects a moderate and helpful establishment, once hit me for $18 for washing three shirts, undies and socks.

You can rinse them out yourself in the hotel bathroom and hang them over the shower rail, but if you're leaving early the next morning, you've simply replaced a smelly lump with a soggy lump in the corner of your suitcase.

When you're moving round a lot in a foreign country, you need a laundry strategy. Mine is to decide in advance what will be the least interesting places on my itinerary, and allocate an afternoon in each of them for the sole purpose of finding and using a laundromat. Apart from the cleanliness, it's a novel way to explore a town.

In America, Salt Lake City, Utah, was my laundry town. I was only there to make the connection with the Rio Grande Zephyr, a lovely old train which winds through the Rockies between Salt Lake City and Denver. I had a Sunday afternoon to kill, and you don't have to be a genius to figure out that the world centre of the Mormon Church is not exactly going to be hotsy-totsy city on a Sunday afternoon.

So out came the washing bag. Following the directions of the hotel receptionist, I set off to walk the five blocks to the nearest laundromat along South Temple Street, which, according to the brochure the receptionist gave me, seemed to contain all the main sights of the city.

First you pass the 28-storey glass and steel headquarters of the Church of Jesus Christ of Latter Day Saints. This contains the great genealogical library in which the Mormons are trying to chronicle the ancestry of everybody in the world. There are more than 85 million names currently on file. The library is open to non-believers, but the world's 6 million Mormons use it so they can find out the names of all their predecessors and pray for them to be converted to Mormonism in the afterlife.

Then you pass the monument to Brigham Young, the man who, in 1847, led the first band of Mormons from persecution in the eastern states across 1,500 kilometres of prairie to the base of the Rocky Mountains, where he supposedly stopped and said 'This is the place'.

Next there's Brigham Young's elegant two-storey home. But more interesting is the peculiar wooden building adjoining it, guarded by a wooden lion over the doorway. The top floor of the building has 20 attic windows, each with its own gable. It looks like Cape Cod gone mad. Why such a confection would be built is a mystery until you learn that this was the residence of Brigham Young's 20 wives. The design ensured that each bedroom was private.

(The Mormons have a pamphlet to cover the unusual marital circumstances of their pioneer. God revealed to the leader of the Mormon Church last century that polygamy was His will, but Brigham Young was unhappy about it. The pamphlet says that shortly after he heard of the new doctrine, he saw a funeral cortege passing down the street, and 'he is reported to have said that he would gladly trade places with the man in the coffin than face this doctrine'. Nevertheless, Brigham Young loyally set about obeying God's will. Later the Mormon Church abandoned polygamy after the US Supreme Court declared it illegal. Some naughty Mormons still do it but they risk excommunication.)

As you cross Salt Lake City's streets you are assailed by bird noises, loud chirpings and cuckooings. They are, it turns out, devices attached to the traffic lights to help blind people cross the road. A cuckoo means a green light in an east–west direction, and a chirp means a north–south green light. (I don't know how blind people are supposed to tell the direction. They could hardly look at a compass.)

The streets and footpaths are very wide, as if the city in times past was inhabited by a race of giants (and if so, what mutation occurred to turn the original Mormons into the brown-suited midgets who now parade the streets?). In fact, the street width is another piece of far-sighted urban planning by Brigham Young. He insisted that streets had to be wide enough to turn a bullock team. Nowadays this makes them ideally suited to the metal and glass behemoths which Americans describe as modest family saloons.

My arrival at Vogue Cleaners was an anti-climax. It was closed. The brochure informed me there was a shopping centre four blocks to the east, so I waited for the cuckoo and trudged there through the autumn leaves. The shopping centre turned out to be an elegant complex converted from barns which once housed the city's trolley cars, full of antique shops, ethnic food, patchwork quilts, candlemakers and all the rest of the upmarket kitsch you can find in the Argyle Arts Centre in Sydney or the Jam Factory in Melbourne. But no laundromat.

Dusk was gathering, so I headed back towards the hotel and ended up in Temple Square, which is the dead centre of town. Just inside the gates of the square, I was greeted by a one-armed man who asked if I'd like to join a walking tour of the temple area. So that the afternoon wouldn't be a total loss, I agreed.

There were about 15 of us, innocently expecting to glance at the world's biggest organ in the Mormon Tabernacle, give the architecture the once over and get out to dinner. This was not to be.

After a brief wander round the square, during which we were told that no-one who was not 'in good standing with the Church'(i.e. paying a tithe of 10 per cent of income) was allowed to enter the temple itself, we were led into a modern building called The South Visitors' Center. Down the stairs we found ourselves in a theatrette.

The lights dimmed, the curtains opened to reveal a set of waxwork figures in Biblical garb, and an impressive voice boomed from all around us. We were listening to Lehi, the leader of the tribe of Israel which sailed in a reed boat from the Middle East to America 600 years before Christ. This is the basis of the Mormon faith – that America is just as much the promised land as Israel.

But there's more. We moved to a second theatre where other waxworks told us how Jesus Christ made a four-day visit to America around AD 28. Then in AD 400, an American prophet named Mormon inscribed the whole story of God's Americans and Christ's visit on metal plates, and buried the plates in a stone box near what later became New York.

In 1827 a man named Joseph Smith dug them up, translated them with the help of an angel, and produced The Book of Mormon, what the faithful call 'the companion volume to the New Testament'.

An hour had passed, and here we were moving into a third theatrette. And this time, the guide locked the door behind us. We saw a movie in which a Mormon archeologist did a tour of South American ruins which proved that Christ really had been in America.

It was enough to make you give up Eric Von Daniken for life. But my mind wasn't really on it. I kept thinking: 'Surely they can't keep us here. There must be laws about this. They must let us out sometime.' And then, answering myself: 'Yes, but this is Utah, where 70 per cent of the population is Mormon. They can pass any laws they like.'

The lights went up. The tourists eyed the guide nervously. He began a speech on why he personally found The Book of Mormon so accurate. He handed out cards and asked us to fill in our names and addresses. There was no way I was going to do that. They can keep me here forever, I thought, but they're not getting my real address. I filled in fictitious details and handed him the card with shaking hand.

With agonising slowness, he walked to the door and turned the key. I brushed past him more rudely than I should have. But I had washing to do. I have never been more relieved to see a hotel handbasin.

Postscript: Not all Mormons are scary. I went back to Salt Lake City a few months after this experience to write a story about the imminent death of the president/prophet of the Church of Jesus Christ of Latter Day Saints. I discovered that the Mormon Church is split into factions, one of which is described as 'liberal'.

The liberal Mormons turned out to be delightful people, although just as earnest as their conservative opponents. At the time of my visit, the liberals were worrying that a far right winger named Ezra Taft Benson, aged 86, would become the new president/prophet of their church. They feared he would politicise the church, and possibly even try to tell Mormons how to vote. (And eventually it came to pass that Benson did become president of the church, suggesting that God may be a conservative. So far Benson has kept a low profile.)

Peggy Fletcher, editor of a Mormon philosophical magazine called *Sunstone*, says it isn't easy being a liberal. She says her magazine's view is that 'criticism and analysis can only help the faith', but officials of the church regard her as an inconvenience. She finds herself under informal but constant observation, and funny rumours tend to circulate about her – that she was seen smoking, or drinking Coca-Cola.

'In this city, the way to discredit someone is to point at behaviour that is unorthodox,' Peggy Fletcher says. 'If people could discover that

I drink coffee or that I smoke, or I don't go to church every week, then they could discredit the ideas in the magazine.

'So I don't give them any reason to do that. I'm very careful about even drinking cocoa or something that might look like coffee. I wear dresses to work now, when I used to wear Levis. It seems a silly thing, but I don't want anyone to have that easy way out. I want them to come to grips with the issues in the magazine. You have to decide "do I want to fight the Levi battle or the nuclear disarmament battle?" I know what's more important.'

Beyond Superdome

'The Big Easy' is the latest nickname New Orleans has adopted for itself, designed to convey an image of hedonism to potential visitors. The image is important, because tourists and conventioneers are now the principal source of income for a nearly bankrupt city. New Orleans wants them to think only about lacy balconies, spicy food, hot jazz and loose women.

But for residents, life in New Orleans is far from easy. What seems like a relaxed, desegregated and pragmatic town is, below the surface, rigidly stratified according to family background, race and money.

Take the institution known as Mardi Gras. This isn't just a couple of weeks of fun and games in early February. It dominates the functioning of New Orleans all through the year. Everything depends on what 'krewe' you belong to.

Ostensibly a krewe is a group of people who get together to organise one of the carnival parades, meeting occasionally during the year to plan floats and costumes. In fact, the krewes are like lodges, near-secret societies whose members help each other politically and financially, and where more important deals are made than in any boardroom or council meeting.

The two oldest and most powerful krewes, dating back to the 1850s, are called Rex and Comus. You can only become a member of Rex or Comus by invitation, and no black, Jew or woman has ever been invited to join. The black mayor of New Orleans, Ernest Morial, once put out feelers to some members of Rex, knowing he would have far more access to the top business people in the city if he could meet them in one of their krewes. He was told he would not be welcome to join.

Then he put out feelers to a krewe called the Zulus, which represents the most influential black businessmen in the city. But racism can cut both ways. Mayor Morial was told he would have great difficulty being acceptable to the Zulus, because they represent men of pure African descent, and he had rather too much white blood in his background.

The social rules by which New Orleans runs were laid down 150 years ago, and not even economic collapse can change them. The French first settled the swampy ground near the mouth of the Mississippi River in 1718, but soon gave the land to the Spanish, who started building beautiful terrace houses in what is now the French Quarter. The French got New Orleans back towards the end of the 18th century, but in 1803, Napoleon sold it to America as part of the $15 million Louisiana purchase.

The Americans may have paid good money for the city, but they weren't welcomed by the French and Spanish speaking citizens (known as Creoles). The Creoles wouldn't let the Americans move into their part of town, so the Americans built their own townships upriver, determined to prove they could create even more magnificent mansions than the Europeans – and introduce even more snobbish rules about who was eligible to enter them.

The wealth of New Orleans as America's second largest port allowed the competition between the Americans and the Creoles to reach ever more fanciful extremes during the 19th century. The Americans went in for giant houses with mock Greek columns and landscaped lawns in what they called The Garden District, while the Creoles went in for compact terraces decorated with iron lacework overlooking fountained courtyards, in what they called 'le vieux carré'. The result is a wonderful experience for the modern visitor – two vast collections of 18th- and 19th-century architecture, separated these days by a small 20th-century business district, and surrounded by sprawling ghettoes occupied by the descendants of the slaves who once served the mansion owners. (One of these ghettoes, incidentally, is called Desire. Tennessee Williams wrote about it. Desire no longer has a streetcar, but it does have one of the highest crime rates in the city.)

New Orleans stagnated in the 20th century as its port declined in importance, and in the 1960s the city authorities decided its future lay in becoming America's convention city. They kept building bigger and bigger convention centres, surrounded with hotels and old warehouses renovated into shopping malls. The nation's conventioneers responded. The reputation of The Big Easy attracted planeloads of dentists, accountants, engineers, salesmen and other groups keen to talk all day and seek sin in the French Quarter all night.

What should have been the ultimate convention centre was the Superdome, a massive creation which squats on the edge of the French Quarter like the mothership of an interplanetary invasion. The Superdome can hold 97,000 people for sporting events, but still the city authorities say it's not big enough for some of the conventions they think are out there just waiting to pour their money into New Orleans.

So if you're visiting New Orleans in the late 1980s, don't expect to find a quaint French village. Expect a humid, dirty, crowded city, whose population of a million is matched by about as many visitors each year. Expect lots of French names but no-one actually speaking French; tourist rip-offs everywhere; a high crime rate; narrow streets full of crumbling beauty; and some of the world's most original food.

Cajun popcorn and dirty rice

When the people of New Orleans aren't eating food or talking about food, they are queuing up for food.

Their obsession isn't surprising, given the unique cuisine which has evolved from combining French, Spanish and African styles with the abundance of local seafood. The queueing results from the addition of American democracy to the mixing pot. Galatoire's, the city's second most famous French restaurant, takes no reservations, so everyone is equal when they start queueing around 6 pm. Outside Antoine's, the city's most famous French restaurant (since 1840), the queueing starts about 6.30 pm. At either place, it usually takes about 45 minutes to get a table.

But at Antoine's, the democracy is diluted. If you belong to one of New Orlean's old money families – the kind who have been horrified by the growth of tourism – you don't need to queue. You arrive in a car as big as a bus, and glide straight inside past the puzzled crowd stretching along St Louis Street.

The rich know the special rules, as explained to me by a New Orleans matron: 'You must have your own waiter at Antoine's, and he is the only one who looks after you each time you go. In my family, we phone him a few days before we want to go, discuss our menu, and arrange our time. Then he has the table waiting for us.' Those who make reservations in this way eat in a different room from those who queue up – a room that's quieter, with more subdued lighting and more leisurely service.

Both rooms have the same menu, featuring world famous dishes created at Antoine's, like Oysters Rockefeller. The menu is in French, even down to the advice that good food takes time to prepare. But that doesn't guarantee that the waiter will actually *speak* French. A Parisian family at the next table to me looked increasingly desperate as the waiter explained one of the dishes in the broadest of Southern drawls:'Weyull, thet's a feeyush in a creeyum sos with lil shreeyumps all wrapped up in a paypuh bag.'

He was referring to the pompano en papillote, which I was eating at the time. I must say I can't recommend it on that tasting – a pleasant local fish had been swamped in a floury sauce containing tasteless prawns, served in greaseproof paper. The Oysters Rockefeller had suffered similar overkill – big fresh oysters on the shell were buried under a mound of what looked like green mashed potato. The ingredients in the Rockefeller sauce are secret, although there's clearly watercress and pepper in it, and, the waiter insisted, *no* spinach.

I thought the second most famous restaurant, Galatoire's (209 Bourbon Street) handled the Oysters Rockefeller much more deftly, and indeed scored over Antoine's in everything but history.

A couple of blocks from Antoine's and Galatoire's, you'll see an equally long queue outside a restaurant called K-Paul's. But this crowd looks quite different – no coats and ties here, just jeans and T-shirts. Yet K-Paul's offers by far the best food I had in New Orleans.

The owner and chef, a bearded mountain named Paul Prudhomme, is a descendant of the Cajuns (local pronunciation of Arcadians) – French Canadians who settled the swamps round New Orleans 200 years ago. He used to be the chef at an excellent restaurant called the Commander's Palace, but got bored with having to cook the same menu every day. So he set up his own restaurant in much more humble surroundings, determined to let his imagination fly.

K-Paul's is a big, noisy room with revolving fans, no credit cards, no bookings and a different scribbled menu every day. Paul Prudhomme says he cooks a spicy mixture of Cajun food and Creole food.

'Cajun cooking is old French cooking that my ancestors had to adapt when they came to Louisiana,' he says. 'They started using a lot more white, black and cayenne peppers, and the peppers are the key to the flavour. Creole style is more sophisticated, because it comes from Spanish, French and Italian cooking adapted by the African servants who moved between the kitchens of the big New Orleans houses.'

If you're lucky you'll find on K-Paul's menu a gumbo (thick peppery soup of prawns, oysters, celery, capsicums and rice); or a jambalaya (stew of chicken, spicy sausage, okra and ham); or crawfish etouffee (yabbies in a sauce of tomato and tabasco); or blackened redfish (a moist piece of seafood with a hot crunchy coat that was invented by Prudhomme and copied round the world).

As side dishes there might be 'cajun popcorn' – Prudhomme's joke name for tiny crawfish tails in batter – or 'dirty rice' – rice in a gravy made from chicken livers and onion. You pay about $20 a head for a full meal (plus wine served in old jam jars).

Paul Prudhomme got worried when I said I wanted to write about his restaurant for Australia, and said ominously: 'If I start getting tourists in the line outside, I'll have to issue my regulars with cards so they can get in first.'

Take the risk: he's at 416 Chartres Street.

ENCOUNTERS

The celebrity safari: Woody Allen; Dennis Hopper; Gloria Steinem; Clint Eastwood; Jack Lemmon; Isaac Asimov.

The worst-kept secret in New York is that on most Monday nights during the summer, Woody Allen plays clarinet with a band called The New Orleans Funeral and Ragtime Orchestra at a place called Michael's Pub in midtown Manhattan.

I say *most* Monday nights because sometimes Woody Allen doesn't turn up, and the band plays on without him. But it seemed to me that Michael's Pub, on a Monday night, would be the place where I'd have the best chance of breaking my run of bad luck in celebrity-watching.

Everybody but me seems to run into famous people in Manhattan. My friends boast of seeing Meryl Streep or Bill Cosby or Diane Keaton or Madonna in restaurants, in the street or in the local deli. One person I know claims that Mick Jagger lives in the same block as he does. He says Mick Jagger, escorted by bodyguards, pushes a pram past his house regularly.

But I've never seen anyone. Well, I tell a lie. I saw Carl Bernstein once in Fifth Avenue, but he's only a journalist.

I live opposite the Dakota apartments, outside which John Lennon was shot, but I haven't seen Yoko Ono once. My co-workers in the office taunt me with the fact that Sigourney Weaver, star of *Alien*, lives on the 9th floor of my apartment block. She'd be hard to miss, because she's immensely tall, but hours hanging round the lifts and the lobby have yielded not a glimpse.

Just around the corner from where I live is a restaurant called Columbus, which is part-owned by the dancer Mikhail Baryshnikov

and which always has big black limousines double-parked outside it at night. I took a friend there for dinner with high hopes, especially when I saw a burly man who was obviously a bodyguard leaning against the wall just inside the entrance.

Peeping over my menu, I scrutinised the crowd. A balding man in a striped shirt looked familiar. I was pretty sure he was an actor. This conversation ensued:

Me: 'Isn't that Robert de Niro?'

Friend: 'Robert de Niro's not bald.'

Me: 'He could be. He might have come out without his wig. He's in a Broadway play at the moment, so he's in town.'

Friend: 'I'm sick of this. I'll ask the waiter.'

She asks the waiter if the man is Robert de Niro. The waiter studies the man for a long time, then says: 'Robert Duvall'. Now Robert Duvall is a fine actor, but he doesn't really rate with Mick Jagger (or Robert de Niro, for that matter).

In desperation, I purchased a publication which, according to its cover, is entitled: *The New York Map to the Stars' Homes! Tips on Where to Find Stars. What to do if You See a Star, Dating the Stars – Yes You Can! See the Stars' Homes Up Close, 2 Complete Walking Tours!*

My New York friends considered this publication rather tasteless, the sort of thing you'd expect to find in Los Angeles but not in cool Manhattan. Here, they told me, celebs are supposed to be ignored. The instructions on the map take a different philosophy. They advise:

'Celebs in Manhattan can often be seen walking, jogging, eating at popular restaurants and dancing the night away in the hottest clubs. Remember that stars are people too, so don't overlook parks, the stalls in public bathrooms, telephone booths, theaters and the Clinique counter at Bloomingdale's.

'Stars don't use public transportation. Don't waste valuable time looking for them on subways and buses. They never dine out on Saturday evenings, so that everyone will think they're at a fab industry party. They always eat after 9 pm.'

I used the book for a casual stroll up the west side of Central Park and down the east side of it, two streets which seem to house most of New York's famous. On Central Park West I passed the alleged apartment blocks of Mia Farrow and her 10 children, Mary Tyler Moore, Raquel Welch, Faye Dunaway and Bianca Jagger. Around Fifth Avenue, where the REALLY rich congregate, I saw the habitats of Jackie Onassis, Neil Sedaka, and the high security fortress of Bob

Guccione, publisher of *Penthouse*. But not a single glitteratus.

I decided to be systematic about my star search. I went to Elaine's Restaurant on the upper East Side. *The New York Post* is always publishing reports of the big names who eat at Elaine's. It said that Shirley Maclaine ate there three nights in a row, with a different man each time. That same week, Andy Williams, Neil Diamond and Willie Nelson were also spotted there by the *Post's* spies.

I had actually been to Elaine's once before, in 1982, when I was interviewing Andrew Anspach, the manager of the Algonquin Hotel. He suggested we meet at Elaine's, and promised he'd introduce me to Woody Allen if he happened to be there. Of course, he wasn't. (I'd spent hours worrying about how one would converse with a comic genius, and had formed a theory that a good way to get on a relaxed level would be to ask him where he buys his socks. So it's probably just as well we weren't introduced.)

I did learn two things from that visit: (a) Elaine's food, which purports to be Italian, is disgusting; and (b) you must never let them seat you in the annexe on the right of the door, because that is Siberia, where the stars never sit.

My second visit was on a Friday night in mid-1987 and I was seated in the main room, which is dark and untidy and lined with faded photos and posters. I learned two more things this time:(a) Elaine's food has got even worse; and (b) famous people in Manhattan don't go to trendy restaurants on Friday or Saturday nights because they don't want to mix with what they call 'B and Ts'. B and T stands for Bridge and Tunnel, and B and Ts are residents of Brooklyn and New Jersey who come looking for a good time in Manhattan at weekends.

Pondering the problem over the ensuing weeks, I concluded that while some people are blessed with animal magnetism, I am cursed with celebrity repulsion. Whenever I go anywhere, powerful forces operate to keep famous people away from that spot.

And of course, soon after that visit, I read in *New York* magazine that Woody Allen has stopped going to Elaine's. Now he goes more often to Elio's, an Italian restaurant with better food, run by the former head waiter of Elaine's. There is considerable bitchery between Elaine Kaufman and Elio Guaitolini, who worked together in Elaine's for 15 years. She says he stole her customers, and he says he was the main reason they went to Elaine's in the first place.

I decided the odds of seeing Woody Allen were better at Michael's Pub than at Elio's. I phoned during Monday afternoon and asked if

Woody Allen was playing. 'He's expected,' said the host, 'but it's up to him.'

The show was due to start at 8 pm. The place, more a restaurant than a pub, is packed, mainly with conservative young people who look like they're just out of college. The food is almost as bad as Elaine's and twice as expensive, but nobody is here for that.

At 8.40, a man in a navy blazer wanders onstage and starts setting up a drum kit. The crowd quietens. At 8.50, Woody Allen hurries in, wearing a pale blue suit and looking anxious. He sits at a table with a tall blonde woman (not Mia Farrow or Diane Keaton), and frowningly unpacks his clarinet.

In New York, the game is to look cool. The crowd ignores Woody Allen. He takes off his coat and walks onstage with the rest of the band, all in navy blazers except a lady trombonist in a grey pinstripe suit.

The numbers are all bouncy, complicated versions of jazz and blues evergreens. No one in the band addresses a single word to the audience, not even to introduce the numbers. Each musician gets plenty of solos (during which Woody Allen stares at the floor and pulls at his lower left eyelid), but all the arrangements are built around the clarinet (I can't imagine what they do on the nights when Woody doesn't show up).

The surprise is that Woody Allen's playing is not just competent, it's spectacular. He makes the clarinet squeal and yelp and bray and buzz like a didgeridoo. He is the Jimi Hendrix of the woodwind. The crowd are bouncing in their seats, tapping the tables with their palms, whistling and smiling.

The show ends at 9.40. Woody Allen returns to his table. Two girls go over and ask for his autograph. Woody Allen doesn't smile, but he doesn't look irritated either. Then another person comes over, and another, until there's a queue of 25 autograph seekers snaking round the nearby tables. Woody signs them all in silence.

How uncool, I thought. They weren't here for the music at all. They probably came to Michael's Pub purely for the chance to see Woody Allen. Some New Yorkers aren't that different from me.

Postscript: Having failed to see celebs in my role as normal citizen, I was finally forced to use my role as journalist, and try to arrange interviews with them. The results of some of these arranged encounters make up the rest of this chapter.

Of course, any veteran starspotter will tell you that this is cheating. You get no points for organised meetings with the rich and famous. The only valid sightings are those that happen by chance. So I remain ever vigilant.

'I chose cocaine because it was the drug of kings'

Nobody plays a better psychopath, a better junkie, or a better alcoholic than Dennis Hopper. That's because he *is* all those things. He'll tell you so himself. He'll tell you that it was drink, drugs and madness that kept him from working in America for most of the 1970s and early 1980s.

And now, it's drink, drugs and madness that are making him the busiest actor in Hollywood. At the age of 52 Dennis Hopper is every director's favourite lunatic.

During 1986 and 1987 he made 12 movies. In the preceding 12 years he made only 5 movies, including *Apocalypse Now*. Hopper says he has now replaced drug addiction and alcoholism with workaholism.

He was nominated for an Academy Award for one of his comeback films, *Blue Velvet*. In it, Hopper plays a drug dealer who has been turned into a paranoid psychotic by cocaine. It's the most terrifying role he's done. If Hopper's best known movie, *Easy Rider*, could be said to have started the fashion for cocaine, then *Blue Velvet* could be the movie that ends it.

In the 1950s Dennis Hopper was one of Hollywood's hottest young actors, spoken of in the same breath as James Dean, with whom he starred in *Giant* and *Rebel Without A Cause*. With *Easy Rider* in the 1960s, he was the hero of the hippy generation. But through the 1970s, he had most of Hollywood's directors terrified. He was unreliable, moody, argumentative, stubborn and violent. That reputation stayed with him until 1985. Then his life changed.

I spoke to Dennis Hopper at a press conference organised by Orion Pictures to promote *Hoosiers*, in which he plays an alcoholic who helps to coach a small town basketball team.

Nattily tailored in a grey plaid coat and blue shirt and tie, Hopper looked remarkably healthy for a man who says he nearly destroyed himself with drugs and drink. He also loves to talk, as if celebrating having regained control of his mind. I asked him why he'd suddenly started making so many movies.

Hopper: 'I moved back to Los Angeles. And got sober, and I stopped doing drugs. It was better than hearing voices and being incarcerated. When you bottom out like I bottomed out, you either die, or go insane, or both, or get sober and decide to live.

'I'm an alcoholic drug addict. So when I stopped doing drugs and doing alcohol, I realised it wasn't Los Angeles that I hated, and it wasn't Los Angeles that necessarily hated me, but it might be my problem.

'I'd lived in Taos, New Mexico, for years, up in the mountains wondering why I wasn't working and why I could only work in Europe. And so I went back to Los Angeles and my friends were there, and my peer group were behind the desks in the offices, and I went to work. I started doing everything that was offered me. I just kept doing the next job. The most time I've had off was about a week.'

Q: *What caused you to stop taking drugs?*

'In the 70s people used to ask me about my drug intake, and I'd say, "I only use drugs to cover up the fact that I'm an alcoholic, ha ha ha." I didn't believe I was an alcoholic. I just drank all day long. The most difficult thing for a drug addict or an alcoholic is to say, "I'm a drug addict or an alcoholic."

'I stopped drinking for one year, during 1983, thinking that alcohol was my problem, and I started using cocaine like I drank beer. And a year later I was doing half an ounce of cocaine every three days, by myself, just snorting it.

'At the end of that I was hearing voices, my friends were being murdered in the next room, the telephone wires were talking to me, the radio was talking only to me. I committed myself to an institution because I was totally insane. I was there for three months. Since I came out of that I haven't had an aspirin.'

Q: *What caused your dependence on alcohol, do you think? Was it the pressure of work in your early film days?*

'Well, I could say it was the combine I worked on as a kid in Kansas when we drank beer because there was so much heat, it was 125 degrees, and you drank beer and salt and you were 7 years old.

'I enjoyed it, you know. It wasn't the pressure. It was something that I justified because all the people that I admired were alcoholics – John Barrymore, all the writers, the actors of the past, they were as famous for their drinking as for their acting, even up to Richard Burton and Peter O'Toole.

'I drank because I thought I'd become more creative perhaps, and it was stylish. People drank Beefeater martinis straight up with an olive. I thought that was the most horrible thing I'd ever tasted when I was 18. They said, "It's an acquired taste," and I acquired that taste real fast.'

Q: *Do you think all the work you are doing now is another kind of addiction?*

'Some of us are addictive personalities and I'm one of those people. So it probably is work that I'm addicted to now, but it's a lot healthier, and if I can stop smoking I might make it another few years.'

Q: *Do you feel concerned now that some of the early films you made, especially* Easy Rider, *encouraged drug use, given the damage that drugs did to you?*

'I have to accept that *Easy Rider* helped to make cocaine a popular drug. I chose cocaine because it was the drug of kings and I always thought it was too expensive for anybody to use. And we all assumed, and the medical profession backed me up, that it was not a habit-forming drug. I thought it was a lot better than smoking heroin, which we knew was habit-forming and we'd seen a lot of lives destroyed. We hadn't seen any lives destroyed by cocaine at that time.

'The only time I'd ever seen it was when big band leaders had had it, men that I'd gotten high with. It was not on the streets. But two years after *Easy Rider*, you could buy it a lot easier than you could get heroin, on the street. It was being passed around on silver trays in Hollywood.

'I used it. I'm a drug addict. My saying, "Hey, I feel it's okay, it should be made legal and then we can control it," all that bullshit was rhetoric that came out of the '60s, and I was there.'

Q: *There have been reports that you are making a sequel to* Easy Rider. *Is that just a myth?*

'I think it's a myth now. There is a script. There are three rewrites so far. Peter Fonda decided he didn't want to do it, because he didn't like the director and because he felt it made fun of his character, and that one of the only images he had in his career was Captain America and if nothing else he'd rather go with that than make some money. I, on the other hand, had signed for the picture and was ready to go with anybody. But I don't think it's going to happen.'

Q: *What is the plot of it? Weren't the two heroes killed on the road at the end of* Easy Rider?

'It starts in biker's heaven. This man drives in on a big golden Harley with tears in his eyes, and there are all the bikers roasting swans and stuff like that, and he says he's just been to the United States.

'He says it's a terrible thing because it's 200 years after the nuclear war – yes, the United States did win, yay, we got those Russians – but there's nothing but a bunch of mutant bike gangs running around, they've got no colours, they've got no flag, no leaders. We've got to restore their colours, their flag.

'And all these bikers volunteer, but he says "No, no, on a road down there, in Florida somewhere, there are two guys who never made it to biker's heaven . . ."'

Beautiful and serious

The most surprising newspaper photograph of 1987 was Gloria Steinem in a miniskirt, proudly showing off two long slim legs. She posed for the photo to break a stereotype about feminists, and to prove that women can choose to do anything they want – including look sexy. And she certainly did.

Steinem also wrote a book about another great sex symbol, Marilyn Monroe, and that was my excuse for meeting America's most interesting feminist. She wasn't wearing the miniskirt for our interview in the cluttered offices of *Ms* magazine. She was wearing a long black wool dress which is apparently her work uniform.

She says Monroe has a lot to teach women and men in the 1980s. 'I think women can learn from her because she's an exaggerated version of what can happen to us,' says Steinem. 'We're valued for who we are on the outside and not for our heads and hearts. So we have a harder time with ageing and with self-confidence.

'And I think she would be instructive to some men who may have thought that women were really enjoying our own denigration, rather than just pretending to.'

Steinem's impression of how some men might react to the Monroe book was confirmed by the only negative review the book received – written by a man in *Vanity Fair* magazine. The reviewer accused Steinem of being 'another sob-sister making money off poor dead Marilyn'. (In fact, all the royalties from the book go to the *Ms* Foundation, which gives away about $400,000 a year to women's groups around America.)

'If I had to get inside the reviewer's head, which I think we have some obligation to do,' Steinem says,' I think he would have wanted to believe that Marilyn Monroe enjoyed her life. Because if you find somebody sexual and attractive and interesting and so on, you don't want to know that they are unhappy and they've been shitting you all this time. I think he was feeling that I was a messenger who brought an unwelcome message, so he was killing the messenger.

'This image some men hold of the woman as an all-giving, all approving person who asks nothing in return, is very seductive and unchallenging, but it's not what happens in a friendship with another grownup. So for me to come along and say: "Listen, this woman was not telling the truth, she was really quite miserable, she wasn't enjoying sex, she probably really did commit suicide, she wasn't done in by the Kennedys", that's an unwelcome message.'

At 53, Steinem is the best known symbol of the American women's movement. She says she learned a lot about herself by studying Marilyn Monroe. Like Monroe, Steinem was a neglected child. Her parents were divorced and she had to care for a mother suffering a series of nervous breakdowns.

She became a journalist and author, got involved in a series of radical causes in the 1960s, and founded the National Women's Political Caucus and *Ms* magazine. These days she spends much of her time lecturing on women's issues and organising to prevent the Reagan administration from rolling back gains women have made in the past decade.

She lives in a small New York apartment, works out of *Ms* magazine's offices in Manhattan's garment district, and conducts a reasonably public romance with a millionaire property developer named Mort Zuckerman.

Steinem says she realised recently that she had better start saving a bit of the money she earns for her old age. 'By getting immersed in Marilyn Monroe's life, I saw the way my childhood upbringing affected my adult life,' she says. 'I saw that many things I thought I had chosen freely, like giving money away and never owning anything and never getting my clothes from the cleaners, were not freely chosen. I did them because they felt like home and that was the way I was brought up. Marilyn was more extreme, but she also never saved money, never took care of herself, never fixed up the places she lived, repeating this childhood neglect pattern.

'When you find yourself repeating the same old patterns you have to try to figure out whether this is good for you. I may well continue to feel better giving away more money than the average person, but on the other hand I don't want to end up a bag lady. So I ought to see to it that I look after myself.'

Q: *Do you see another parallel between you and Marilyn in that you became a sort of physical symbol in the way she did? In the '70s, your image – the long blonde hair and the aviator glasses – was used by cartoonists and so on to represent the sort of respectable feminist.*

Steinem: 'It's an accident who gets to be recognisable and who isn't. I think the role I play can be a sort of bridge for people who might be coming to their first feminist event. People are curious.'

Q: *So you don't see any parallel in the way you became known for a particular look and Monroe became known for a particular look?*

'Well, here's the difference, Marilyn Monroe went to great lengths to look like Jean Harlow. She used the same woman to bleach her hair, she adopted the same appearance, she curtailed the way she moved in order to have this sexy walk.

'There wasn't somebody in my life with long hair and glasses for me to model a look on. In fact women were not supposed to wear glasses, they were not supposed to wear blue jeans. So, for better or worse, I chose it myself.'

Q: *'Is it an advantage being so recognisable, so much of a symbol?*

'Yes and no. Yes, because it encourages people to come along, so it's like sending out a signal. You don't have the power to make anybody do anything but you have the power to persuade sometimes. On the other hand you get a lot of the shit because you also symbolise something that people oppose. There may be a feeling that if they could just get rid of you they could get rid of the movement, which isn't true of course.'

Q: *Do you get the sense that these days there isn't so much rage from men against feminism as there was 15 years ago?*

'Yeah. There is much more of both an acceptance and an understanding that maybe this is good for men too, that having two incomes, for example, means that men can get to know their kids instead of discovering 18 years later that they don't know who their kid is. There's more recognition that if women become full human beings, men can too.'

Q: *Is the women's movement in America in a healthy state at the moment?*

'Well, the unanimity among the various groups is deafening. Sometimes I think there's too much unanimity. You need to fight out tactics and be willing to disagree. The weak link is the mechanism to get out the vote. The reason for the success of the right is that they used their own mechanisms to get out the vote. There are 9,000 fundamentalist Baptist churches and in the basement they have a card file with voter information. We haven't done it.

'So even though our numbers are bigger, the ability to turn out the vote is not as big as it should be. We have to learn to do that. In every community there's a battered women's shelter, a rape crisis centre and so on. We're trying to say to each other that whenever a woman comes in for help, you have to ask her if she is registered to vote.

'But it's a long process. A lot of these women feel real estranged from the electoral system. "What has it got to do with my life," they say.'

Q: *You have said that women get more radical as they grow older while men get more conservative. Have you become more radical?*

'If radical means going to the root of the issues, I have. In the beginning a lot of us felt that the injustices were so clear that if you just pointed them out to people, they would want to fix them. But you figure out it's more difficult because there are a lot of people benefiting from these injustices. Equal pay may seem like a simple demand but if there are big industries with huge pools of female labour, it's not going to be easy to change.

'Gradually you begin to see the problem of distribution of wealth in this country, so you no longer think of it as something I'm going to do for two years and then I'm going back to my real life. That's the way we used to think in social movements. Now we know it IS your life.'

Clintville-by-the-Sea

As Clint Eastwood was leaving the mayoral chair at the end of the meeting of Carmel City Council, an old lady in the audience remarked: 'Your hair looks lovely today.' Mayor Eastwood beamed. 'Thank you,' he said, 'I washed it an hour before the meeting.' That's one more vote secured if he should stand for the next local government elections.

Not that Mayor Eastwood needs any more votes. There's no doubt about it – Carmel, California, population 5,000, is Clint Eastwood's town.

In the main street, there's a shop called Clintville-by-the-Sea, devoted exclusively to Eastwood memorabilia. You can pick up a

T-shirt showing Mayor Eastwood pointing a large revolver, with the slogan: 'I said Curb Your Dog!' Or you might prefer an original oil painting of Mayor Eastwood meeting the Pope. Or something from the range of ladies' cotton underwear bearing the words: 'Go ahead, make my night.'

Up the street from Clintville-by-the-Sea is the Hog's Breath Inn, a pub-cafe which Mayor Eastwood owns. It's a rustic-looking retreat with open fires, rough-hewn oak tables, and a menu offering such delights as the Dirty Harry Burger, the Magnum Force Omelette, the Eiger Sandwich and the Sudden Impact Polish Sausage Roll.

The Hog's Breath Inn is crammed with customers, most of whom have still or movie cameras on their laps, hoping that Clint might drop in to check on business. But the mayor has other matters on his mind today – the monthly council meeting.

At precisely 4 pm he bounds on to the stage of the Carmel Women's Club, where meetings have been held since his election because there isn't enough seating space at the council chambers. He looks a little plumper than in his movies, and demonstrates a preference for shades of brown . . . dark brown shoes, tan pants, brown tweed jacket, light brown shirt, dark red tie, deeply tanned face, topped by tousled grey hair. There are about 100 people in the audience, plus a TV camera crew, and 6 press photographers.

First order of business is the pledge of allegiance to the flag – 'one nation under God, indivisible, with liberty and justice for all' – during which Eastwood is the only one among the five council members to hold his hand over his heart.

He announces community service awards to the local librarian and the tree care specialist in the public works department, remarking with a smile that 'during winter storms, Cliff can be seen swaying in our large pines'. Then it's down to regular business. I'd like to be able to report that a council meeting chaired by Clint Eastwood is more exciting than a council meeting chaired by your local mayor, but I'd be lying.

His leadership style is taciturn. He leaves it to other council members to comment on issues like whether a local camera store should be allowed to put up a larger sign (unanimous 'no' vote because Carmel is keen to retain its beauty), and whether a dentist should be allowed to extend his office space into an adjoining house (majority 'yes' vote – council isn't totally anti-business). Eastwood doesn't like discussion to go on too long. When a citizen affected by a decision wants a right of reply to a planning officer, Eastwood says: 'Okay, but let's not have a debate, please.'

By the time he opens the meeting for general public comments, the audience has shrunk to about 40. The only person who comes forward is an old lady who asks if the mayor would autograph a photograph taken of him talking to her late husband. He says: 'Oh, thank you, I'll do it when we adjourn.'

The meeting is over in an hour. The mayor takes off his tinted aviator glasses, and puts his papers in a dark brown briefcase. Stepping down from the stage, he agrees warily to answer a few questions for the Australian journalist.

It is hard work studying all the details necessary to be mayor? – 'Well, I've lived here a long time. I really don't know any more than the next person. I try to learn a lot about it because I enjoy it.'

Is he still making movies at the same rate? – 'Yes, I have two projects at the moment, one for next year, and one to direct and not be in.'

What has been his greatest accomplishment since taking office? – 'I think probably my greatest accomplishment is having much larger public interest than there was in past administrations. In past administrations, sometimes the council meetings would have two or three people in the audience. There's more participation.'

Does he think people are mainly coming to the meetings to see a film star? – 'I think for the locals that's long worn off. They're here for the issues. You get a few tourists, but the majority of people here tonight were locals.'

What have been his main disappointments with the job? – (Eastwood starts moving towards the door at this point) 'I have no disappointments. Naturally, I'd love to do things yesterday, but that's just my nature. Sometimes it takes a little longer than I would like.'

And then two burly gentlemen whom I haven't noticed before, but who have bodyguard written all over them, step between the mayor and the media and he strides off into the sunset.

The politicised Lemmon

It's a terrible thing to have to admit, but Jack Lemmon made me get drunk. It wasn't intentional, I'm sure. He was drinking what looked like Coke and ice (although it may have been rum and Coke and ice) and I was drinking white wine. The waiters in the boardroom of Columbia Pictures kept bringing glasses for both of us, and both of us kept drinking them.

Jack Lemmon needed the fortification, because he was in the midst of a five hour interviewing session with a small but intense group of foreign correspondents, for the purpose of promoting the international release of a film called *That's Life*. My only excuse is that Jack Lemmon was so entertaining that I didn't notice how much I was sipping.

I remember thinking during the interview that this was exactly the sort of event that I had come to New York to experience. Jack Lemmon has been a hero of mine for 15 years, ever since I started to take movies seriously. To find that in person he's intelligent, funny, planning to live part-time in Italy, and an active left winger, is, as they say in New York, a goosebump experience.

Jack Lemmon, famous for playing nervous wrecks, gives every indication of being a cheerful, relaxed man. He said he can now choose his own films, instead of doing them for the money, and doesn't mind waiting months, even years, till the right script turns up.

He is 62, but he says he didn't suffer any crisis about turning 60 like the hypochondriac architect he portrays in *That's Life*. He's happily married to Felicia Farr (who co-stars in *That's Life* as a fortune teller who gives him a dose of crabs).

Nevertheless, the role he does best – 'the modern urban worrier' – is a major part of his own personality, he says. So what *does* Jack Lemmon worry about?

'Who knows what Reagan's going to do, or what Khomeini's going to do, or some other nut?' he said. 'I worry about the grandchildren I don't have yet. I worry about what it might be like to communicate with a 10-year-old grandchild who has lived in nothing but an armed camp. We not only have covered the planet with bombs and rockets and guns and germs, but we're filling the air with them now too.

'I think one of the reasons why I respect what I do, and any of the arts, is that we cannot learn by studying politics or science, because all we've done through that is retrogress, practically back to the dark ages and living in caves with clubs. But art can enlighten, can make us think.

'If we do not get out of the arts a better understanding of human behaviour and of other ideologies, at least enough to live with them instead of conquering them, then we will destroy the world.'

Is this getting all too serious for you? Don't worry, we'll get to Marilyn Monroe soon.

Lemmon considers *The China Syndrome* (about a cover-up of a nuclear reactor accident) and *Missing* (about the US government helping a right wing coup in Chile) to be among his most important films, but he denies that they are 'anti-American'.

'*Missing* attacked what can be done within any government, and certainly within ours,' he said. 'It argued that the state department was behaving in a way that is basically un-American.

'The most important thing about the film really is that it was made in this country. When I visited Cuba I was surrounded by people from communist and non-communist governments and they were saying, "Aha, *Missing*, that shows the kind of thing that America does." And I was saying, "Wait a minute, it's fascinating that Russia didn't make it, Cuba didn't make it, America made it." Nobody here would dream of coming in and saying you can't make it, or you can't show it.

'Unfortunately some Americans said, "How dare you? What the hell are you doing, criticising the government and letting the whole world see it?" This country wouldn't exist without self-criticism. That's what's made us so great so fast.'

Lemmon was abused in America for going to a film festival in Cuba in 1984, and for praising the achievements of Fidel Castro. He had letters from fans saying they would never go to another Lemmon film, a reaction he describes as 'assinine, and I can't worry about people like that'.

'The praise was that in 25 years Castro has taken a country that was just devastated, 90 per cent of the population without clothes, shoes, to a point where there is nobody starving there now,' Lemmon said. ' I keep wishing that we would stop merely stiff-arming Cuba and try to get together with them, have more cultural and economic interchange. They no more want to do business with Russia than I do, but they have to.'

What Jack Lemmon films did the Cubans show at the film festival?

'I was sure they would want *Missing* and *China Syndrome*, but they said to me, "You can pick any of your films that you want, but there's one that we insist on – *Some Like It Hot*." It's the most popular foreign film in Cuba, and also in Russia, incidentally.'

While we were talking, I was noting down on my pad that Jack Lemmon was smoking thin brown cigars, wearing a black suit, yellow shirt and black wool tie, and that his hair was a fluffy white mane like

Gough Whitlam's. Either he's telepathic or he can read upside down, because he suddenly broke off his train of thought and said: 'I want to explain I don't wear my hair like this normally. It's getting a little Einsteiny. I've been doing a play, *Long Day's Journey Into Night*, for 7 months now, and that's why the long hair – the hammy old actor at the turn of the century.'

This led to a diversion onto Lemmon's view that film actors are better if they've had stage training. 'It is almost impossible to learn how to act on film,' he said. 'You're doing little bits and pieces, out of sequence, with all kinds of people hollering and screaming at you, and you've never had enough rehearsal.

'You look at the fine younger actors in America now – de Niro, Jack Nicholson, Dusty Hoffman – you find that almost without exception they are stage trained.'

So where does that leave Marilyn Monroe? She was a star, not an actor, Lemmon argues.

'Working with Marilyn was very interesting, because she was not trained, but she desperately wanted to be,' he said. 'She would stop in scenes all the time that were seemingly going along fine. We liked each other offscreen, respected each other, but there was no contact onscreen. I didn't feel she was acting with me, so much as acting at me.

'But when I thought nothing was happening between her and me, something sure as hell was happening between her and the lens. I'd say, "I don't know why Billy Wilder is printing that scene" and then I'd go to the rushes and I couldn't see myself. She was all you could look at.'

Asimov's meaning of life

Most New Yorkers' idea of helping the homeless is to toss the occasional coin to the ragged bundles of humanity who congregate in shop doorways and subway entrances all over central Manhattan. But if you're a rich New Yorker, you're not in the streets very often, and you don't come into contact with the homeless. You need to find another way to deliver your charity.

So it has become fashionable to help the homeless by holding a dinner pary. Not for the homeless themselves, of course, but for a literary celebrity. You then invite your friends to pay $125 to visit your home, meet the celeb, consume a gourmet meal and leave with a warm feeling of having alleviated human suffering.

I decided to pay $125 to dine in a large apartment on Manhattan's Upper West Side with Isaac Asimov. I could have dined in apartments all over New York with authors like Jane Brody (healthy cooking), William Caunitz (police thrillers), Tama Janowitz (trendy bohemiana), Dan Greenburg (Jewish humour) or Dominick Dunne (society scandals), all of whom had donated their time to attract contributors to the cause. But I chose Asimov because 20 years ago his stories filled my teenage imagination with wonder.

Asimov, formerly Professor of Biochemistry at Boston University, is 68. He has written 365 books, and is in *The Guiness Book of Records* as America's most prolific author. Most of them were science fiction or science fact, but he's also covered religion, linguistics, limericks, ancient history, mathematics, humour, crime, Shakespeare, health, and poetry. He is a 20th-century Renaissance Man (and he's written about that too).

Asimov is best known (to me anyway) for creating the three Laws of Robotics, for *Fantastic Voyage* (miniaturised scientists exploring the human bloodstream) and for the *Foundation and Empire* series (a future history of the galaxy). It seemed to me that if anyone was ever going to tell me the answer to the Ultimate Question about Life, The Universe and Everything, it would be Isaac Asimov. So I took along my tiny tape recorder.

The evening began with drinks in the parlour and a welcoming speech by our hostess, Betsy Newell. She said a group to which she belongs has taken over a derelict hotel on the Upper West Side and is renovating it as a shelter for the 300 homeless people who normally sleep in Central Park.

'This party is to raise money to fix up that building, to buy beds and linen and curtains and equipment for those rooms, so those homeless people won't have to spend another winter in the park,' Mrs Newell said. She invited us to take our food from the buffet and join our author at table. There were 8 of us in the Asimov group.

Isaac Asimov proved to be a small man with a big head, made larger by fluffy muttonchop whiskers, and a strong Brooklyn accent (he pronouces 'this' as 'dis' and 'third' as 'toid'). He seemed brusque at the beginning, giving single sentence answers to our nervous questions, but as the two hour meal rolled on, he turned into a hilarious raconteur.

Excerpts from the evening . . .

David (a journalist): 'Did you see the film *Robocop*, where they use your Laws of Robotics?'

Asimov: 'I didn't see it. That's the trouble with being a prolific writer – you sit there facing a typewriter all day. Are you Australian? I saw *Crocodile Dundee*. Loved it.'

Leo (an insurance executive): 'What did you think of *Star Wars?* (Leo meant the movie, but Asimov deliberately misconstrued the question to mean Ronald Reagan's proposed space-based defence system.)

Asimov: 'We shouldn't spend the money on it. It won't work. This stupid president we've got. You get something into his head with a crowbar, you can't get it out. Once you build it, how will you know if it works, unless the Russians co-operate and send about a thousand nuclear monsters and we see if we can stop them?'

Ian (an investment banker): 'Do you think we'll ever be able to travel through time?'

Asimov: 'No it's theoretically impossible. Not in real life.' (Disappointed silence all round the table. Asimov tries to cheer us up . . .) 'Well, not in the sense of getting into a machine. But if you travel at close to the speed of light, go way out and come back, you may find that much more time has passed on earth than has passed from your point of view.'

Ian: 'That reminds me of a limerick: "There was a young lady called Bright, Whose speed was much faster than light, She set off one day In a relative way, And returned on the previous night."'

Asimov: 'Oh limericks. What's your name, honey?'

Beth (computer analyst): 'Beth.'

Asimov: 'Okay. Aah . . . There is a young lady named Beth, Who has me quite out of breath. She had me one night, And boy what a fright. I thought she would screw me to death.'

David: 'Why do you write so many books?'

Asimov: 'Because I can't think of anything else to do. I once gave a talk and after the talk I called for questions. One question was "Dr Asimov, if you had to choose between writing and women, which would you choose?" And I said, "Well, I can type for 12 hours at a time."'

Ian: 'But you like women too?'

Asimov: 'Oh yes. But you know what gets me about women? They are so down on these artificial colours in food, and then they take this lipstick, God knows what's in it, and they put it all over their lips and lick it off. Why? If they took that stuff from lipstick and put it into food, they'd refuse to eat it.

'And lipstick is so stupid. You show me a girl with lipstick on and I'll show you a girl that married men are afraid to kiss. Fortunately my wife is used to me coming home with lipstick all over my face, because I tell her the fans are overwhelmed and delighted.'

Ian: 'You're known for witty lines. What's the cleverest comeback you ever did?'

Asimov: 'As in the case of Dorothy Parker, my most quoted remarks I never said. There's one that went around that I was overheard to say to a young lady in an elevator: "Look upon me as a father, I incest." I don't recall saying that.

'I remember much better the lines that I was on the receiving end of. Once I was attending a meeting of a club that I go to every week. One guy hadn't showed up for three or four weeks. He had some cockamamie excuse – his wife was in the hospital, near death, something like that.

'I said to him with conscious virtue: "The only reason I wouldn't show up for a luncheon was if the young lady in bed with me wouldn't let me get out." Whereupon the guy says: "Which accounts for Asimov's perfect attendance record."'

David: 'Do you worry that people don't read books as much now as when you first started writing?'

Asimov: 'Yes, but there is hope. My son, who is no great brain – he's 36, a gentleman of leisure with an assured income – would never read any of my books. Then one day he rushed home and got *Fantastic Voyage* to read, because he's seen the picture. So for some people, watching televison makes them want to read the book.'

Mary Lou (travel consultant): 'Do you get a lot of people writing to you, asking questions?'

Asimov: 'Not questions. What I get are answers. There are more people who have the exact answer to all the problems of the universe.

'I get crazies. A guy sent me a taped monologue and so I gave it to my wife and said listen to it. He was telling me a very common story, that there are people who are controlling him by radio waves, and that unless I do something about it, he's going to kill himself. My wife's a psychiatrist, she said I shouldn't write back. She said no matter what you say you'll end up in worse trouble.'

David: 'Dr Asimov, what is the meaning of life? Do people ask you that a lot?'

Asmiov: 'Yes they do, but they never get an answer. I can't tell you the meaning of life, but I can tell you the meaning of *my* life. The meaning of my life is to write.'

15

CITIES

New York: improvements underground; the mayor fights back.

I'll never forget the morning I rode to work in a clean, airconditioned subway carriage.

The doors didn't fly open as the train was going at top speed. No windows fell out. The train didn't stop for minutes in a tunnel and then roar through the scheduled station without stopping.

No beggar or busker shuffled through the carriage demanding money or screeching painfully on a saxophone. The sign on the side of the carriage actually corresponded with where the train was going. The lights stayed on for the whole journey. No-one was stabbed or shot. No purses were snatched.

I had heard rumours that carriages like this existed somewhere in the New York subway system, but this was my first encounter with one. The other passengers were as overcome by this dreamlike experience as I. We sat there in awed silence, staring round the shiny walls of the carriage, searching for graffiti. There were none. We could even understand nearly all the announcements over the public address system.

My trip of 30 blocks took 6 minutes. As I got out of the train at Times Square, I began to think that the New York Transit Authority might not be lying in claiming that its efforts to civilise the most chaotic underground railway in the world (3.5 million passengers a day) are achieving success.

I wondered if the authority might actually be telling the truth when it says that more than 4,000 of the subway's 6,000 carriages are now graffiti free and fully airconditioned. Maybe subway crime has been reduced since the introduction of special 'transit cops' in the most dangerous stations and trains (to only 4,853 robberies, 468 assaults and 5 murders in 1987).

Maybe it **has** cleaned up and renovated some stations to such an extent that you can see the original art nouveau tilework from around 1910. Maybe it's true that less than 10 per cent of subway trains now have incorrect direction signs, and that there were only 47 'DOE incidents' – 'Doors Opening En Route' – in 1987.

But the week after that amazing experience I rode the subway again with David Hill, former head of the NSW State Rail Authority. Things were a little different.

'Jesus, smell the urine,' Hill said as we descended the steps into the station. That comment on the permanent perfume of the subway stations (which are home to thousands of derelicts) was the most complimentary remark he made all day.

We put our tokens into the turnstile (standard price $1 for any journey – a system which Hill says can't be introduced in Sydney because the distances are too great), and made our way through a labyrinth of tunnels to what may have been the right station. There were of course no route maps on the platform. The maps are displayed inside the carriages, so you have to board a train in order to find out that it is not going to your destination.

There's little point in asking directions, because everybody has a different language for the routes. Old time New Yorkers use descriptions like 'the BMT line' and 'the IRT line', which are the names of the private companies that ran the competing subway systems before the city took them over – BMT means Brooklyn-Manhattan Transfer, and IRT means Interborough Rapid Transit. Newer citizens use numbers, colours or letters to describe the lines, depending on which attempt to simplify the system has caught their allegiance. They always fail to indicate which trains are the expresses and which are the all-stations, so you find yourself whisked away to Brooklyn before you've had a chance to study the map in the carriage.

A train roared in, covered from airvents to axles in swirling multi-coloured graffiti. New York subway graffiti are unlike any other. However closely you examine them, they contain no meaning or message. They are purely visual extravagances.

Hill, it turned out, was an expert. The graffiti, he said, are symbols or 'tags' identifying various gangs who break into the subway garages and spend hours working with spray cans. In our carriage, he was able to decipher signatures that said 'SAZ', 'HOW', and 'SCORE'. I said I thought some of the graffiti were almost beautiful.

'I've got no sympathy with that bullshit about it being folk art,' said Hill. 'If they want to draw on the walls, let them do it at home. Passengers find a vandalised carriage intimidating, it raises their anxiety.'

The floor of the carriage showed the remains of a multitude of spilled cans of Coke and what was probably vomit. 'This is just horrible,' said Hill. As the train picked up speed Hill complained that the driver kept accelerating and braking too abruptly, and said: 'Hear that clackety clack? They haven't made proper connections between the sections of rail. And where's their sound insulation?'

Over the noise it was impossible to hear most of the announcements coming from the public address system, which in any case were delivered in an accent which seemed to eliminate most consonants. The voice seemed to be saying 'nestah finiceree, chayfuh aybeeseenkay lah mah clone dough'. I guessed, since I'd ridden the line before, that this meant 'Next stop 59th Street, change for A, B, C and K lines. Mind the closing doors.' Hill said inaudibility was a common problem with rail announcements, but in Sydney it was possible for passengers to look at indicators on the platforms.

When we got out of the train, Hill approached a transit policeman, leaning against the wall with a pistol, baton and two-way radio hanging from his belt, and asked how many transit policemen were employed in the system. The man said there were 2,200 special transit cops, and in addition 3,000 of the regular city police made special patrols of the subway.

Hill noted that the Sydney system gets by with a little less than 300 security guards. But then again, incidents of violence in the Sydney system run at only 20 a month.

I asked Hill if there was anything the State Rail Authority could learn from the New York subway system. He paused for a long time, then said: 'Every rail system in the world has something to teach us, but in the case of New York, I'm still trying to find what that is.'

Surviving the scandals

Ed Koch, mayor of New York, thinks he and his city are the victims of an international bum rap. There's this ridiculous myth around the world that New York is a dangerous, dirty metropolis run by a mayor who has surrounded himself with crooks.

In fact, Ed Koch knows that he ought to rate as one of the most successful politicians in the world. Controlling a budget of $23 billion (four times that of the state government of NSW), and a workforce of 230,000 public servants, he finished the 1987 financial year with a surplus of $666 million. When he took over as mayor of New York 10 years ago, the city was bankrupt.

Koch said he would spend the surplus giving the people what they want – 2,000 extra policemen, 1,200 extra teachers, as well as more street-cleaners, ambulances, AIDS treatment facilities and shelters for the homeless.

But does he get any gratitude, any respect, any adulation? He does not. All he gets is constant carping about corruption.

Every week the media would bring up some new allegation about city officials taking bribes, or doing expensive favours for powerful friends. No-one has demonstrated that Koch is personally corrupt, but he seems to have been astonishingly naive about activities going on quite close to him.

The scandal the citizens enjoyed the most was one involving Bess Myerson, a former Miss America whom Koch appointed as New York's cultural affairs commissioner. During Koch's 1985 election campaign, Myerson was photographed holding the mayor's hand at social occasions. Before that, the mayor had been the subject of rumours that he was a homosexual.

As it turned out, Myerson was never involved with Mayor Koch. Her real lover was a married gentleman named Andy Capasso. In 1987 he was jailed for tax evasion, and Myerson had to resign when she was charged with arranging city contracts for Capasso's construction company, and influencing a judge who was presiding over Capasso's divorce hearing. Presumably Mayor Koch will have to find another lady to hold his hand during the next election campaign.

After being re-elected in 1985 with the support of 77 per cent of the voters, Ed Koch in 1987 faced a *New York Times* opinion poll in which 55 per cent of voters ticked 'it is time to give a new person a chance to run the city' and only 37 per cent ticked 'Mr Koch has performed his job as mayor well enough to deserve re-election'.

In the same poll 66 per cent said they believed the city government 'is run for a few big interests looking out for themselves', while only 25 per cent said it was run 'for the benefit of all the people'.

Ed Koch finds this unfair, since he says 75,000 extra public service jobs and 390,000 extra jobs in private industry have been created in New York since he took office 10 years ago.

Koch says he has adopted a policy of never complaining about the media 'because it doesn't help'. When he wants to get his side of a story out, he expresses it on his weekly TV program or he writes a book (he has three autobiographies to his credit, one of which was turned into a musical). But ask him one question – 'how have the corruption scandals affected your ability to manage the city?' – and all the pent-up anger pours out.

I will transcribe his answer here in full because it gives you a sense of Koch's style, which is to talk any difficult subject to death. Picture a tall, bald, rotund man of 63, regularly raising and lowering his eyebrows, thrusting his head forward and gesturing with his right hand as if catching a slow baseball. Picture a man who could get a job as a stand-up comic if he's voted out of office in 1989.

'One hundred people have been referred to under Reagan as under suspicion or indicted or part of some scandal. There are corruption scandals going on in Boston, Washington, Chicago. The mayors of those towns are doing pretty good. I'm not in any way telling you that any of those mayors or myself are pleased and happy that you have corrupt people. But they are there, and regrettably not uncovered soon enough.

'Look back at the number of people who have been in any way indicted or removed in New York, and it probably runs to three dozen at the outside. If you look at the number who have been convicted, it's a handful, a handful. Now I'm telling you that whether it's one, it's one too many. And whether they've been indicted or convicted or whether you just think they're corrupt, it's sad that they were there to begin with. But people are not very careful in how they describe this sort of thing.

'So when someone will ask me "Do you take responsibility?" – sure I take responsibility. Then I say "What do you want me to do when I take responsibility? What does it mean?"

'What it means is that I like to believe that people in this town say I've been a good mayor – and, well, I'm only one of three mayors in the history of New York that's been elected three times. So when I run for a fourth term, people will have to decide: what I've done over the last 12 years, does it sufficiently outweigh what others will attack me for?

'If I were not to prevail, undoubtedly the reason would be because people would say that the corruption of the people who have been corrupt in some way tarred me. I understand that. It's always possible. I hope not.'

One other issue gets Mayor Koch equally het-up. It's the suggestion that New York is a dangerous city because of a high crime rate, particularly in the subways. He says New York gets a negative image because it is the constant focus of attention by the international media. He believes New York is so much a part of people's fantasies, that tales about it take on mythical proportions.

'Last time I looked at it, roughly 3 per cent of the felonies committed in a day in this city were committed on the subway,' Koch said. 'You might say that means a lot because New York is a dangerous city. No. The FBI puts out an index of the top 25 cities for crime in terms of population, and we are 14th down. It used to be Detroit was number one, and I hope I'm not doing Dallas a disservice, but I think it's number one now, or if it's not number one, it's up there. Then you have LA, Chicago, Boston, Washington DC, Denver. These are cities that have far greater crime than we do, according to the FBI.

'Why do our subways get so much attention? The story I'm going to tell you now is a true story, and it could have happened in any city in the world. I was in Tokyo, and the Governor of Tokyo, a very smart man, he said to me, "Mayor, I understand you get a lot of crime in the subways?" And I said to him, "Why do you think that? How would you know that?" And he said "I read about it in the Tokyo papers." So I said, "Well, apparently you have no crime in Tokyo, because I never read about it in the New York papers."

'Now there's a little message there. Obviously we'd like to eliminate all crime, but what I'm saying is that it's a bad rap. Whatever happens in New York City is of huge interest to the people around the world.'

16

GATHERINGS

*A collection of organisations whose ideas set them apart
from the mainstream: the Amish; the Bohemian Club; the
liberals; the doctors versus the lawyers; the unions.*

It's harvest time in the Amish country around Lancaster, Pennsylvania. The fields are full of men with braces, blue shirts and Abraham Lincoln beards, loading corn on to horse-drawn carts. Amish people are welcoming each other in the evenings to feasts of fresh vegetables and meat in their homes, the reward for a hard day's labour.

But this hospitality is not extended to the Lapp family. Anne and John Lapp have been excommunicated by the people with whom they grew up and with whom they celebrated their wedding 18 years ago.

The Lapps are being 'shunned'. No other Amish person will speak to them, do business with them, eat with them, travel with them or even accept anything from their hands. This includes John Lapp's parents. 'They don't shun the children, only us,' says Anne Lapp. 'But, when John's mother comes to visit the children and she wants to hold the baby, someone else – not me – must pass her the baby.'

The Lapps' 14-year-old daughter, Geraldine, interpolates: 'My Grandma doesn't like shunning my Mum and Dad but she has to.'

The story of the Lapps shows a less idyllic side of the Amish people than was displayed in *Witness*. In that Oscar-winning film, they gave only kindness to an outsider who needed their help. In reality, the 14,000 Amish in Lancaster County are fierce in their desire to keep the outside world away. The Amish man who gave technical advice for the 'barn-raising' sequence in *Witness* is also being shunned, for revealing their secrets.

The 'sin' of the Lapps was much worse. It wasn't simply that they decided to drive a car and have electricity connected to their home; they wanted to share their Christianity. The issue is difficult for outsiders to understand – as is so much of the Amish culture – but Anne Lapp tries to explain: 'As Amish people grow up, we attend services in the home, conducted in high German – even though the language we speak between ourselves is a German dialect called Pennsylvania Dutch. So maybe half the people at the service don't understand it, just as many Catholics never understood the services when they were conducted in Latin.

'The Amish feel that they are saved by good works, by doing things the hard way. After we got married, John started reading the scriptures in English and he found that we are saved by faith in Jesus Christ. The Amish way became very frustrating for him. He didn't want his children to go through what he went through, to be raised without understanding.

'I'm not saying none of the Amish people are saved. But they would consider it boastful to be talking about your religion, so they don't share it. They want to keep it to themselves, to make it difficult. We believe in mission work.'

Two years after they were married, in a joyous 14-hour ceremony attended by 350 other Amish, John Lapp found that his talk about spreading the gospel was earning the disapproval of his bishop.

When he and Anne joined a group which held meetings in a separate church building instead of a home, and which supported missionaries in other countries, the shunning began. 'It was very difficult at first,' Anne says. 'Our family turned their backs on us. We had to get a whole new set of friends.'

Since then, the Lapps have had 8 children, the oldest of whom has returned to the Amish and teaches in a one-room Amish school. John and Anne Lapp have become part of a new sect numbering about 300 people. They call themselves 'Amish-Mennonite' because they are more liberal than the Amish but not as liberal as the Mennonites, from whom the Amish split in the late 17th century.

They still believe in pacifism and adult baptism. The women still wear plain dresses, aprons and white lace 'prayer caps' and the married men still wear beards without moustaches. But they may drive cars, watch television and have curtains in their homes (condemned by the Amish, along with all non-functional items, as being 'for fancy'). And the Amish-Mennonites may speak freely to 'the English' – the term the Amish use for all outsiders.

The Amish desire to keep the world away arises from their bitter experience of persecution in the 16th century. They began as a Protestant sect called the Anabaptists in Switzerland, and they were frequently tortured and imprisoned by agents of the Catholic Church and by other Protestant groups. At first, they were all Mennonites – named after one of their leaders, Menno Simons – but, in 1693, an elder named Jacob Amman complained that the Mennonites were becoming too worldly and formed a breakaway group.

Both groups were offered land and religious freedom in America in 1710 by William Penn, an English Quaker who eventually gave his name to the State of Pennsylvania. The Mennonites have changed since, along with American society, while the only concessions made by the Amish have been to permit the use of stoves and refrigerators powered by propane gas, and of public telephones in emergencies.

Anne Lapp still admires the Amish for their determination. 'In the winter, when you only have one fire and one kerosene lamp in one room, you can imagine the close family ties that will create,' she says.

Men are brought up to work on the family farm – mostly concentrating on dairy cattle, corn and tobacco. Women are brought up to make clothes and cook food in vast quantities.

'I've brought up my daughters to be able to cook for 40 people, short order,' says Anne Lapp. 'In the Amish community, it's not unusual on a Sunday night for three or four buggies to pull up at your house at the dinner hour without warning and all of a sudden you've got 30 people to cook for. My girls, if I'm not here, should be able to handle that.'

The Amish community is one of the fastest growing religious sects in the United States (the Amish population has risen from 50,000 to 90,000 in the past 10 years), mainly because the birthrate is so high and the pressures to conform are so intense.

Two serious problems afflict the Amish in Lancaster County, which was their first settlement in America.

The first is inbreeding. Among the 14,000 Amish in the area, there are only 14 family names (the most common are Stolzfoos, Lantz, Blank, Schmucker and Lapp). Abnormalities are starting to appear in newborn babies, particularly extra fingers on one or both hands. To remedy this, the Lancaster Amish are seeking greater contacts with communities in Ohio, Indiana and Canada – sending younger people 'courting' further afield.

The second problem is tourism. The popularity of *Witness* and publicity by the local Visitors' Bureau have lured busloads of 'English' to the area, particularly at weekends. They drive up and down past the farms, snapping away despite warnings that the Amish believe photography breaks the biblical commandment against the making of 'graven images'.

Local souvenir shops sell Amish dolls, mugs, doorstops, paperweights and miniature buggies. The gimmicks sell well because the Amish are so attractive to Americans who yearn for freshness and innocence in their own lives – but none of the money goes to the Amish.

They don't mind that; they just wish they could be left alone.

Nude nymphs in the forest

The Bohemian Club of California is so secretive, so powerful, and so strange, that collecting rumours about it is much easier than collecting facts. However, here are a few facts about the Bohemian Club:

• It owns 1,100 hectares of redwood forest north of San Francisco, where its members go for a two-week 'retreat' each year. During the retreat the members dress up as wood sprites, perform playlets, and burn effigies in front of a 13-metre high statue of an owl.

• It has been in existence for more than 100 years and now has 2,300 members, all men, who pay $8,500 to join and $110 a month in fees.

• Members include Ronald Reagan, Richard Nixon, George Schultz, Henry Kissinger, several former CIA bosses, the chief executives of many of America's richest companies, authors like Herman Wouk and Irving Stone, several former astronauts, and an assortment of leading figures in the media, science and the arts.

• Club officials describe its purpose as 'celebrating the arts' and say that members never discuss business on club property, adhering to the motto: 'Weaving spiders come not here'.

• The club is currently under legal attack because of its refusal to admit women as members, and to employ women in any staff capacity.

Now here are a few rumours about the Bohemian Club of California:

- During retreats, some club members go around naked, some dress as women, and many urinate on trees, to celebrate their escape from the restrictions of society and from their wives.
- Richard Nixon began his political comeback with an address to club members during the 1967 retreat. Several members agreed to back him for another run for the presidency.
- The deals which made Dwight Eisenhower a Republican presidential candidate were done when he attended a Bohemian Club retreat in the early 1950s.
- At one retreat in the early 1940s a few members decided around a campfire to develop the atomic bomb.
- The Bohemian Club is where much of the real business of America's conservatives has been conducted for most of the 20th century.

The club was founded in San Francisco around 1880 by a group of journalists and artists who wanted a place where they could drink and talk. Its original rules said rich men could not join, but within a decade of its founding the club was dominated by businessmen and politicians.

Past members have included the authors Mark Twain and Jack London, the composers Victor Herbert and Arthur Sullivan, the media baron William Randolph Hearst, the performers Ray Bolger and Bing Crosby, the Supreme Court Judge Earl Warren, and the presidents Theodore Roosevelt and Herbert Hoover.

Before the Second World War, everyone knew it was pointless to fill in a membership application if you were Jewish, black or a Democrat, but more recently the club has made an effort to broaden its social mix. In the early 1980s, the Jewish author Herbert Gold and the black author Ernest Gaines were invited to attend an 'evening of entertainment' at the Bohemian clubhouse in San Francisco. The entertainment turned out to be four club members in blackface performing Mills Brothers songs. Both authors declined an invitation to join the club. Gold says: 'The brandy, the cigars, the men congratulating themselves on being there – I found it boring. The word bohemian is most inappropriate.'

But California's former Democratic governor Edmund Brown was an active member, and despite liberal views on most subjects, was adamantly opposed to women joining. He said he had the habit of walking nude between his tent and the showers at club retreats. This would not be possible if women were admitted to the retreat. 'If I want to sit around in a pair of shorts and listen to stories that I don't want to listen to when my wife is there, I should have that right,' he said.

Ironically, the anti-discrimination legislation which Brown helped to pioneer is now being used against the Bohemian Club. The Californian Fair Employment and Housing Commission has obtained a court order declaring the club's policy against hiring women to be discriminatory. The club is appealing to the US Supreme Court. And a body called the Centre for Law in Public Interest has taken a case before the Alcoholic Beverage Control Commission asking that the club's liquor licence be revoked until women are allowed to be members.

These two cases have brought to light much more information about the club's activities than its members would like. In one hearing, a member who works for one of San Francisco's staidest law firms told how he wore fairy's wings and a body stocking for his role as a woodnymph in a musical comedy called 'Low Jinks' held during a retreat. He said the retreats always begin with members dressing up in red robes and burning an effigy called 'Dull Care' in front of a giant statue of an owl.

Members divide into about 120 separate 'camps', each with its own name and artistic emphasis. Ronald Reagan is a member of a camp called Owl's Nest. Richard Nixon is a member of Cave Man. This is a list of the members of the camp called Mandalay, generally agreed to have the most comfortable quarters at the retreat:

Stephen Bechtel (head of Bechtel, the biggest construction company in America); Charles Black (businessman and husband of Shirley Temple); Leonard Firestone (tyre magnate); Gerald Ford (former president); Najeeb Halaby (former head of Pan Am); Edgar Kaiser (steel tycoon); Henry Kissinger (former secretary of state); John McCone (former head of the CIA); Herman Phleger (former diplomat); George Schultz (secretary of state); William French Smith (former attorney-general).

The best attended retreat in recent times seems to have been in 1981, when members were able to celebrate the election of Ronald Reagan (although he was not present in person). The retreats are heavily guarded from outsiders, but an agenda was leaked to the media by a member who found it all too much.

There was a comedy revue performed by the US Supreme Court judge Potter Stewart, the broadcaster Walter Cronkite, the attorney-general Edwin Meese, the conservative columnist William F. Buckley, and the former chairman of the Bank of America, Leland Prussia. Casper Weinberger delivered a talk entitled 'Re-arming America'.

Arthur Hailey spoke on 'Joys and Anguish of the Author'. The former astronauts Frank Crippen and John Young explained the Space Shuttle. The president of Caltech, Marvin Goldberger spoke on 'Space Wars: Fact vs Fantasy'.

Some of the subjects dicussed seem to have turned up later in the policies of the Reagan administration, and several club members have become members of the Reagan cabinet. But according to the information sheet which the club gives to inquiring journalists, this would be mere coincidence. The document says:

'One of the exaggerated notions about the Bohemian Club is that it is a gathering and decision-making place for national and international "power-brokers". In fact, the club is a refuge from decision making and other pressures and strivings of business and the "market-place" . . .

'Worldly fame impresses the club's members far less than the gifts of talent, time and effort that individual members provide for the club's own unique activities.'

The perils of the progressive

It's not easy being a liberal in Ronald Reagan's America, and its even tougher being an organised liberal. Norman Lear, founder of an organisation called People For The American Way, learned during 1987 that he had been placed on the death list of a neo-Nazi group called The Order. This was revealed in the trial of 9 members of The Order for the murder of a radio reporter in Denver.

That's the strongest negative reaction that People For The American Way have so far inspired, but it's typical of the way the New Right has reacted.

Pat Robertson, a TV evangelist who ran for the US Presidency, branded People For The American Way as agents of communism, satanism, drugs and immorality. The chief spokesman for the US Justice Department, Terry Eastland, was a little more moderate in his comments: 'What they are is an uncivil organisation. I think People For The American Way has helped lower the level of public discourse in this country.'

This is all pretty hurtful to John Buchanan, a Baptist minister and former Republican Congressman who is now Chairman of People For The American Way. He says his group, which has 250,000 members and an annual budget of $8 million, is not radical. It is simply working to protect the first amendment to the American Constitution, which supposedly guarantees freedom of speech and freedom of religion.

But when it has modest successes – like persuading the US Senate Judiciary Committee to reject a Reagan nominee for judge because he was both extremist and incompetent, or persuading the Texas School Board to reinstate a chapter on evolution in a biology textbook – some people get angry.

'They don't like us because we celebrate the pluralism and the diversity we believe are the strengths of our society,' John Buchanan said. 'That means we monitor those who oppose those freedoms, we try to make the American people aware of the nature of this new political force that is the far right and the religious right, and we try to create a counterforce.'

I asked Buchanan if there was not an argument that the American people, in voting overwhelmingly for Ronald Reagan, had indicated they favour conservatism, and therefore that People For The American Way was opposing the will of the majority.

'If you look at polls of people's opinions on issues, you find the American people disagree with Ronald Reagan on all sorts of issues, but they happen to like him as a man,' Buchanan said. 'There is no mandate for the far right's agenda.

'See, we have no problem with the old kind of conservatives, who believe in things like fiscal responsibility and limited government. But the far right have a strange new agenda which they want to force on everyone. They are a militant minority who can have a serious impact on school boards, on government, on leadership positions in political parties, on the judiciary.

'It isn't just that they want to censor books. In Indiana, they succeeded in having the child abuse legislation weakened because they argued that parents have an absolute right to impose Biblical discipline on children. That was in a year when 8 children in Indiana were beaten to death by their parents.'

People For The American Way started in 1980 as the result of a television commercial made by Norman Lear, who had been the producer of satirical shows like *All In The Family* and *Maude*. Lear was horrified by what he saw as the intrusion into politics of some TV evangelists, and made a commercial which showed a construction worker getting out of a truck and saying: 'I saw a preacher on TV the other day telling everybody what the Christian position is on a bunch of political issues. I agreed with him on everything, so I'm 100 per cent Christian. But my boy disagrees with that preacher on about half the things, and my boy's just as good a Christian as I am. And my wife disagrees with that preacher on almost everything and my wife's the best Christian in our family. You can't really judge a person's morality or their Christianity based on what they believe about a bunch of political issues. That's not the American way.'

Lear received support from officials of the Baptist, Lutheran, Methodist, Jewish and Catholic churches, and from a number of business, media and political leaders, so he formed an organisation which took its name from the last line of the commercial. Now People For The American Way employs 60 researchers full-time, monitoring the activities of the far right and undertaking campaigns through media, mail or public speaking.

It issued a report which shows that during the 1985–86 academic year, there were 130 incidents in which right-wing pressure groups tried to censor books, films or curricula in schools and libraries. This was a 35 per cent increase on the previous year.

It sponsored a series of TV commercials starring the actor Lloyd Bridges, who argued that unbiased, expert federal judges were essential for democracy to work, and attacked two right-wingers of limited legal experience who had been nominated to judicial positions by Ronald Reagan. One of the nominees was rejected by the Senate Judiciary Committee and the other was accepted by a vote of 49 to 47 of the whole Senate.

During the 1986 election for some members of the Senate and House of Representatives, People For The American Way wrote to all candidates to remind them of the constitutional separation of church and state. John Buchanan said: 'We were asking them to avoid the use of religious intolerance, and specifically not to claim better qualifications based on their religious affiliation or imply God's endorsement for their candidacy.'

Not all candidates accepted the advice. In Los Angeles, one Republican candidate wrote to local ministers saying 'God did a rather unique thing – he called on me to run for congress'. In Nebraska, a Republican candidate for governor said in a fund raising letter, 'I have God. I know I can count on God. Can I count on you?' And Joe Morecraft, a Republican candidate in Atlanta, called on his voters to pray to God to 'remove' the Supreme Court judges who voted for the legislation of abortion.

John Buchanan has bitter personal experience of the dangers of holding liberal views and of the power of the far right. After he had been the member of congress for Birmingham, Alabama, for 16 years, the Moral Majority organisation took exception to his views on women's rights, racial equality and public education (Buchanan opposed the removal of 'secular humanist, Godless' books from school libraries).

The Moral Majority campaigned successfully to deny him the Republican Party's nomination – 'they beat my brains out with Christian love,' Buchanan said. But he feels there is some poetic justice in the fact that 'the man who replaced me as the Republican candidate, a former member of the John Birch society, was then defeated by an excellent opponent who was both a Democrat and a Jew'.

That reinforced his belief in the potential of American voters to behave 'nobly' if they were given full information about their choices. 'People are hungry for strength and purity in public life, and that's what sometimes gives the religious right some support,' he said.

'The American people will respond if someone appeals to their rages, their prejudices and their fears, their worst side. But if someone appeals to their nobility, their idealism and their best selves, they can respond to that. We base our activities on the belief that the American people are capable of honour.'

Malpractice makes profit

If one in every five American doctors is sued for malpractice by a patient each year, and if the average court award to a patient is $1.1 million, there are three possible explanations:

1. America has a lot of incompetent doctors.

2. America has a lot of paranoid patients.

3. America has a lot of greedy lawyers exploiting a legal system weighted in the patient's favour.

Doctors will tell you that number (3) is true, and that it causes number (2). Lawyers will tell you that there's some truth in all three explanations, but that even a non-greedy lawyer has a duty to assist victims of medical incompetence and to keep the pressure on doctors who might take shortcuts in care.

Everyone agrees that the explosion in malpractice cases has massively increased the cost of health care in the United States. The average general practitioner in New York pays a malpractice insurance premium of $20,000 a year. Doctors in the most vulnerable specialities – obstetrics, orthopaedic surgery and neurosurgery – pay $100,000 a year. The cost of malpractice insurance has been rising by 30 per cent a year, keeping pace with the rise in damages awarded.

The American Medical Association, representing the country's 271,000 doctors, estimates that doctors now spend $15 billion a year on 'defensive medicine' – using elaborate technology to do unnecessary tests so they can prove they took all possible precautions if they get sued. The AMA says many fine doctors are getting out of medicine because they can't stand the constant anxiety that they may be dragged through the courts over a result they could not control.

What the AMA calls 'the malpractice crisis' has brought doctors and lawyers close to total war. The AMA has petitioned the US Congress to ban the lawyers' practice of touting for business among patients and offering a deal whereby they charge nothing if they lose a case, but take a big share of the financial settlement if they win. The AMA and the medical insurance companies have also asked state politicians to place a limit on the size of damages awards, and to make it more difficult to start malpractice actions.

The American Bar Association, representing the nation's 320,000 lawyers, responded with a report arguing that 'the medical profession, in seeking changes to the tort law system, has shown a willingness to trade away the rights of individuals in the hope of easing a perceived burden on itself ... There is no reason to exempt the medical profession from the application of the tort system any more than businessmen or truck drivers or anyone else who has failed to live up to the proper standard of care'.

The lawyers say the doctors are exaggerating the situation. Although one in five doctors is sued for malpractice each year, most cases are settled out of court. And of those that do get to court, juries rule in favour of the doctor 75 per cent of the time. And the average figures for damages awarded are distorted by a few extremely large awards (the record being $29 million).

Nevertheless, doctor-lawyer skirmishes are breaking out all over the country. In the town of Brunswick, Georgia, all the obstetricians got together and voted to refuse treatment to any pregnant lawyer or law clerk and to the pregnant wives of any lawyers whose firms have ever sued any doctor for malpractice.

In Maryland, doctors' wives formed a lobby group called Citizens for Liability Reform. They have a bumper sticker that reads: 'Support

your lawyer. Send your child to medical school.'

In Los Angeles, Chicago and Detroit, doctors have set up what they call a 'Physicians Alert' service. This allows any doctor to phone a hotline and check the name of a new patient against a list of people who are known to sue doctors often. 'Professional plaintiffs do exist,' says David Zeitlin, a spokesman for the Los Angeles County Medical Association. 'If a doctor finds he has one of those, he'll be utterly meticulous with his records. He will take great pains to write down everything. It's another form of defensive medicine.'

But Gary Paul, president of the Los Angeles Trial Lawyers Association, says the Physicians Alert service 'has as its purpose the intimidation of patients, to keep them from filing lawsuits'.

In retaliation, the Trial Lawyers Association has set up a hotline on which patients can find out if their doctor has ever been sued for malpractice. Paul says that the lawyers' service is designed to 'steer the public to doctors with good records. And it may eliminate a number of lawsuits, since 80 per cent of lawsuits are filed against 10 per cent of the doctors. There are doctors in this town who have spent more time in court than I have.'

If the boom in malpractice cases was having the effect of eliminating incompetent doctors from the US health system, then it might be worth the costs it imposes. But it doesn't work that way. The damages are paid by the insurance company, and the doctor continues to practise. In 1985, the latest year for which statistics are available, only 406 medical licences were revoked in the whole of the United States, and most of these were for criminal behaviour rather than malpractice.

According to Dr John Berryman, an obstetrician from Washington, the malpractice laws are functioning as a kind of national compensation scheme for people with serious illness or injury.

'Malpractice used to mean negligence or error,' Berryman says. 'Now it simply means a bad result. If a child is born with a withered arm, all the lawyer must do is get that child before a jury and he'll win an award. The jury may even understand that the doctor is not to blame and see the whole case as simply a withdrawal from a vast fund designed to compensate victims.

'Patients don't realise that one way or another – through their health insurance premiums, their medical bills or their taxes – they are the ones who pay malpractice costs. By far the worst flaw of the system is that it subsidises the incompetents. Bad doctors get to fob off their mistakes onto a pool of funds underwritten by the majority.'

'They want painless unionism'

The American union movement is in big trouble. The statistics prove it. In the early 1950s, union members made up 35 per cent of the US workforce. Now union members make up 18 per cent of the workforce.

President Reagan boasts that 12 million jobs have been created since he came into office. But 60 per cent of these jobs pay the minimum wage – $7,000 a year. Fewer than 10 per cent of the people who got the new jobs are represented by unions.

The prevailing ethos of individualism among Americans, the antagonism of the Reagan administration, and the failure of the union movement to adapt to social change, have combined to bring organised labour to the weakest point in its 100-year history.

But the American Federation of Labor and Congress of Industrial Organisations (AFL-CIO), America's equivalent of the ACTU, has started to fight back. It is trying to reform itself from within, it is developing incentives to attract reluctant workers back to unionism, and, most important, it is going all out to influence who becomes president of the US in 1988.

With 14 million members, the AFL-CIO's endorsement still means something to a politician. So its leaders interrogated all the candidates for the Democrat presidential nomination in search of the one who seemed least antagonistic to labour. The plan was then to go all out in campaigning for him, in the knowledge that if another anti-union president goes into the White House, the AFL-CIO will never again have the numbers to be a significant political force.

There was even talk about endorsing one of the candidates for the Republican nomination, as well as one of the Democrats, so labour isn't completely ignored by the conservatives.

'1988 is a critical time for us,' says Charles McDonald, the AFL-CIO's Chief Organiser. 'If there's a sympathetic administration in Washington, everything else comes together. A union would have to think twice about pouring resources into organising and trying to increase membership now, because the environment is so bad. We just have to wait.'

Are political candidates glad to have the AFL-CIO's endorsement?

'They have to be watchful because the press will tar any labour-supported candidate as being in the special interest group of the trade union movement, given our low esteem in the population at large,' McDonald said. 'But on the other hand we have very strong resources, field workers to help with campaigns, and a reasonably solid block of votes, so they want our help.'

When I told McDonald that the Australian government regularly consults union leaders, and that the current Australian prime minister is a former head of the ACTU, he said: 'That would be our fantasy. There are very few Democrats who see labour's agenda as the most pressing need for the country. They are more sympathetic, but it could never be like having a labour union officer as president.'

Charles McDonald, a 42-year-old lawyer, is in the vanguard of the changes now happening in the AFL-CIO. A report he wrote in 1985, called 'The Changing Situation of Workers and Their Unions', has become the blueprint for reform.

What brought the American union movement to such a low ebb? McDonald and other AFL-CIO officials suggest three reasons.

The bad image of unions: As factories close down all over the country, America is shifting from an economy based on heavy industry to an economy based on services. A lot of the people who are entering the new service jobs are suspicious of invitations to join a union.

'The common stereotype is that a union can only raise things in a confrontational mode,' McDonald says. 'All the attitude surveys we have ever seen and done indicate that there are an awful lot of people who want some form of representation, but they don't want polarisation between the employer and the union.

'They want painless unionism. They don't want a union built on making life miserable for their company. There's a feeling that the union appeals to the lowest common denominator, that it's basically a blue-collar operation, only interested in the 6 per cent across the board increase with no room for merit plans, promotional procedures, professional responsibilities.

'The reality is that the teachers' union, the actors, the football players, a wide variety of unions do represent a more sophisticated approach. We have to change the perception and convince people that a union is very much a customised institution and fluctuates depending on the character of the workforce that it's representing.'

To attract white-collar workers into the union movement, the AFL-CIO is introducing consumer incentives, like low interest credit cards, travel clubs, and cheap health insurance. 'They won't bring in people who are totally opposed to unionism,' says McDonald, 'but they might make the difference with people who have been indifferent about representation up to now.'

The antagonism of the Reagan administration: McDonald says the Reagan government's decision to sack 11,500 striking air traffic controllers in 1981, and replace them with untrained non-union workers, was a signal to managements 'that nothing is too ruthless in your resistance to trade unions'.

He says the government has failed to enforce laws that are supposed to protect workers, and has introduced new rules that make it difficult for workers to join unions and elect representatives.

US employers now spend $500 million a year hiring consultants who are nicknamed 'union busters' and who specialise in exploiting the labour laws to prevent unions from entering workplaces. McDonald estimates there are about 1,200 professional 'union busters' operating in the US, and he encounters them in 90 per cent of the AFL-CIO's organising campaigns. 'The legislation that affects labour relations is the prime reason we are having such a damn difficult time organising people.'

The Reagan administration blocked a union-sponsored Bill which would have required companies to give 90 days' notice before closing factories, and it is seeking to exempt military contractors from having to pay union rates to their employees.

The AFL-CIO hopes things will improve now that the Democrats have a majority in the Senate. But McDonald points out that President Reagan still controls the National Labour Relations Board, the agency that supervises union elections and gives unions permission to represent new workers. McDonald says that board operates so slowly and bureaucratically that it is 'a major irritant'.

Inflexibility in the unions themselves: The AFL-CIO is fighting to stamp out two old habits in its 90 affiliated unions: competing among themselves for members, instead of trying to attract new members, and going on strike without first consulting the AFL-CIO on whether it is the most effective tactic.

McDonald argues that strikes are out of date as an industrial weapon and, in the current American climate, are more likely to destroy a union than gain improved working conditions. Unions can no longer afford to operate individually to try to resolve grievances.

'In this country we have a 7 per cent unemployment rate and a seemingly inexhaustible patience by the employer when we go out, and a willingness to hire permanent replacements for people on strike, which the law allows,' McDonald says.

'We are experimenting with tactics which will hurt employers economically so they will change their attitudes, while not endangering the employees. You might consider consumer boycott pressures, or shareholder actions, or singling out individual executives for criticism, or you might try to figure out how the company's being financed and see if you can develop a relationship with the bank.

'At the workplace there might be demonstrations, protests, working to rule, raising grievances and complaints with the employer at every opportunity, all designed to convince the employer that it's more peaceful and productive to recognise the union and talk to us.'

The AFL-CIO is computerising data about companies to learn where they are most vulnerable, and offering itself as a centralised resource on tactics for its affiliated unions. As the federation president, Lane Kirkland, puts it: 'We must be part of the general staff at the inception, rather than the ambulance drivers at the bitter end.'

The process of changing attitudes, both inside unions and outside them, is slow, but McDonald predicts that total membership of the AFL-CIO will start to rise in 1989, and approach 15 million by 1990. 'I think we've seen the bottom,' he says.

But what if a sympathetic Democrat is not elected president in 1988?

'Who the hell knows?' McDonald says. 'Nobody can operate on that scenario right now.'

17

LAST HORIZONS

The most memorable moment of my journey on the Lakeshore Limited from Grand Central Station, New York, to Union Station, Chicago, was waking up and seeing the snow. I do not mean the snow outside the window. I mean the snow which covered half my sleeping compartment. It had blown in during the night through the toilet bowl, which was conveniently located next to my bunk, but which was unusable because of ice damage.

Now I knew why I'd kept waking up with my left side frozen and my right side sweating. The heat came out of ducts under the window, but didn't reach as far as the toilet. The brochure about The Lakeshore Limited opens with the words, 'If you like seeing water, this is the train trip for you'. I don't think they meant the icy puddles on my floor.

Over the loudspeaker system, the 'onboard services director' said good morning, apologised for the train being two hours behind schedule, warned that passengers must not use the toilets in the front two carriages, and reported that the temperature outside was 10 degrees Fahrenheit or minus 12 degrees Celsius. I was beginning to have serious doubts about my decision to leave New York by train.

But as I type this chapter, I'm sitting on another train – The Southwest Chief from Chicago to Los Angeles, also known as The Atchison, Topeka and Santa Fe. This is an altogether different proposition. I'm in a wide, padded seat which converts to a comfortable bunk, in a well-warmed double-decker carriage. The toilets are downstairs, and they work. The snow is outside, covering the wheatfields around Dodge City, Kansas. Farewelling America with a cross-continent rail journey now seems a brilliant idea.

It's mid-January, 1988. I've sent the rest of this book off to the publishers, but I decided to save the last chapter to write on the train, because the three-day journey would give me time to reflect on my term in America.

I started this book with a set of generalisations based on being in New York for 11 days. Now I'm trying to articulate a set of equally shameless generalisations based on living in the United States for 21 months. I'll recount this last train journey between the generalisations. Here's the first one:

1. Americans are more idealistic than Australians. Or, put another way, Australians are more cynical than Americans.

Corrupt behaviour by a public official still shocks Americans, while in Australia, we almost expect it. Americans are moral people, with a profound belief in the existence of good and evil. There may be differences in defining those terms between the right-wing fundamentalists and the liberal left, but they are united in demanding high standards in those who represent them. (The unique exception to this may be New York City, which has lately been showing an almost Australian tolerance for corruption scandals.)

During 1987, a judge nominated for the US Supreme Court had to withdraw because it was revealed that he had smoked marijuana 15 years ago. Another nominee was rejected because he appeared to have extreme conservative views which might bias his judgements. A candidate for the presidency had to withdraw from the race because it was revealed he was playing around with women to whom he wasn't married.

Another presidential candidate had to withdraw because he was caught pinching parts of his speeches from other politicians. In Australian terms, this is staggering. Have we ever cared what our politicians say in their speeches? We assume it's a pack of lies anyway, so where the words come from is irrelevant. Not so for Americans. They expect their politicians not only to be monogamous and ethical, but also to expound a Vision for the future of the country. And the Vision must be original, not borrowed.

Back on the rails . . . The Southwest Chief may be a much smoother train than the Lakeshore Limited, but they have one element in common – their food. Amtrak, the US government agency which runs all inter-city passenger trains (20 million people a year over 38,000 kilometres of track), seems to have taken suburban cuisine of the 1950s as the inspiration for its menu, and Rumanian airlines as the inspiration for its dining car design. We eat baked chicken or sirloin steak or swordfish or a 'regional special' of chicken Kiev, with tinned vegetables, off-pink polyester plates on blue and yellow plastic tablecloths.

All meals start with a green salad. Joy of joys, we have a choice of dressings, a ritual I discussed in Chapter 1. They are Olive oil and vinegar, Honey French, Bleu (!) cheese and Thousand Island. They come in plastic sachets, and at last I am able to divine the mysteries of Thousand Island, since the ingredients are printed around the label. Thousand Island dressing is made of 'soybean oil, cucumbers, water, tomato paste, vinegar, hi-fructose corn syrup, eggs, sugar, salt, modified food starch, lemon, herbs and spices, onion, and xanthan gum (food fiber)'.

Amtrak has not forgotten the great dining car tradition, started last century on the Orient Express, of having a single flower in a slender metal vase on every table. In this case, a label is attached to each stem which says, 'Formosa Silk Flower. Made in Taiwan'. The flower is welded to the vase.

2. Americans are more democratic than Australians, sometimes to the point of absurdity.

You might say that Australians participate more in the political process than Americans, since 95 per cent of us vote in our major elections, while only 65 per cent of Americans vote, even for the presidency. But those Americans who choose to participate have tremendous control over the way their country, state or district is run.

Collect enough signatures and you can place any referendum question on the ballot – referendums in parts of California, for example, required the government to cut property taxes and to ban electroshock therapy in mental hospitals.

Americans get to vote for judges, state treasurers, sheriffs, members of the board of education, attorneys-general, parks supervisors, even dogcatchers. This can lead to abuses. Few voters know all the individual candidates, so they tend to vote the ticket of the party they support, Democrat or Republican. This gives the local party boss the power to pick officials who suit not only his political vision but sometimes his financial needs. But is it worse than the alternative chosen by Australia – judges appointed by politicians without even a public inquiry into their suitability?

At a national level, Americans believe in telling their elected representatives what they want all the time. They don't just give a prime minister a majority in the parliament and leave him to do what he likes, occasionally nibbled by an ineffectual opposition and a media muzzled by libel laws.

Members of the US House of Representatives have terms of only two years, so that the minute they are elected, they start running for re-election. There is no official leader of the opposition. But then, every congressman is his or her own leader of the opposition, out to score off the president at every chance.

The balance of powers and duties between the president, the senate and the House of Representatives ensures that no one megalomaniac can determine the future of the United States. That's why Americans could feel comfortable electing Ronald Reagan on the basis of his charm rather than his intelligence – they know that hundreds of other politicians are part of the process of government, and each politician has a large staff working to find out what the public wants.

During my day between trains in Chicago, I met up again with Bruce Kraig, the greatest living expert on the hot dog (see Chapter 6). It turns out Kraig's food fascination is not confined to wieners and Rosen buns. He took me to a wonderful little restaurant called The Bird, way out in Chicago's western suburbs, where a chef named Benny Moy does extraordinary variations on Chinese standards like egg roll stuffed with shrimp; chicken wings stuffed with a minced spiced pork; 'mock squab' (Cornish hen marinated in cognac); and squid in wine sauce. Now I must think of Chicago not only as the hot dog and pizza capital of America, but as the site of the best Chinese meal I've eaten in this country.

After moving round this country a bit, I've developed a very superficial rating system for cities one might visit. I'm inclined to rate Chicago as a city that can hold your interest for three days. On this scale, I rate Los Angeles as a two-day town (mainly to visit Santa Monica and Venice Beach and eat at Spago and St Estephe, but longer if you insist on seeing Disneyland and Universal Studios); San Francisco as a four-day town; New Orleans three days; Boston one day; Salt Lake City two days (long enough to get kidnapped by the Mormons and escape); Washington two days (or one day if congress is not in session); Atlanta only as long as it takes to change planes and go somewhere else; and New York at least two weeks.

If I were planning a holiday in the USA, I'd arrive in LA or San Francisco, and take the train from there to Chicago. I'd examine the architecture and Art Institute, and eat deep dish pizza and Benny Moy's new wave Chinese creations. Then I'd fly to New York.

3.   America is a far more open society than Australia.

I'm about to leave a journalist's paradise. Information is everywhere. Phone a public servant with a question, and he or she gives you an answer. It's a requirement of their job. There's no 'I have to clear this with the minister', 'I'm not at liberty to discuss that' or 'That's not supposed to be public information'.

America is built on the concept that citizens have a right to know what their paid officials are doing. An official who refuses to answer must have something to hide. Australia is built on the concept that public servants function best in secrecy, and anyone who asks questions is a nuisance. In effect, our administrators still treat us as convicts.

The Southwest Chief left Chicago at 5.30 pm on Thursday. Now, as it passes through Wagon Mound, New Mexico, about 5 pm Friday, I have just learned that it is four hours behind schedule. And they're playing Muzak in my carriage. I withdraw some of my earlier praise.

They've also announced that there will be a 'happy hour' in the lounge car, during which margaritas will cost $1.50, a trivia quiz will be played, and there will be free guacamole. Later they'll show the movie *Secret of My Success* on the TV sets at each end of the lounge car.

The fascination of trains like the Southwest Chief and the Lakeshore Limited lies more in their past than in their present. Between 1902 and 1967, the Lakeshore was called The Twentieth Century Limited. It had showers, and its lounge car had a barber and a secretary to take passengers' dictation (which would have been a fine way to write this chapter). During the 1940s, the Twentieth Century Limited made the trip from New York to Chicago via Cleveland in 16 hours. In 1988, its supposedly refurbished carriages and locomotives keep collapsing in the cold, and my journey took 20 hours.

The Southwest Chief, originally The Super Chief, was the train that carried the Hollywood stars between the East and West coasts. Walt Disney is supposed to have created Mickey Mouse while riding it in 1929. It had a luxury dining car called The Turquoise Room, and a glass-roofed observation car with wood-inlaid Navajo motifs. Now the lounge car is stainless steel with orange curtains and formica top tables. This is called progress. But the view I'm seeing of the Sangre de Cristo Mountains and the Cimarron River is sensational.

4.   Americans are more diverse than Australians. They are also more conformist.

The American system supports differences – racial, geographical, socio-economic, linguistic. The constitution assumes variety and is designed to prevent any one group from forcing its views on others. What makes this society exciting is when you think you've understood one part of it, there are a hundred parts still to examine.

But within his social group, an American will obey the silliest dictates of fashion. When Eddie Murphy starts wearing a gold chain round his neck, every black in the street has one next week. When *New York* magazine writes up a new restaurant in Manhattan, it's crammed with Yuppies for 6 months (until the next discovery is announced). At baseball games, when the electronic scoreboard flashes 'Cheer the winner!', the crowd do it. When the scoreboard says 'Louder!', they obey. Can you imagine the reaction at Sydney Cricket Ground if a scoreboard tried to tell the spectators how to respond?

The Amtrak brochure says the Southwest Chief stops in Albuquerque, New Mexico (pronounced albakerky), long enough for passengers to stretch their legs and buy Indian crafts from stalls set up along the platform. We pulled in at 9 pm Friday to find the Indian traders had got tired of waiting in the cold, and just one stall remained, displaying some attractive silver and turquoise jewellery. But before most passengers could get near it, we were recalled to the train.

It also seems that we are being robbed of our Indian guide. The brochure promises that a representative of the Inter-Tribal Indian Ceremonial Association will board at Albuquerque to 'point out scenic highlights and discuss regional history, culture and folklore' of the Apache, Zuni, Navajo, Acoma and Hopi tribes. His or her failure to appear is understandable, since in the pitch dark we are unlikely to appreciate such formations as Pyramid Rock, the Kneeling Nuns, and the Red Cliffs of New Mexico, described in the brochure as 'noted for their changing colors in the bright desert sun'.

5.   America is unable or unwilling to look after its poor.

The richest nation on earth should not have beggars lining the streets of its big cities.

I awaken Saturday morning to find all the snow has vanished. I'm looking at a scrubby pink tundra with purple mountains in the distance. The only sign that humans may exist out there is a bundle of grey logs (rail sleepers?) next to the line. This, presumably, is the Mojave desert, in which, according to the Amtrak brochure, 'with temperatures often the hottest in the country, a person can last only two days'. Slightly longer with an Amtrak breakfast of eggs easy over and hash brown potatoes.

As we pass through San Bernadino, the conductor tells me the temperature outside is 70 degrees Fahrenheit (21 degrees Celsius). This is winter in California. We'll be hitting Los Angeles around noon. It will take nearly two hours to get through the sprawling suburbs of LA. From there, Australia is just a short hop across the Pacific. I can pop back anytime.

6. Americans are impossible to generalise about.

Index